Katherine Mansfield and Elizabeth von Arnim

KATHERINE MANSFIELD STUDIES

Katherine Mansfield Studies is the peer-reviewed, annual publication of the Katherine Mansfield Society. It offers opportunities for collaborations among the significant numbers of researchers with interests in modernism in literature and the arts, as well as those in postcolonial studies. Because Mansfield is a writer who has inspired successors from Elizabeth Bowen to Ali Smith, as well as numerous artists in other media, Katherine Mansfield Studies encourages interdisciplinary scholarship and also allows for a proportion of creative submissions.

Series Editor
Dr Delia da Sousa Correa, *The Open University, UK*

Editors
Dr Gerri Kimber, *University of Northampton, UK*
Professor Todd Martin, *Huntington University, USA*

Reviews Editor
Dr Aimee Gasston, *Birkbeck, University of London, UK*

Editorial Assistant
Dr Aimee Gasston, *Birkbeck, University of London, UK*

International Advisory Board
Elleke Boehmer, *University of Oxford, UK*
Peter Brooker, *University of Sussex, UK*
Stuart N. Clarke, *Virginia Woolf Society of Great Britain, UK*
Robert Fraser, *Open University, UK*
Kirsty Gunn, *University of Dundee, UK*
Clare Hanson, *University of Southampton, UK*
Andrew Harrison, *University of Nottingham, UK*
Anna Jackson, *Victoria University of Wellington, New Zealand*
Kathleen Jones, *Royal Literary Fund Fellow, UK*
Sydney Janet Kaplan, *University of Washington, USA*
Anne Mounic, *Université Sorbonne Nouvelle, Paris 3, France*
Vincent O'Sullivan, *Victoria University of Wellington, New Zealand*
Josiane Paccaud-Huguet, *Université Lumière-Lyon 2, France*
Sarah Sandley, *Honorary Chair, Katherine Mansfield Society, New Zealand*
Ali Smith, *author*
Angela Smith, *University of Stirling, UK*
C. K. Stead, *University of Auckland, New Zealand*
Janet Wilson, *University of Northampton, UK*

KATHERINE MANSFIELD SOCIETY
Patron
Professor Kirsty Gunn
Honorary President
Emeritus Professor Vincent O'Sullivan, DCNZM
Honorary Vice-Presidents
Emeritus Professor Angela Smith
Emeritus Professor C. K. Stead, ONZ, CBE, FRSL
Honorary Advisory Chair
Dr Sarah Sandley

COMMITTEE
Chair
Dr Gerri Kimber
Vice-Chair
Professor Janet Wilson
Membership Secretary
Professor Todd Martin
Treasurer
Ralph Kimber
New Zealand Treasurer
Kevin Ireland
Secretary
Dr Sarah Ailwood
Assistant Secretary
Dr Helen Rydstrand
Chair of Katherine Mansfield Studies Advisory Board
Dr Delia Da Sousa Correa
Newsletter Editor
Dr Martin Griffiths
Marketing Secretary
Dr Jessica Gildersleeve
Conference Committee Chair
Professor Gina Wisker
Postgraduate Representative
Joe Williams

Katherine Mansfield and Elizabeth von Arnim

Edited by
Gerri Kimber, Isobel Maddison and Todd Martin

Editorial Assistant
Aimee Gasston

EDINBURGH
University Press

Edinburgh University Press is one of the leading university presses in the UK. We publish academic books and journals in our selected subject areas across the humanities and social sciences, combining cutting-edge scholarship with high editorial and production values to produce academic works of lasting importance. For more information visit our website: edinburghuniversitypress.com

© editorial matter and organisation Gerri Kimber, Isobel Maddison and Todd Martin, 2019
© the chapters their several authors, 2019

Edinburgh University Press Ltd
The Tun – Holyrood Road, 12(2f) Jackson's Entry, Edinburgh EH8 8PJ

Typeset in 10.5/12.5 New Baskerville by
Servis Filmsetting Ltd, Stockport, Cheshire.

A CIP record for this book is available from the British Library

ISBN 978 1 4744 5443 8 (hardback)
ISBN 978 1 4744 5445 2 (webready PDF)
ISBN 978 1 4744 5444 5 (paperback)
ISBN 978 1 4744 5446 9 (epub)

The right of Gerri Kimber, Isobel Maddison and Todd Martin to be identified as the editors of this work has been asserted in accordance with the Copyright, Designs and Patents Act 1988, and the Copyright and Related Rights Regulations 2003 (SI No. 2498).

Contents

List of Illustrations	vii
Acknowledgements	viii
Abbreviations	ix
Introduction: Complementary Cousins *Isobel Maddison*	1

CRITICISM

After Life – Expressions of Mourning in Elizabeth von Arnim and Katherine Mansfield *Juliane Römhild*	11
Tracing Garden Networks: Katherine Mansfield and Elizabeth von Arnim *Bonnie Kime Scott*	27
'Our own little grain of truth' *Angela Smith*	41
Writing Toward a New World: Awakenings in Katherine Mansfield's 'Bliss' and Elizabeth von Arnim's *The Enchanted April* *Noreen O'Connor*	54
'*Ces femmes avec ces fleurs!*': Flowers, Gender and Relationships in the work of Elizabeth von Arnim and Katherine Mansfield *Karina Jakubowicz*	70
Strange Monsters: The Struggle for Women's Validity as Artists in the Writings of Elizabeth von Arnim and Katherine Mansfield *Richard Cappuccio*	86
'Not a Feminist, but …': Elizabeth von Arnim and Female Resistance *Alison Hennegan*	99

Digging Out Characters: Elizabeth von Arnim in Virginia 115
Ann Herndon Marshall

'[P]assionate, magnificent prose': Tracing the Brontës in the Friendship and Writings of Elizabeth von Arnim and Katherine Mansfield 132
Charlotte Fiehn

CREATIVE WRITING

Short Story

Sarah Laing: Vessel 147

Poetry

Nina Powles: If Katherine Mansfield Were My Best Friend 159

CRITICAL MISCELLANY

Of Bliss and Blushing: Cities and Affect in Katherine Mansfield and Jean Rhys 163
Andrew Thacker

Beatrice Hastings in Paris 181
Chris Mourant

REVIEW ESSAY

Katherine Mansfield's Many Forms 195
Derek Ryan

Notes on Contributors 205
Index 208

List of Illustrations

Frontispiece. Elizabeth von Arnim with her dog, Coco, early 1920s, on the terrace of the Chalet Soleil, Crans-Montana, Switzerland. With kind permission of Ann Hardham.   x

Figure 1. Chalet des Sapins, Crans-Montana, Switzerland, 1921. Katherine Mansfield's Swiss home '1/2 an hours scramble' away from her cousin, Elizabeth. Katherine Mansfield Collection, Harry Ransom Center, The University of Texas at Austin.   2

Figure 2. Chalet Soleil, Randogne-sur-Sierre, Switzerland, home of Elizabeth von Arnim. With kind permission of Ann Hardham.   3

Figure 3. Portrait of Katherine Mansfield, 1921. PAColl-6826-1-20-2. John Middleton Murry Collection, Alexander Turnbull Library, Wellington, New Zealand.   43

Figure 4. Elizabeth von Arnim and Billy at Bonnie Hall Plantation, home of Nelson Doubleday in Yemassee, South Carolina, USA, 1940. With kind permission of Ann Hardham.   123

Figure 5. The borrower's card of Katherine Mansfield from the library of Sylvia Beach's bookshop, Shakespeare and Company. Image reproduced courtesy of the Firestone Library, Princeton University.   165

Figure 6. Index card from the library of Shakespeare and Company showing volumes by Mansfield for borrowing. Image reproduced courtesy of the Firestone Library, Princeton University.   165

Figure 7. Amedeo Modigliani, *Beatrice Hastings*, 1915, oil paint on paper, 40 x 28.5 cm. Private Collection. © Bernard Bonnefon/akg-images.   182

Acknowledgements

The editors would like to extend particular thanks to the judging panel for this year's Katherine Mansfield Society Essay Prize: Professor David Trotter, University of Cambridge and Chair of the Judging Panel, Claire Tomalin, renowned biographer and author of *Katherine Mansfield: A Secret Life*, and Professor Susan Sellers, University of St Andrews. The winning essay, 'After Life – Expressions of Mourning in Elizabeth von Arnim and Katherine Mansfield', by Dr Juliane Römhild, is featured in this volume.

The editors would also like to thank the following organisations and individuals: Jennifer Walker, for her invaluable help and advice throughout the volume, and particularly with the von Arnim images; David Thompson at Tate Images; Ann Hardham, for permission to publish all the images of Elizabeth von Arnim, including the Frontispiece; Jamie Ritchie and Ann Hardham, for permission to quote from the unpublished family archives in their possession which feature in Juliane Römhild's essay; and the Firestone Library at Princeton University for permission to publish reference cards from the Sylvia Beach papers.

Abbreviations

Unless otherwise indicated, all references to Katherine Mansfield's works are to the editions listed below and abbreviated as follows. Diaries, journals, letters and notebooks are quoted verbatim without the use of editorial '[sic]'.

CW1 and CW2
The Edinburgh Edition of the Collected Works of Katherine Mansfield: Vols 1 and 2 – *The Collected Fiction*, eds Gerri Kimber and Vincent O'Sullivan (Edinburgh: Edinburgh University Press, 2012)

CW3
The Edinburgh Edition of the Collected Works of Katherine Mansfield: Vol. 3 – *The Poetry and Critical Writings*, eds Gerri Kimber and Angela Smith (Edinburgh: Edinburgh University Press, 2014)

CW4
The Edinburgh Edition of the Collected Works of Katherine Mansfield: Vol. 4 – *The Diaries of Katherine Mansfield, including Miscellaneous Works*, eds Gerri Kimber and Claire Davison (Edinburgh: Edinburgh University Press, 2016)

CP
The Collected Poems of Katherine Mansfield, eds Gerri Kimber and Claire Davison (Edinburgh: Edinburgh University Press, 2016)

Letters **1–5**
The Collected Letters of Katherine Mansfield, 5 vols, eds Vincent O'Sullivan and Margaret Scott (Oxford: Clarendon Press, 1984–2008)

Notebooks **1–2**
The Katherine Mansfield Notebooks, 2 vols, ed. Margaret Scott (Minneapolis: University of Minnesota Press, 2002)

Elizabeth von Arnim with her dog, Coco, early 1920s, on the terrace of the Chalet Soleil, Crans-Montana, Switzerland. With kind permission of Ann Hardham.

Introduction: Complementary Cousins

Isobel Maddison

'I would like to write one story really good enough to offer you one day'; 'please let all the pride be mine that you are my cousin.'[1]
Katherine Mansfield to Elizabeth von Arnim, 1922

Elizabeth von Arnim is probably best remembered as the author of *Elizabeth and Her German Garden* (1898) and *The Enchanted April* (1922), and as the elder cousin of Katherine Mansfield. In recent times, fresh scholarship has begun to reinstate von Arnim into the cultural *milieu* of which she was a significant part, while research into the complex relationship between Mansfield and her cousin has done much to shed light on the familial, personal and literary connections between these unlikely friends.[2] Although their lives appeared to be very different (Mansfield's largely one of penurious poor health, von Arnim's chiefly one of robust privilege), we know each experienced the other as an influential presence. They read and commented on each other's work, and Mansfield's critical assessments became part of the wider reception of von Arnim's writing, while von Arnim's skill as an author seeped into her cousin's youthful aspirations and into her first collection of stories, *In a German Pension* (1911).[3]

Of particular interest is the period between May 1921 and July 1922, when Mansfield and von Arnim lived on the same Swiss mountain '1/2 an hours scramble away' from each other (Figs 1 and 2). Here, Mansfield wrote to Ottoline Morrell, she and her cousin exchanged 'Chateaubriand and baskets of apricots' and had 'occasional long talks', 'ruminative, and reminiscent' like those Mansfield imagined as typical in the 'afterlife'.[4] Familial links were deepened during this period, and glimpses into their everyday lives taken from letters reveal personal affection, occasional tension, but primarily a love for literary expression. In December 1921

Fig. 1 Chalet des Sapins, Crans-Montana, Switzerland, 1921. Katherine Mansfield's Swiss home '1/2 an hours scramble' away from her cousin, Elizabeth. Katherine Mansfield Collection, Harry Ransom Center, The University of Texas at Austin.

John Middleton Murry and Mansfield were reading copies of Jane Austen they had borrowed from von Arnim's Swiss chalet,[5] while in March 1922 von Arnim claimed to have taught Mansfield to play chess or, at least, to have been 'the remote cause' of it, fearing her cousin would 'play it dreadfully well' and she'd want, amusingly, to 'brain her with the Queen'.[6]

Writing to Dorothy Brett in 1921, Mansfield reveals her affection for von Arnim:

> [Elizabeth] appeared today [. . .] . She looked like a garden walking, of asters, late sweet peas, stocks, and always petunias. She herself wore a frock like a spider web, a hat like a berry [. . .] . I have gathered Elizabeth's frocks to my bosom as if they were part of her flowers. And when she smiles a ravishing wrinkle appears on her nose – and never have I seen more exquisite hands [. . .] . The point about her is one loves her and is proud of her [. . .] . But no doubt Elizabeth is far more important to me than I am to her.[7]

Clearly, by this point, relations in the Swiss mountain air were warm and the feeling was mutual. Later, von Arnim expressed similar pride in Mansfield: 'I'm fearfully proud of her – just as if I had hatched her.'[8]

Introduction

Fig. 2 Chalet Soleil, Randogne-sur-Sierre, Switzerland, home of Elizabeth von Arnim. With kind permission of Ann Hardham.

In Switzerland the cousins appeared to be in tune with each other most of the time; it was also a period of important literary activity for both writers. Mansfield completed 'At the Bay', 'The Doll's House' and one of her best-known stories, 'The Garden Party', while von Arnim wrote her most radical novel, *Vera*, which Mansfield considered 'extraordinarily good'.[9] The lives of these authors remained enmeshed until the end of Mansfield's poignantly short life in 1923. The final letter Mansfield wrote was to von Arnim, and, just a few months after his wife's death, Murry would go on to dedicate his first edited collection of Mansfield's poems to her cousin. The epigraph reads: 'To Elizabeth of the German Garden who loved certain of these poems and their author'.[10]

This volume develops current scholarship by offering a comparative reading of Mansfield's short stories and von Arnim's novels in order to augment our understanding of writing in the late nineteenth and early twentieth centuries, while adding welcome nuance to the ways in which we have frequently approached both authors and their writing. By tracing the resonances found in the work of Mansfield and von Arnim, the volume offers fresh considerations and original insights into a variety of texts rarely brought together. The first such reading is by Juliane Römhild, whose essay, 'After Life – Expressions of Mourning in Elizabeth von Arnim and Katherine Mansfield', was the deserving winner of the Katherine Mansfield Essay Prize in 2018. Underpinned by new archival material, it considers loss following the Great War as it is rendered in von Arnim's novels *Christine* and *In the Mountains*, which are read alongside Mansfield's stories of mourning, including 'The Fly' and 'The Canary'. Römhild draws comparisons between the personal losses suffered by both authors and writes convincingly of their significance in the work of these cousins. Bonnie Kime Scott's essay, 'Tracing Garden Networks: Katherine Mansfield and Elizabeth von Arnim', switches to an exploration of the use of gardens in their writing, and draws attention to the historical and horticultural contexts within which both women were working. In her wide-ranging essay, Scott identifies gardens as places of 'renewal and becoming' that unite women and exist apart from 'androcentric, male-dominated spaces and expectations' (p. 39). In her illuminating essay, Angela Smith considers Mansfield's reading of R. O. Prowse's *A Gift of the Dusk* and von Arnim's *Vera* as 'triggers' that push Mansfield's imagination into uncompromisingly new directions. Discussing abjection and trauma in the work of these authors, Smith's essay, 'Our own little grain of truth', also acknowledges Mansfield's 'glinting wit', which, she argues, adds sparkle to her most daring psychological stories, just as it adds to 'von Arnim's artistry' (p. 53). Noreen O'Connor's essay, 'Writing Toward a New World: Awakenings in Katherine Mansfield's "Bliss" and Elizabeth von Arnim's *The Enchanted April*, is an original reading of one of Mansfield's best-known stories alongside von Arnim's best-known novel. O'Connor argues that these texts are 'gently revolutionary' in revising the traditional marriage plot while offering accounts that are not easily organised into 'pre-war narrative forms or the alienated individuality we have come to expect from modernist works' (p. 68). Karina Jakubowicz's contribution returns to garden literature in her essay '"*Ces femmes avec ces fleurs!*"', which considers flowers, gender and relationships in the work of von Arnim and Mansfield. Situating both writers in the wider context of the popularity of nature poetry and sentimental flower books, Jakubowicz argues that the passion for flowers presented by both authors reveals an intertextual dialogue that provides a 'window' into their work, as well as the wider cultural and literary *milieu* (p. 83). The judges of the 2018 essay prize highly commended Richard Cappuccio's essay, 'Strange Monsters: The Struggle for Women's Validity as Artists in the Writing of Elizabeth von Arnim and Katherine Mansfield'. Noting that both writers were accomplished musicians, Cappuccio suggests that the representation of the female artist in von Arnim's *Christine* and several of Mansfield's short stories provides an index to the struggle for female autonomy at the time of their writing. Reading the inclusion of specific pieces of music as intertextual clues, Cappuccio unearths hidden resonances to establish new and revealing connections. Alison Hennegan's essay, '"Not a Feminist, but …": Elizabeth von Arnim and Female Resistance', develops the discussion of gender and raises a series of questions about the role of women in the society inhabited by von Arnim, Mansfield and beyond. Situating the discussion in its historical and literary contexts, Hennegan ranges across several of von Arnim's novels using Mansfield's work as a counterpoint, while offering a detailed scholarly discussion of von Arnim's novel *Father*. Ann Herndon Marshall also presents fresh information about von Arnim. Her essay, 'Digging Out Characters: Elizabeth von Arnim in Virginia', charts the period around 1939 towards the end of her life at Clover Fields, Virginia, in the United States. Marshall establishes connections, both personal and literary, with the novelist Amélie Rives and, through painstaking research of von Arnim's journals of 1939–40, reconstructs von Arnim's last years, her nostalgia for people and places, and her fear of the looming Second World War. Charlotte Fiehn brings the first section of the volume to a close with her essay, '[P]assionate, magnificent prose: Tracing the Brontës in the Friendship and Writings of Elizabeth von Arnim and Katherine Mansfield'. Identifying the importance of the Brontës for both authors, Fiehn establishes resonances between *Jane Eyre* and von Arnim's *Vera* in particular, as well as with Mansfield's 'Bliss' and 'The Little Governess', bringing these literary cousins closer together in new and interesting ways.

There follow two excellent pieces of creative writing: a striking story by Sarah Laing, titled 'Vessel', about a car crash and memories of Katherine Mansfield's Wellington before the 1855 earthquake, and an impressive poem by Nina Powles that muses on the idea 'If Katherine Mansfield Were My Best Friend'. The Critical Miscellany section showcases Andrew Thacker's essay, 'Of Bliss and Blushing: Cities and Affect in Katherine Mansfield and Jean Rhys', which opens with an imaginary journey to Paris and Sylvia Beach's Shakespeare and Company bookshop before Thacker airs the tantalising possibility of a meeting between Mansfield and Rhys. Scrutinising the very real borrowers' cards for the bookshop housed in the Beach archive at Princeton University, Thacker explores the reading material of several writers, including Mansfield, in this fascinating essay that sketches some of the 'complex ways that two colonial outsiders [Mansfield and Rhys] experienced Paris', capturing 'the mood of the spaces in which they moved' in their writing (p. 178). This is followed by Chris Mourant's essay, 'Beatrice Hastings in Paris', which highlights the significance of Hastings to the art of Modigliani, with whom she had a brief affair, and her own significance as an editor of the influential British periodical, *The New Age*, which included so many of Mansfield's early stories. Mourant traces Hastings's movements, relationships and feminist contributions, and reinserts her into the intellectual environment of which she was an important part and from which she has frequently been omitted.

Derek Ryan closes the volume with an illuminating review essay on 'Katherine Mansfield's Many Forms', focusing on fresh scholarship in books by Gerri Kimber and Janet Wilson, and by Vassiliki Kolocotroni and Olga Taxidou, plus new work by Chris Mourant, John Newton and C. K. Stead.

It has been a pleasure to work on this volume in collaboration with so many excellent scholars and, as always, it is wonderful to showcase the work of Katherine Mansfield and Elizabeth von Arnim together, forging new associations and prompting fresh thinking for future research.

Notes

1. Katherine Mansfield to Elizabeth von Arnim, 1922. Quoted from Leslie de Charms, *Elizabeth of the German Garden* (London: Heinemann, 1958), p. 232.
2. See Erica Brown, *Comedy and the Feminine Middlebrow Novel: Elizabeth von Arnim and Elizabeth Taylor* (London: Routledge, 2012); Isobel Maddison, *Elizabeth von Arnim:*

Introduction

Beyond the German Garden (Farnham: Ashgate, 2013); Jennifer Walker, *Elizabeth of the German Garden: A Biography of Elizabeth von Arnim* (Leicester: Book Guild, 2013); Juliane Römhild, *Femininity and Authorship in the Novels of Elizabeth von Arnim: At Her Most Radiant Moment* (Madison, NJ: Fairleigh Dickinson, 2014); Isobel Maddison, 'Complementary Cousins: Constructing the Maternal in the Writing of Elizabeth von Arnim and Katherine Mansfield', in *Middlebrow and Gender, 1890–1945* (Leiden: Brill/Rodopi, 2016); Isobel Maddison, Juliane Römhild and Jennifer Walker, eds, *Re-Evaluating Elizabeth von Arnim*, in *Women: A Cultural Review*, 28 (22 June 2017).

3. See Isobel Maddison, 'Worms of the Same Family: Elizabeth von Arnim and Katherine Mansfield', in *Elizabeth*, pp. 85–103.
4. *Letters* 4, p. 252.
5. See *Letters* 4, p. 339, Mansfield to von Arnim, 15 December 1921.
6. Quoted in Maddison, *Elizabeth*, p. 2. In *Letters* 5, p. 70 (21 February 1922), Mansfield writes to von Arnim: 'John, after his beating at chess has had the satisfaction of teaching me,' which implies that it was Murry who was taught chess by von Arnim, and not Mansfield.
7. de Charms, p. 225.
8. Quoted in Maddison, *Elizabeth*, p. 103.
9. de Charms, p. 228.
10. John Middleton Murry, ed., *Poems of Katherine Mansfield* (London: Constable, 1923).

CRITICISM

After Life – Expressions of Mourning in Elizabeth von Arnim and Katherine Mansfield

Juliane Römhild

The only person whom we see is my Cousin Elizabeth who lives ½ an hours scramble away. We exchange Chateaubriand and baskets of apricots and have occasional long talks which are rather like what talk in the afterlife will be like, I imagine ... ruminative, and reminiscent – although dear knows what it is really all about. How strange talking is – [1]

Katherine Mansfield's description of her conversations with Elizabeth von Arnim in the Summer of 1921, perched high in the Swiss mountains, is intriguing. What could those two writers have been ruminating and reminiscing about? It seems to me that they must have talked, among other things perhaps, about their Beauchamp family connections and their memories of pre-war life. In 1921, few people could talk about friends and family without reminiscing about those they had lost in the war. Conversations about loved ones would turn into ruminations on the loss of pre-war love and life. As cousins, Mansfield and von Arnim shared a long family history.[2] Mansfield had stayed with von Arnim's parents in England, where she had met and taken a particular liking to von Arnim's youngest daughter, Felicitas. Mansfield and Felicitas, whose family nickname was Martin, shared a sense of rebelliousness and imagination,[3] and von Arnim's brother had acted, not very effectively it seems, as Mansfield's legal guardian in England. Both writers shared the experience of recent loss in their close family circle. In 1915, Mansfield had lost her much-loved brother Leslie in the war, while von Arnim had lost her nephew, John Waterlow, as well as Martin, who had died of pneumonia in 1916 in Germany. However, Martin was not the only daughter von Arnim had 'lost' to Germany. Martin's older sister Beatrix, usually called Trix by the family, had married a German officer in 1919, and von Arnim keenly felt that Trix, too, was 'lost' to her.

While the reflections of grief in Mansfield's writing are quite well explored, much less has been written on von Arnim's wartime novels *Christine* (1917) and *In the Mountains* (1920).[4] At first glance, this is surprising, since the close links between her life and writing have been fascinating to scholars. However, this gap becomes perhaps more explicable when considering some of the cultural boundaries around grief in the wake of the Great War that have affected scholarship as well. As a result, 'how civilians were mourned', in particular women and children, remains an under-researched field.[5] It seems to me that von Arnim's two novels are inspired by a similar impulse to what Mansfield famously called her two '"kickoffs" in the writing game'. In an oft-cited letter to John Middleton Murry, she explained,

> *One* is joy – real joy – [. . .]
> The other 'kickoff' is my old original one [. . .]. Not hate or destruction [. . .] but an *extremely* deep sense of hopelessness – of everything doomed to disaster – almost wilfully, stupidly [. . .] – *a cry against corruption* that is *absolutely* the nail on the head. [. . .] and I mean corruption in the widest sense of the word, of course –[6]

Von Arnim's works, too, show a supreme capacity for joy, but some of her strongest work is, like Mansfield's, motivated by states of deep pain and, at times, anger about the corruption of human relationships. The major 'kickoff' for *Christine* and *In the Mountains* is grief. Accordingly, I propose to read these novels through the double lens of wartime mourning and biographical research that has been so productively applied to Mansfield's works and life. As it turns out, in spite of their obvious artistic differences, both writers share certain characteristics in their responses to loss.

Mansfield's New Zealand stories are inscribed with her grief for a sibling as much as for her homeland and her childhood. However deep and at times desperate as her grief for Leslie was, Mansfield could rest in the knowledge that she was joining the ranks of the many mothers, sisters, wives and fiancées who had lost a soldier for a great cause – as compromised as that cause might have turned out to be under the progressively disillusioned gaze of British mourners. There was nothing dishonourable in losing a brother handling dangerous weaponry. Von Arnim's grief, however, was more complicated. She was not mourning a British soldier but a daughter who lived in Germany and who strongly identified with the German cause. Martin's musicality and lively intelligence had made her particularly dear to von Arnim, but in 1915 she broke off contact with her teenage daughter, not only over allegations that Martin had stolen money (untrue, as it later turned out), but also because of Martin's political views, as she explained to Trix: 'Imagine, I had to tell Martin not to write me anymore, her invectives had become so tactless. [. . .] I don't want to hear about her political nonsense.'[7] In contrast, von Arnim had written to Hugh Walpole in 1914 about those 'hateful Germans [. . .]. Oh, I wish I were a man – wouldn't I be off to the port! I have a wholly barbarous desire to kill at least one German before I die! The satisfaction of it Hugh!'[8] Von Arnim was, of course, not alone in her initial support of the war; in fact, 'there had never been such a demonstration of loyalty' among writers 'as this one of 1914. [. . .] British writers of all persuasions were at this time uncritically united behind the Allied cause.'[9] However, this kind of patriotism also led to a strong nomenclature surrounding and regulating all expressions of grief. During the war,

> women seem to have felt the pressure of male codes of behavior, to the extent of being unable or unwilling to show grief openly [. . .]. Public grief would have been unpatriotic, feminine, weak. [. . .] Suppression becomes a characteristic mode for women in wartime.[10]

Von Arnim's admonishments to Trix's older sister Elizabeth, called Liebet, 'to help by being absolutely quietly courageous'[11] about Martin's death, and her assurance to Trix 'that you and I, my dear little one, have to be brave',[12] demonstrate how public discourse found its way even into private correspondence. Even women grieving for soldiers did not always meet with sympathy or understanding, as Mansfield experienced in her own marriage.[13] Under these circumstances, it was impossible for von Arnim to voice grief for a Germanophile daughter in public.

Thus, in her acute state of grief and guilt, von Arnim sought ways of legitimising Martin's death in *Christine*. She wrote to Liebet that 'Martin's death is just as directly the result of the war as Johnnie's,'[14] a phrase we find almost exactly repeated in the Preface to *Christine*, where Christine's mother, Alice Cholmondeley (von Arnim's pseudonym for the book), claims, 'The war killed Christine, just as surely as if she had been a soldier in the trenches.'[15] Indeed, Christine, who sets off to study music in Berlin, where she witnesses the outbreak of the war, travels in enemy territory with a great deal of courage. In scenes that are reminiscent of Mansfield's story 'Germans at Meat', she withstands the heckling by the German guests at her Berlin pension without resorting to national prejudice or jingoist stereotype against her hosts. In her depictions of the German bourgeoisie and upper classes, von Arnim mobilises the prominent discourse on British civilisation versus German *Kultur*.[16] Similar to Mansfield in *In a German Pension*, von Arnim also sets 'the international status of music [. . .] against the tide of incipient nationalism'.[17] However, in spite of her love of German musical culture, Christine remains a thoroughly civilised English girl at heart and embodies the presumed decency and fairness of the English soldier abroad.

Christine's death in Germany references sacrifice as the most prominent trope in the iconography of grief during World War One. Christine's innocence and goodness mark her out as the sacrificial lamb. Like Martin, she dies of pneumonia, which she – unlike Martin – catches through the cruel neglect of a callous German officer as she tries to leave the country by train. Her death is all the more tragic because 'her great gift, which was extraordinary [. . .] has been lost to the world, broken and thrown away by the war'.[18] Christine's name already associates her with God's son. Like Christ, she endures the jeers of the crowd as she stands under guard on a railway platform for hours, suffering from thirst and the heat. Her mother presents her letters to the public as precious relics and explains, 'the love in them [. . .] made them sacred things in days when we each still hoarded what we had of good'.[19] Carol Acton has shown how '[p]rescribing and controlling grief through consolatory rhetoric [. . .] emphasises the meaning of the death in the service of the state' and 'thus becomes an essential element in the overall "manufacture of consent"' to the war.[20] Alice Cholmondeley hopes Christine's letters 'may have a certain value in helping to put together a small corner of the great picture of Germany'.[21] She appeals to a community of consenting mourners when she explains, 'We no longer in these days belong to small circles, to limited little groups. [. . .] We live in a great relationship. We share our griefs.'[22] Through the persona of Alice Cholmondeley we can sense von Arnim's own desire to 'share' her grief and write herself into 'the great relationship' uniting England's grieving mothers.

The creation of a literary space that is 'me' and 'not-me'[23] explains the rather porous border between fact and fiction in *Christine*, but also in Mansfield's response to the death of Leslie. Von Arnim modelled her protagonist on her dead daughter in a number of ways. As already mentioned, Martin and Christine both die of pneumonia, and both play the same instrument, the violin. In a letter to Trix, von Arnim remembers her daughter's musical gift: 'Along came Martin, that little Beethoven head, and how delightful was her play even back then [. . .] . How strangely mature. I always listened entirely enchanted.'[24] Martin's 'Beethoven head' reappears in the novel where Christine's teacher, Herr Kloster, exclaims, 'But you have the real Beethoven brow – the very shape – and I must touch it.'[25] Like Martin, Christine enchants her German audience: 'whenever I play to them they all grow kind.

It's rather like being Orpheus with his lute.'[26] However, unlike Martin, Christine is a model daughter. From her pension at Lützowstraße – coincidentally von Arnim's old address in Berlin – Christine promises her mother, 'I'm going to be your son, and husband, and everything else that loves and is devoted, and I'm going to earn both our livings for us, and take care of you forever.'[27] Christine fulfils a fantasy von Arnim also repeatedly expresses in her invitations to Trix when she asks, 'don't you want for a bit to be with me & take care of your little mother?'[28] Finally, perhaps von Arnim's deepest fantasy of saving her daughter is fulfilled in *Christopher and Columbus* (1919), a novel about Anglo-German twin sisters. One of the sisters is named Anne-Felicitas and makes a lucky escape to America. Similarly, Mansfield's passionate wish 'that her brother's last thoughts had been of her'[29] also led her to blend reality with fantasy when she inserted her own name into Leslie's dying words. In a letter to her friend Samuel Koteliansky, she quotes her brother in a grief-stricken passage, 'and just before he died he said "Lift my head, *Katy* I can't breathe –" To tell you the truth these things I have heard about him blind me to all that is happening here.'[30] Among Mansfield's biographers, only Kathleen Jones mentions Mansfield's transgressive move. Expressions of grief are messy: 'bereavement is particularly well placed to contest conventional wartime binaries of home and front, masculine and feminine [. . .] of "ally" and "enemy other"'.[31] It can also, we may add, transcend the binary of fact and fiction.

In a situation where the public discourse flattens any direct expression of the unruly and conflicting emotions and desires associated with grief,[32] the exploration of those feelings through writing can function as 'a genuine expression of remembrance and grief as opposed to an attempt to create cultural memory by committee' in the shape of memorial shrines.[33] In women's writing on the war, 'we find bizarre manifestations of guilt and grief, a sense of mourning that is forbidden and incomplete'.[34] In such a reading, the lustful cruelty of the mourning boss in Mansfield's story 'The Fly', who admires the plucky little fly while leaning 'his thick wrist on the blotting-paper' to drop 'another great heavy blot' of ink precisely on the body of the struggling animal,[35] becomes a vehicle for working through some of the contradictory feelings Mansfield had for her own father and brother. At the same time, the story acts as an exorcism of suffering,[36] and, what is more, by enacting 'a Freudian shift from mourning to melancholia' with the suppression of the son's memory, it shows the dangers of blocking off grief.[37]

Similarly, the cruelty of Christine's death can then also be read as a way of working through the ambivalent feelings of grief, guilt, anger and love that von Arnim may have experienced about the unruly Martin, which haunted her, while Martin herself remained painfully out of reach.[38] This ambivalence is inscribed in the novel's play with genre: *Christine* is an epistolary novel that was marketed as non-fiction, and von Arnim strictly denied authorship.[39] Letters express both the presence and the absence of the correspondent, particularly in wartime. 'Even the simplest letter' from the front still 'bore witness to the physical existence of the writer',[40] yet at the same time each letter served as a painful reminder of their absence. The unbearable tension of presence and absence, of memory and loss, spills over into the imaginative destruction of the lost daughter, revealing how the loved object needs to be fully externalised before it can leave the potential space and become irrevocably other: 'an object comes into existence only as it is lost', as Toshiaki Komura puts it.[41] Accordingly, we may read *Christine* as a long and complicated farewell letter in which von Arnim re-enacts the ultimate loss of the beloved child in order to idealise the fraught relationship with her daughter into a perfect union.

The potential estrangement from her children had been of concern to von Arnim for some time. Already in *The Pastor's Wife* (1914), the English protagonist, who has followed her German husband to the outer reaches of Pomerania, has to watch helplessly as her children turn into little Germans in spite of her best efforts.[42] Like Martin, Trix had a mind of her own, and von Arnim tried to steer her daughter's ship from afar:

> I am sure [she wrote in 1915] you will [. . .] always think of me when you do something like spending money or anything else. 'Would Mummy think this is right?' [. . .]. Since you have been so far from me for such a long time, my spirit must be with you.[43]

The letters following Martin's death show von Arnim's desperate attempts at keeping her surviving daughter close: 'Oh Trixie darling [. . .], I would give anything, anything in the world to take you on my lap and kiss away all the sorrow and grief!'[44] and 'Your mummy has only one thought: to be with you and the other dear children again.'[45] Von Arnim wanted Trix to join her older sisters Liebet and Evi in the United States, but Trix resisted while von Arnim's admonitions became more urgent: 'You have to [. . .] do anything I tell you without questions. You may and should think whatever you want, and what you don't understand now won't hurt you. Later you will understand everything.'[46] However, Trix refused to leave the country she considered her homeland. In September 1916, von Arnim travelled to the United States alone to be with Liebet and escape her increasingly unbearable second marriage.

Any letters von Arnim wrote to Trix between 1917 and 1918 are lost. The surviving correspondence resumes in 1919, the year that Trix married the German officer Anton von Hirschberg. This was a difficult situation for von Arnim. Anti-German sentiment was still rife, and von Arnim feared the difficulties that might arise for her should word get out about her new son-in-law. Moreover, their different experience of the war, opposed political allegiances and also their exposure to five years' worth of propaganda had caused a deep rift between mother and daughter. In her letters, von Arnim tried to separate her political views from her personal feelings for Trix with mixed success. In April, von Arnim wrote,

> I'm sorry you should say in your last letter 'you seem to hate us' – I expect when we meet the stupid old war will be rather a barrier between us, but love & honesty should be able to get round it.[47]

Seeing that the engagement to von Hirschberg was progressing, she resigned herself and gave her blessing in June:

> Of *course* get married as soon as you like – how well I understand your longing for your own home [. . .] and I send you my very loveliest blessing & shall pray that you may be very happy all your dear little life.[48]

However, she made clear her feelings about von Hirschberg's nationality: 'of *course* I feel at present rather bad that you should be marrying one of them. This is as natural in me as it is in you that you should want to.'[49] Her resistance to meeting von Hirschberg at her Swiss chalet and her refusal to attend the wedding were hurtful to the uncomprehending Trix:

> How funny you are, little Trix, not to understand & be so much astonished that, after all the dreadful horrors of the war, we are not ready at once to fall on your necks & embrace you! When I say 'your' I of course mean your nation. But can't you understand that, as I don't know your fiancé, & only know he was an officer & the adjutant of a person for whom we have rather an active dislike, I should feel disinclined to see him at present? [. . .]. And why should I? You say Pappa was a German, but what has that to do with me? I never was, & you very well know that the moment the war started I took steps to be repatriated.[50]

Von Arnim's fierce political stance in the letters stands in stark contrast to the decidedly reconciliatory tones of *In the Mountains*, which she was writing in the same year. It seems to me that von Arnim's anti-German feelings stemmed at least partly from her feeling of fighting a losing battle for Trix. She had not been able to persuade her to leave Germany during the war; now her daughter's marriage made her fear she would 'lose' her to Germany entirely. Her appeals to Trix's sense of her English heritage remained fruitless. Trix refused to write in her 'mother tongue' and continued to correspond in German. With some bitterness, von Arnim eventually resigned herself to the fact that Trix was 'now so German (as is natural) that she might just as easily not have had me for a mother at all'.[51] Leading up to their reunion visit in Switzerland in late September 1919 (without von Hirschberg), she asked the newly married Trix to travel under her maiden name one last time for practical reasons as much as for emotional ones: 'Come to me for this once & this last time as my own little girl – & after that le déluge! For that same reason I shall send no telegram to you on your wedding day.'[52] To von Arnim, this visit would be a farewell as much as a reunion.

The painful process of letting go, of grieving and healing, is the central topic of *In the Mountains*, in which the nameless diarist returns to her Swiss chalet in order to mend her broken spirit after the war. She takes in two itinerant English sisters, Dolly Juchs and Mrs Barnes, who draw her back into life. In her grief, once again, von Arnim plays with fact and fiction. Dolly bears a certain resemblance to Trix, with whom she shares an irrepressible sense of humour. In fact, Dolly's last name, Juchs, means 'joke' or 'lark' in German. Dolly is the widow of two German husbands, of whom she has fond memories. Yet neither grief nor hardship has been able to change her sunny disposition, and she lacks all political instinct. According to the narrator, Dolly 'is of no age – she never was and never will be forty'.[53] In Dolly, von Arnim can forgive and even like a number of characteristics that she found difficult in her daughter. She wrote to Liebet, 'Trix is *very* happy & adores her man & from what she told me he does sound good & kind. [. . .] She is still exactly the same & extraordinarily *confus*, seeing all that she has experienced.'[54] However, von Arnim had changed during the war. And, like her narrator, she experiences a sense of *déjà vu* when she returns to her chalet after five years of absence: 'This place is exactly as it was when I left it in August 1914. Not a book out of its place, not a *nippes* [nick-nack]. The clocks all going, the cat purring, Coco smiling, Auguste as wonderful as ever.'[55] In the novel, the friendly dog Coco will appear as Mou-Mou, and the housekeeper Auguste will be renamed Antoine. When the narrator returns to her study, she finds 'there on the table, spotlessly kept clean by Antoine but else not touched, [. . .] all the papers and odds and ends of five years back exactly as I must have left them.'[56] This eerie pre-war still life points towards the broader context of the novel as an elegy for the end of an era as much as for a younger, pre-war self. These gently apocalyptic overtones resonate with the general preoccupation with eschatological models in (post-)war writing.[57]

As a typical characteristic of grief, identification with the lost object[58] creates a situation where the painful feeling of permanent separation from the lost one can, at least temporarily, be suspended. Dolly's propensity for marrying Germans is, of course, shared by von Arnim and her narrator, who points out the obvious: 'Twenty years ago I might have done it myself.'[59] What is more, Dolly had been Henning von Arnim's nickname for his wife. More dramatically, Mansfield experienced intense moments of identification with her dead brother in the year after his death. In her diary, she records nightly visions of him: 'I woke and was he, for quite a long time. I felt my face was his serious, sleepy face. I felt that the lines of my mouth were changed, and I blinked like he did on waking.'[60] Kate Kennedy explains these moments of identification as a form of hysterical mourning in which the ambivalent feelings towards the lost object are partly repressed in an instance of 'becoming' the object and enacting their imagined experiences.[61] Both Kennedy and Mary Burgan explore the 'sexualized link' that the hysteric fantasises 'as a means of crossing an emotional or physical divide'.[62] In their responses to loss, both Mansfield's and von Arnim's mourning 'runs the gamut of object relations from libidinal approach through attachment to the loss of the love-object'.[63] While we can easily trace the sexual element in Mansfield's nightly hauntings, it seems harder to hypostasise such a libidinal note in a mother–daughter relationship. However, in *In the Mountains*, there is a noticeable romantic element between Dolly and the narrator. Acting like a desperate suitor, the narrator confesses, 'I've loved you from the moment I saw you [...] in your funny petticoat.' In response, Dolly and the narrator, 'kissed each other, – not once, but several times; fell, indeed, upon each other's necks'.[64] At a nightly visit to Dolly's bedroom, the narrator points out that Dolly 'had never in her life been in love' with a man.[65] Dolly agrees and kisses her again.

Mansfield's and von Arnim's experiences of identification and haunting can be contextualised within the widespread fascination with the supernatural during the immediate post-war years and the strong spiritual bent in war writing.[66] Beset by Leslie's ghost, Mansfield's writing becomes 'the medium through which she attempts to alleviate her survivor's guilt and grief, or, to use her terminology, to effect her redemption'.[67] Incidentally, redemption is also a trope in von Arnim's literary responses to the war. While *Christine* was at least partly driven by the attempt to alleviate guilt and grief, *In the Mountains* chronicles a spiritual recovery. Von Arnim's narrator has not been devastated by 'only the war' or by a broken heart. With a certain pathos, she confesses, 'I've lost my faith. It has been like losing God, after years of trust in Him.

I believed with all my heart. And I am desolate.'[68] On her birthday, the narrator takes stock of all the ghosts that populate the empty rooms of her Swiss cottage, among them a much-loved brother – perhaps as an oblique reference to Mansfield's loss. However, also on that day, Dolly and her sister appear out of nowhere. Looking rather like ghosts themselves, '[t]hey [. . .] just stood and stared'.[69] The complications of their presence drag the narrator out of the past and into the present. Unwittingly, they act as midwives for the narrator's new post-war self. At the end of the novel, the narrator climbs down from her mountain and returns to life in England. On a not entirely dissimilar note, pregnancy and birth also play a prominent role in Mansfield's New Zealand stories. Tied up as they are in Mansfield's family dynamics, they also indicate the healing and recuperative function of these stories, which shifts the eschatological stage from apocalypse to a new beginning. Burgan asserts that 'Mansfield's writing is a willed resistance to the chaos of hallucinatory dementia' and refers to her 'great New Zealand stories' as a 'therapeutic project'[70] at the end of which Mansfield can 'rejoice "that a man is born into the world"'.[71] Ultimately, writing is a paradoxical form of mourning because '[t]he varied and rich appeal to a traditional eschatology, to a sense of the world coming to an end, shows precisely the opposite'[72] by inspiring acts of narrative creation, including stories of rebirth and healing.

If *In the Mountains* is a fantasy of healing and renewed stability, it is also a fantasy about (re)gaining control. As with many novels by women after the war, in von Arnim's text 'feminine power and vulnerability [. . .] hinge on an almost shamanic power to rescue and to heal'.[73] The novel acts as a counter-narrative to von Arnim's very real feelings of helplessness about Trix. Firstly, the narrator acts as a saviour by giving shelter to Dolly and her sister, thereby providing the refuge that von Arnim could not give Trix during the war. Secondly, she also provides Dolly with the right husband. Dolly's first marriage was the result of her youthful infatuation with Siegfried, a student at her father's boarding school. Still under age, Dolly ran away with him. The episode is reminiscent of an episode from Trix's childhood that von Arnim remembers in 1919:

> Do you remember when you started off alone leaving father & mother & brethren & home, to go keep house for Herr Braun [the tutor]? And I waylaid you at the bottom of the garden & brought you safe back to the flock? It's very like that what you are doing now – but alas I can't waylay you & bring you home now![74]

Only in her novel does von Arnim have the power to bring the errant Dolly home by introducing her to a proper husband in the shape of the narrator's uncle, a dean, who (like Trix's husband) is significantly older than his bride. Unlike Anton von Hirschberg, however, this husband will not be 'an insoluble problem'[75] – he will be the solution by shepherding the lost sheep back into Albion's fold. Unlike Trix, Dolly has never become a German at heart and will easily make a creditable asset to the deanery. Like in other war novels by women, marriage thus 'shores up [...] national stability' and 'stabilises the discourse surrounding Empire, nation, and Edwardian and Georgian ideals'.[76] Once again, von Arnim's choice of genre enables this fiction of healing and renewed stability. Unlike the letter, which embodies the vagaries of war, the diary is a way of regaining control over potentially overwhelming emotions by ordering and 'shaping one's emotional expression [...] by the physical act of writing'.[77]

However, while Mansfield and von Arnim shared the ambivalent feelings of grief, guilt and the spiritual need for recovery as a 'kickoff', aesthetically their literary responses to loss took different forms. While von Arnim's narrator produces, with melancholic irony, a – probably fictitious – fan letter by Henry James as a marker of her pre-war prominence in *In the Mountains*, the much younger and less established Mansfield had no desire to return to the pre-war literary order. In her famous castigation of Virginia Woolf's *Night and Day*, she writes,

> There *must* have been a change of heart. It is really fearful to me the 'settling down' of human beings. I feel in the *profoundest* sense that nothing can ever be the same – that as artists we are traitors if we feel otherwise: we have to take it into account and find new expressions new moulds for our new thoughts and feelings.[78]

Did von Arnim have 'a change of heart' and, if so, how did it manifest in her writing? The new decade coincides with a new phase in her work. *In the Mountains* was von Arnim's last German diary novel. From now on, her stories would be set in England. Her next book, *Vera* (1921), is a marked departure from her previous work and garnered high praise from Mansfield and Murry in particular, who called it a '"Wuthering Heights written by Jane Austen"'.[79] However, 'new expressions' and 'new moulds' did not necessarily lead her in the direction of outright modernist experiment. As Winter notes, '[t]he overlap of languages and approaches between the old and the new, the "traditional" and the "modern", the conservative and the iconoclastic, was apparent both during and after the war' and could also involve a 'self-conscious return to nineteenth-century forms and themes.'[80] We can see this in *Vera*, which transforms the Bluebeard tale into a modern Gothic novel. Similarly, in *In the Mountains* modernist features, such as the use of musical elements like rhythm, repetition and motif,[81] stand in contrast with a rather conventional – and somewhat contrived – ending. Walker calls it 'reminiscent of the finale of an opera',[82] thereby evoking an art form whose stylised use of extravagant emotions is closely associated with the nineteenth century. Von Arnim habitually struggled with her conclusions, since most of her novels raise complex problems that defy easy answers. Accordingly, her more radical novels like *Vera* and *The Pastor's Wife* have disconcerting open endings. With *In the Mountains*, however, von Arnim apparently felt the need to tie her plot into a neat bow. Her biographers Kirsten Jüngling and Brigitte Roßbeck sense a 'certain stylistic blockage' and do not quite know what to make of it.[83] Reading *In the Mountains* as an expression of some of von Arnim's deepest wishes might help us understand the exuberant ending of the book. The contrived set-up, it seems to me, has written into it a tacit acknowledgment of the obvious impossibility of her wish. Moreover, the reconciliatory spirit of the novel can then also be understood as a safe 'potential space' for exploring a mind-set that can afford to look beyond the narrow horizon of anti-German feeling. The novel, we might say, is a rehearsal of forgiveness.

Although Nouri Gana rightly points out that '[m]ourning is a function of the pursuit of happiness',[84] it remains unclear whether the process of grieving can ever be fully completed. Freud remained ambivalent on this point.[85] Indeed, Mansfield's choice of the word 'ruminative' resonates with the repetitive, even obsessive, aspects of mourning. In Mansfield's writing, we can see this reflected in her use of imagery and symbols. Her diaries, for example, record repeated references to dying flies,[86] while her 'lonely suffering surfaces in the images of windows and mirrors used almost obsessively in her fiction'.[87] Meg Jensen argues that 'such compulsive reliance on key tropes signals a private desire unfulfilled, a public episode of mourning that never ends'.[88]

Similarly, von Arnim remained ambivalent about Germany and was clear-sighted about the dangers of Hitler's rise to power. She described estranged mother–daughter relationships in *Love* (1925) and *The Jasmine Farm* (1934), a reflection perhaps on von Arnim's disappointment that none of her surviving daughters took after her in character or artistic sensibility. In spite of this lingering sense of unease, Trix and von Arnim managed to rebuild their relationship – a testament to their shared heritage of resilience and generosity. After she eventually met him, von Arnim also quickly grew to like and trust Anton von Hirschberg. In contrast, Mansfield died in January 1923 without another chance to revisit New Zealand and reconnect with her father after Leslie's death. Without an immediate opportunity for closure and with her health rapidly declining, Mansfield's preoccupation with loss and grief continued. Two of her last stories, 'The Fly' and 'The Canary', are about mourning. While 'The Fly' deals with repression, 'The Canary' is a first-person monologue of open grief and comes to the conclusion that our sadness stays with us, 'it is there, deep down, deep down, part of one, like one's breathing'.[89]

Notes

1. *Letters* 4, p. 252.
2. For an overview, see Jennifer Walker, 'The Beauchamp Connection', in Janka Kascakova and Gerri Kimber, eds, *Katherine Mansfield and Continental Europe: Connections and Influences* (London: Palgrave Macmillan, 2015), pp. 154–68.
3. Jennifer Walker, *Elizabeth of the German Garden: A Literary Journey* (Brighton: Book Guild, 2013), pp. 164, 166.
4. See Isobel Maddison, *Elizabeth von Arnim: Beyond the German Garden* (Farnham: Ashgate, 2013); Jennifer Walker, 'Elizabeth and Her Mountain Garden', *Women: A Cultural Review*, 28 (2017), pp. 40–55; Juliane Römhild, *Authorship and Femininity in the Novels of Elizabeth von Arnim: 'At Her Most Radiant Moment'* (Madison, NJ: Fairleigh Dickinson, 2015).
5. Joy Damousi, 'Gender and Mourning', in Susan R. Grayzel and Tammy M. Proctor, eds, *Gender and the Great War* (Oxford: Oxford University Press, 2017), pp. 211–92 (p. 226).
6. *Letters* 2, p. 54.
7. 19 February 1915. While von Arnim generally wrote in English, her letters during the First World War were in German, presumably to please the German censors. All translations of these letters are mine; unless otherwise stated, they are in a private collection and are reproduced here with kind permission.
8. 16 November 1914. Countess Russell Papers, Huntington Library.
9. Peter Buitenhuis, *The Great War of Words* (Vancouver: University of British Columbia Press, 1987), p. 15. For a detailed discussion of *Christine* in the context of anti-invasion literature, see Maddison, *Beyond the German Garden*.
10. Jenny Hartley, 'Introduction', in Jenny Hartley, ed., *Hearts Undefeated: Women's Writing of the Second World War* (London: Virago, 1994), pp. 1–10 (p. 7).
11. 7 June 1916, in Leslie de Charms [Elizabeth (Liebet) Butterworth], *Elizabeth of the German Garden: A Biography* (London: Heinemann, 1958), p. 179.
12. 22 June 1916.
13. Kathleen Jones, *Katherine Mansfield: The Story-Teller* (Edinburgh: Edinburgh University Press, 2010), pp. 254–5.
14. Von Arnim, in de Charms, p. 179.
15. Alice Cholmondeley [Elizabeth von Arnim], *Christine* (London: Macmillan, 1917), n.p.
16. Adrian Gregory, *The Last Great War: British Society and the First World War* (Cambridge: Cambridge University Press, 2008), pp. 58–9.
17. Isobel Maddison, 'Mansfield's "Writing Game" and World War One', in Gerri Kimber, Todd Martin, Delia da Sousa Correa, Isobel Maddison and Alice Kelly, eds, *Katherine Mansfield and World War One* (Edinburgh: Edinburgh University Press, 2014), pp. 42–54 (p. 47).
18. Cholmondeley, n.p.
19. Cholmondeley, n.p.
20. Carol Acton, *Grief in Wartime: Private Pain, Public Discourse* (Basingstoke: Palgrave Macmillan, 2007), p. 3.

21. Cholmondeley, n.p.
22. Cholmondeley, n.p.
23. Von Arnim's use of pseudonyms, most notably her literary alter ego 'Elizabeth', has been explored elsewhere by Jennifer Walker, Isobel Maddison, myself and others.
24. 26 June 1916.
25. Cholmondeley, p. 54.
26. Cholmondeley, p. 157.
27. Cholmondeley, p. 12.
28. 21 February 1919.
29. Jones, p. 148.
30. *Letters* 1, p. 200 (emphasis added).
31. Acton, p. 13.
32. For an overview of grief and the changing perceptions of the Great War in writing, see Janet S. K. Watson, *Fighting Different Wars: Experience, Memory, and the First World War in Britain* (Cambridge: Cambridge University Press, 2004).
33. Sally Minogue and Andrew Palmer, *The Remembered Dead: Poetry, Memory and the First World War* (Cambridge: Cambridge University Press, 2018), p. 12.
34. Kate Kennedy, '"A Tribute to my Brother": Women's Literature and its Post-war Ghosts', *Journal of War & Culture Studies*, 8 (2015), pp. 7–23 (p. 7).
35. Katherine Mansfield, 'The Fly', in *The Collected Stories of Katherine Mansfield* (Harmondsworth: Penguin, 2007), pp. 353–8 (p. 357).
36. Con Coroneos, 'Flies and Violets in Katherine Mansfield', in Suzanne Raitt and Trudi Tate, eds, *Women's Fiction and the Great War* (Oxford: Clarendon, 1997), pp. 179–218 (p. 214).
37. Avishek Parui, '"For the life of him he could not remember": Post-war Memory, Mourning and Masculinity Crisis in Katherine Mansfield's "The Fly"', in Clare Hanson, Gerri Kimber and Todd Martin, eds, *Katherine Mansfield and Psychology* (Edinburgh: Edinburgh University Press, 2016), pp. 113–26 (p. 122).
38. See Elizabeth von Arnim, 'To Teppi Backe', 22 June 1916, quoted in de Charms, p. 180.
39. For more information on the publication details of *Christine*, see de Charms, pp. 188–9.
40. Martha Hanna, 'A Republic of Letters: The Epistolary Tradition in France during World War I', *The American Historical Review*, 108 (2003), pp. 1338–61 (p. 1348).
41. Toshiaki Komura, 'Modern Elegy and the Fiction and Creation of Loss: Wallace Stevens's "The Owl in the Sarcophagus"', *ELH*, 77 (2010), pp. 45–70 (p. 64). For a discussion of externalisation from a Freudian perspective, see Nouri Gana, *Signifying Loss: Toward a Poetics of Narrative Mourning* (Plymouth: Bucknell, 2011), p. 37.
42. For a full discussion of motherhood and cultural stereotype see Isobel Maddison, 'Complementary Cousins: Constructing the Maternal in the Writing of Elizabeth von Arnim and Katherine Mansfield', in Christoph Ehland and Cornelia Wächter, eds, *Middlebrow and Gender, 1890–1945* (Leiden: Brill, 2016), pp. 79–98.
43. 23 May 1915.
44. 26 June 1916.
45. June 1916.
46. 22 June 1916.
47. 14 April 1919.

48. 19 June 1919.
49. 11 July 1919.
50. 3 July 1919. Anton von Hirschberg had been personal adjutant to Prince Heinrich of Bavaria.
51. Diary entry, 1 July 1923, quoted in Walker, *Elizabeth of the German Garden*, p. 290.
52. 5 August 1919.
53. Anonymous [Elizabeth von Arnim], *In the Mountains* (London: Macmillan, 1920), p. 136.
54. 7 October 1919, Huntington Library.
55. 3 August 1919.
56. Anonymous, pp. 30–1.
57. Jay Winter, *Sites of Memory, Sites of Mourning: The Great War in European Cultural History* (Cambridge: Cambridge University Press, 1995), p. 177.
58. Verena Kast, *Trauern: Phasen und Chancen des Psychischen Prozesses* (Stuttgart: Kreuz, 1982), pp. 67–70.
59. Anonymous, p. 131.
60. John Middleton Murry, ed., *Journal of Katherine Mansfield 1904–1922: Definitive Edition* (London: Constable, 1954), p. 95.
61. Kennedy, p. 19.
62. Kennedy, p. 19. See also J. Lawrence Mitchell's speculations about Leslie's homosexual tendencies as a secret bond between the siblings in 'Katherine Mansfield's War', in *Katherine Mansfield and World War One*, pp. 27–41.
63. Gana, p. 27.
64. Anonymous, p. 185.
65. Anonymous, p. 264.
66. See Johnson as well as Winter.
67. Kennedy, p. 12.
68. Anonymous, p. 209.
69. Anonymous, p. 57.
70. Mary Burgan, *Illness, Gender, and Writing: The Case of Katherine Mansfield* (Baltimore: John Hopkins University Press, 1994), p. 93.
71. Burgan, p. 117.
72. Winter, p. 177.
73. Raitt and Tate, p. 5.
74. 14 August 1919.
75. 27 April 1919.
76. Marie Stern-Peltz, 'The Uncertain War a Century On: The First World War in British and Irish Fiction', in Ann-Marie Einhaus and Katherine Isobel Baxter, eds, *The Edinburgh Companion to the First World War and the Arts* (Edinburgh: Edinburgh University Press, 2017), pp. 15–29 (p. 17).
77. Paul C. Rosenblatt, *Bitter, Bitter Tears: Nineteenth-Century Diarists and Twentieth-Century Grief Theories* (Minneapolis: University of Minnesota Press, 1983), p. 107.
78. *Letters* 1, p. 97.
79. John Middleton Murry, quoted in Walker, *Elizabeth of the German Garden*, p. 247.
80. Winter, p. 227.
81. See Walker, 'Elizabeth and Her Mountain Garden'.
82. Walker, *Elizabeth of the German Garden*, p. 53.
83. Kirsten Jüngling and Brigitte Roßbeck, *Elizabeth von Arnim* (Frankfurt am Main: Fischer, 1996), p. 266 (my translation).

84. Gana, p. 32.
85. Freud's views shifted from 'Mourning and Melancholia' (1917), in which he suggested that an end to grief is possible, to a more circumspect position in 'The Ego and the Id' (1923). Judith Butler bases her claim that 'melancholia grounds the subject', since the ego is constituted by 'an incomplete and irresolvable grief', on Freud's later essay. Judith Butler, *The Psychic Life of Power: Theories in Subjection* (Stanford: Stanford University Press, 1997), p. 23.
86. Coroneos, pp. 212–13.
87. Meg Jensen, 'Getting to Know Me in Theory and Practice: Negotiated Truth and Mourning in Autobiographically Based Fiction', *Literature Compass*, 8 (2011), pp. 941–50 (p. 944).
88. Jensen, p. 945.
89. Mansfield, 'The Canary', in *Collected Stories*, pp. 359–62 (p. 362).

Tracing Garden Networks: Katherine Mansfield and Elizabeth von Arnim

Bonnie Kime Scott

Years ago, by way of introducing the set of women writers included in *The Gender of Modernism*, I constructed a 'tangled mesh' or web that traced the connections made by women writers anthologised in that book.[1] Katherine Mansfield was among those included; Elizabeth von Arnim was not. She could well have been, as numerous writers, sometimes labelled 'middle-brow' or 'pre-modernist' and having currents of feminism in their writing, were selected by my contributing editors. Von Arnim's long list of contacts that constitutes her web of modernists includes Mansfield, John Middleton Murry, E. M. Forster, Hugh Walpole, H. G. Wells, Rebecca West, Arnold Bennett, Max Beerbohm, Bertrand Russell, Virginia Woolf, Ethel Smyth, Rose Macaulay, May Sinclair and Somerset Maugham.

Virginia Woolf reminds us that, when a web

> is pulled askew, hooked up at the edge, torn in the middle, one remembers that these webs are not spun in mid-air by incorporeal creatures, but are the work of suffering human beings and are attached to grossly human things, like health and money and the houses we live in.[2]

Webs are spun from within a creature, and the human–natural interface in the garden offers another worthy subject for comparison in these authors. Great gardens are often attached to great houses, which von Arnim could own and design, and Mansfield could only visit, occasionally dreaming of having a cottage garden of her own one day. The letters of both Mansfield and von Arnim share striking, original images of flowers, to which we will return. I do not claim my horticultural choice for this essay as the most important way of comparing these writers. I am quite partial to their capacity for gender-charged drama and satire, though I need not put these aside, as they are supported frequently by garden settings.[3]

Both of our principal authors played around with their names, and the difference between author and persona becomes a special problem with von Arnim. In her deeply researched biography, Jennifer Walker calls her 'Mary' throughout. They usually called each other Katherine and Elizabeth; I say usually because Mansfield called Elizabeth by her Beauchamp nickname, 'May', when writing to her sisters, and may have done so informally as well.

The gardening network I refer to has wide-ranging, if not global, dimensions. Start with the mobility of von Arnim and Mansfield. As adults, each set down in numerous European locations, leaving reports of gardens, and the national differences among them, on a regular basis. The acacias and roses they refer to in English and Swiss gardens represent worldwide horticultural exchange, fed by centuries of exploration and colonisation. Von Arnim's great house in Pomerania, Nassenheide, had as a former owner an explorer and botanist, Graf Henschel von Donnersmarck, who planted the grounds with seeds brought from far-flung locations. Von Arnim would learn about alpine flora in Switzerland. The flora of New Zealand stayed with Mansfield, enriching a number of her best and some more obscure stories. Occasionally, Mansfield may use an English garden to express her feelings of being a colonial outsider, as is the case when she feels judged by a display of geraniums in a garden near her home in Hampstead.[4] The Wordsworths' daffodils were precious to both of them.

They were also aware of other literary and actual gardeners, such as Ottoline Morrell, Virginia Woolf, Vita Sackville-West and Rebecca West. Woolf writes about many gardens, often recording within them passionate exchanges between women, as do Mansfield and (especially in her letters) von Arnim. Also comparable is the range of gardens in Woolf's œuvre. Woolf might be describing a stately garden such as Ottoline Morrell's Garsington or Vita Sackville-West's at Long Barn, or her characters might stroll through public gardens – Kew Gardens, St James's Park or Kensington Gardens – where she had played as a child. In letters and essays, Woolf takes us to relatively small gardens, the 'miniature Kew' of her aunt, Caroline Emilia Stephen, and the 'magic garden' of Violet Dickinson, represented in an essay notably titled 'Friendship's Gallery'.[5] For her 1928 novel, *Harriet Hume*, Rebecca West constructs a back-garden fantasy of three devoted sisters, improbably bound in childhood by a garland of flowers. They eventually turn into trees that survive the ages. Harriet and her antagonist lover are sent on itineraries through several of London's great public gardens. I find this same range in Mansfield's writing, which takes us on a grand scale to the Botanic Gardens in Wellington, or narrows down to a single exquisite tree, as in 'Bliss'. She appreciated Woolf's rendition of an individual flower or snail at Kew. As I have argued elsewhere, the natural aspect of modernist writing has, until recently, been sorely neglected.[6]

The style in which Mansfield and Woolf evoke the natural world has been found comparable by a number of critics, including Patricia Moran, Angela Smith and myself.[7] Moran finds both using 'the natural world as a non-human frame of reference for their characters'. She says, 'They have similar choices of image and construct rhythmic cadences in their renditions.'[8] Smith remarks on the 'moment of suspension' in both writers, 'which is at once a response to the natural world and an impression of their experience of writing'.[9] Perceptions of nature are altered by psychological traits in traumatised characters in both Mansfield and Woolf. These are modernist qualities that I do not find abundantly in von Arnim's writing, though she does use her gardens to evoke her characters and may be found, as Walker has, organising them into musical movements.[10]

Mansfield and von Arnim remarked to each other and to correspondents on their relative styles. As is well known, von Arnim's remark that a recent publication by her was a 'pretty little story' rankled with Mansfield, and it has been suggested that she wrote 'A Cup of Tea' in revenge.[11] Considering how musical both women were, I find it remarkable that Mansfield said, of *The Enchanted April*, 'the only other person who could have written it is Mozart'.[12] In a review of *Christopher and Columbus*, Mansfield selected more floral metaphors:

> In a world where there are so many furies, it is good to know of someone who goes her own way finding a gay garland and not forgetting to add a sharp-scented spray or two and a bitter herb that its sweetness may not cloy.[13]

Indeed, Walker (who is very aware of gardens in her biography), uses this quotation of floral metaphor to suggest that Mansfield considered herself a kindred spirit to her cousin.[14] However, Mansfield disclosed to artist Dorothy Brett that she did not think that her style was similar to von Arnim's, though she did concede, 'There is a kind of turn in our sentences which is alike but that is because we are worms of the same family.'[15] Worms are, of course, important, well-suited creatures in a garden. As many have noted, after reading *Elizabeth and Her German Garden* at the age of ten, Mansfield seems to have determined that she too could aspire to being a writer.[16] She already had a familial string to pull upon and a licence to escape. Aside from style, they had a number of comparable uses for gardens.

Cultivation of Friendships

Lady Ottoline Morrell was a famous networker of modernists, and a friend and correspondent of both von Arnim and Mansfield. Guests at Garsington Manor included Mansfield, John Middleton Murry, T. S. Eliot, D. H. Lawrence, Dorothy Brett, Aldous Huxley, Bertrand Russell, Lytton Strachey, Leonard and Virginia Woolf, and von Arnim. Morrell's guests often sat and talked in the gardens surrounding the mansion. Scholars have noted the similarity of the basic format of Woolf's 'Kew Gardens' to Mansfield's description of people coming and going through the gardens at Garsington, written in a letter to Morrell.[17] When in England, von Arnim regularly visited great gardens and the Chelsea Flower Show. Early in her relationship with H. G. Wells, she visited and appreciated Jane Wells's garden at Spade House. In 1915, she and her daughter drove to Munstead Wood and took tea with Gertrude Jekyll in her famous demonstration garden, and she also visited Vita Sackville-West.

When looking on the positive side of relationships to other women, Mansfield repeatedly associated them with their gardens. Flowers were common currency among women writers. Perhaps to express her regret at missing a party hosted by Mansfield, Woolf had sent her a gift of columbines, which Mansfield describes appreciatively as 'very early favourites – intricate delicate things'.[18] Mansfield visited the Woolfs' walled garden at Asheham in 1917. There they discussed a draft of Woolf's 'Kew Gardens' sketch, as well as details of the approaching publication of 'Prelude' at the Woolfs' new Hogarth Press. Expressing her appreciation of Asheham to Woolf, Mansfield recalls the rambler roses and writes, echoing Wordsworth, 'It *is* very wonderful & I feel that it will flash upon one corner of my inward eye for ever.' Reporting on the flora in her own neighbourhood, Mansfield describes to Woolf

> a most wonderful greengage light on the tree outside and little white clouds bobbing over the sky like rabbits. And I wish you could see some superb gladioli standing up in my studio very proud & defiant, like Indian [*sic*] braves.[19]

In revising her feelings about Mansfield on her death, Woolf recalls a visit to her in Hampstead. She imagines her 'putting on a white wreath & leaving us, called away; made dignified, chosen'.[20]

During her years at the Chalet Soleil in Switzerland, von Arnim visited Mansfield's nearby lodgings on a regular basis, often bringing gifts of fruits and flowers. Of these visits Mansfield writes imaginatively to Brett that von Arnim

> looked like a garden walking, of asters, late sweet peas, stocks and always petunias. She herself wore a frock like a spider web, a hat like a berry – and gloves that reminded me of a thistle in seed [...] I have gathered Elizabeth's frocks to my bosom as if they were part of her flowers.

Flowers are transported to a dress, seen also as a 'spider web', to facilitate a sensual embrace.[21] Flowers also constitute an important part of the women's conversations and bonding. Again, to Brett, Mansfield recalls

> talking about flowers until we were really drunk [...] She – describing 'a certain very exquisite rose, single, pale yellow with coral tipped petals' and so on. I kept thinking of little curly blue hyacinths and white violets and the bird cherry.[22]

For Mansfield, von Arnim's 'love of flowers is really her great charm'. She also opines to Brett that 'no man loves flowers as a woman *can*'.[23] This floral distinction between genders is something she also shares in a letter to von Arnim, 'Breathes there a man [...] who understands a woman's love of flowers?'[24] By the end of the Summer in 1921, Mansfield would thank von Arnim for her gifts: 'I have a whole petunia and nasturtium summer to thank you for' and assures her that she has '"planted out" some of my petunias into a story so they may live a little longer'.[25] Von Arnim's shared petunias are lavished with detail and imagination as Mansfield goes on to picture the challenge of painting them to her artist friend Brett:

> I believe you have been painting petunias – your purple velvety ones. Were they? [...] But they must be difficult, because in spite of the weight of colour there's a transparent light shining through look in them. The look one imagines the fruits had in Aladdin's orchard.[26]

Catalogues

Making up lists may not seem the most complex of writing projects, but James Joyce found it a technique worthy of modernism – a long catalogue of trees being among his most celebrated in *Ulysses*, and rivers accumulating in great numbers in *Finnegans Wake*. In 'Prelude', Mansfield's character, Kezia, investigates vast gardens around the family's new home. Through her, a generous catalogue of plants, their names learned perhaps from her grandmother, is presented. Avoiding a scary tangle of dark native trees on one side of her path, she explores a more organised, domesticated set of plants in a boxwood border: variously coloured camellias 'with flashing leaves', white lilac, and roses in various states and sizes:

gentlemen's button-hole roses [. . .] far too full of insects to hold under anyone's nose, pink monthly roses with a ring of fallen petals [. . .] cabbage roses on thick stalks, moss roses, always in bud, smooth beauties opening curl on curl, red ones, so dark they seemed to turn black as they fell, and a certain exquisite cream kind with a slender stem and bright scarlet leaves.

The discoveries go on to fairy bells, geraniums, verbena, 'pelargoniums with velvet eyes and leaves like moths' wings', mignonette, pansies, daisies and 'little tufty plants she had never seen before'.[27] The list mixes more formal names of plants with colloquialisms such as 'gentlemen's button-hole roses' – apparently a common flower for boutonnieres. The child does more than list types of flowers. She offers dynamic descriptions involving light and decay, as well as adjectives and similes that merge plants with the wings and eyes of animals. She thinks about what it would be like to sniff one that is full of insects. She makes a small assemblage to present as a gift to her grandmother.

While Mansfield had her grandmother's interest in flowers, von Arnim seems to have enjoyed gardening with her father, once he turned to that pursuit during one of the itinerant Beauchamp family's longer sojourns in England. It was she who ran up bills for bulbs, which he tolerated. Probably she selected from printed catalogues, as did other gardeners, including Leonard and Virginia Woolf. Von Arnim would create a number of ambitious gardens in her lifetime, starting at Nassenheide in Pomerania, and including a brief residence at Blue Hayes in Devon, where she moved in 1908. By the 1910s she was building and planting the Chalet Soleil in Switzerland, whose mountainous position still permitted terraced gardens, maintained by her old gardener from Nassenheide. The 1930s found her residing at Mas des Roses in the South of France.

Lists of flowers and panoramic tours of gardens are an important staple of von Arnim's novels and her diary. No doubt they delivered vicarious pleasure to her readership. In her fiction, she takes us to places that she herself has visited or where she has resided, though the reactions to gardens presented in her works, of course, come through personas. Preferring the out-of-doors to household duties, the protagonist of *Elizabeth and Her German Garden* delights in relating a list of established plantings found when the family occupies a long-neglected family home. The extended account, which also situates various plantings in relation to the house, befits a book-length narrative:

The dandelions carpeted the three lawns, – they used to be lawns, but have long since blossomed out into meadows filled with every sort of pretty weed, – and under and among the groups of leafless oak and beeches were blue hepaticas, white anemones, violets, and celandines in sheets [. . .]. Then when the anemones went, came a few stray periwinkles and Solomon's Seal, and all the bird-cherries blossomed in a burst. And then, before I had got used to the joy of their flowers against the sky, came the lilacs – masses and masses of them, in clumps on the grass, with other shrubs and trees by the side of walks, and one great continuous bank of them half a mile long right past the west front of the house, away down as far as one could see, shining glorious against a background of firs. When that time came, and when, before it was over, the acacias all blossomed too, and four great clumps of pale, silvery-pink peonies flowered under the south widows.[28]

Less engaging than this (though of historical and cultural interest) is the list of roses she selects once she begins designing her own garden on the grounds. The length of the list and ambitiousness of the project bespeak the considerable resources of the gardener. Many of the specific names of roses selected by their hybridisers evoke nobility and privilege: Viscountess Folkestone (a tea rose dating to 1886), Duke of Teck (a hybrid dating to 1877), Comtesse Riza du Park (a tea rose dating to 1876), Hon. Edith Gifford (a tea rose dating to 1882) – all still available as vintage roses. One has only to consult a publication such as *The Journal of Horticulture and Cottage Gardener* (7 July 1892) to find similar lists of roses displayed in the show of the National Rose Society in the Crystal Palace. Roses remain a staple of von Arnim's gardening.

Since *Elizabeth and Her German Garden* is constructed like a journal, providing occasional dates, it is possible for von Arnim to list what is in flower in September versus May and to make plans for future planting. Echoing Keats, she reports on 15 September: 'This is the month of quiet days, crimson creepers, and blackberries; of mellow afternoons in the ripening garden; of tea under the acacias instead of the too shady beeches; of wood-fires in the library in the chilly evenings.'[29] She plans her next hundred rose bushes, favouring the Viscountess Folkestones and listing ones that have fared poorly. Von Arnim's German garden may well have been more elaborate in fiction than actuality. E. M. Forster, one of the best known of a series of tutors brought to the family estate at Nassenheide, looked in vain for the garden he had read about.

Von Arnim the author returned to sequential catalogues as a framing device for *The Enchanted April*, a best-selling novel, composed during the period when both she and Mansfield were residing on the same Swiss mountain (1921–2). The principal locale, an Italian castle set on the Mediterranean, is based on her own rental of a *castello* in Portofino. Once again, in this novel a garden provides an escape from indoor domesticity as two young women lease the medieval castle at San Salvatore for the month of April. Week by week, the author provides an inventory of what is in bloom. On first inspecting the grounds, Mrs Wilkins and Mrs Arbuthnot find:

> The wisteria was tumbling itself in its excess of life, its prodigality of flowering; and where the pergola ended the sun blazed on scarlet geraniums, bushes of them, and nasturtiums in great heaps, and marigolds so brilliant that they seemed to be burning, and red and pink snapdragons, all outdoing each other in bright, fierce colour. The ground behind these flaming things dropped away in terraces to the sea, each terrace a little orchard, where among the olives grew vines on trellises, and fig-trees, and peach-trees, and cherry-trees. The cherry-trees and peach-trees were in blossom, – lovely showers of white and deep rose-colour among the trembling delicacy of the olives [. . .]. And beneath these trees were groups of blue and purple irises, and bushes of lavender, and grey, sharp cactuses [. . .]. [T]he periwinkles looked exactly as if they were being poured down each side of the steps – and flowers that grow only in borders in England, proud flowers keeping themselves to themselves over there [. . .] were being jostled by small, shining things like dandelions and daisies [. . .].[30]

Here we have not just an escape into a garden, offering a great variety of plantings and even weeds, but a place redolent with scent, its vitality owed to a looser order of things than the Englishwomen found in their lives at home.

Issues of Class, Gender and Nationality

For the main character of *Elizabeth and Her German Garden*, the garden provides an escape from the indoor responsibilities of the German countrywoman of means and from the Germanic husband she humorously labels 'The Man of Wrath'. Conventions of class and gender dictate that a male gardener perform the actual planting, though Elizabeth tries a few covert motions in that direction. An end result of turning the planting over to a German gardener is neatly laid-out ranks of flowers, rather than the more random placement she, and the typical English cottage gardener under the influence of Gertrude Jekyll, might prefer. She vows to offer more directions to the gardener in the future, merging grass with flowers and massing them for effect. Her decision to plant out tea roses, rather than wintering them in a greenhouse, as she claims was the custom in Germany, demonstrates greater independence in this gardener and continues her resistance to national norms. Indeed, she seems capable of writing the sorts of gardening columns and books that became a staple of Vita Sackville-West.

Class and gender also enter the castle garden at San Salvatore in *The Enchanted April*. The castle has an English owner, but the appearance and functioning of the place are the accomplishment of its Italian gardener, Domenico. Mrs Wilkins and Mrs Arbuthnot are not wealthy or of the nobility, and their escape to a beautiful garden is a rare privilege. The advertisement she reads allows the non-assuming Mrs Wilkins to step outside her sense of limited allowance and privilege. It suggests that the castle is 'for those who appreciate wisteria and sunshine', which she is confident makes her eligible.[31] For greater affordability, the women advertise for two others to share the rent. This yields an elderly widow, Mrs Fisher, who has financial resources but has been leading a restrained, sequestered life in a dark, joyless house. The second is a Lady Caroline, who has seen an abundance of grand gardens and uses the month in Italy as a way of escaping people of her own class, constantly grasping for her attention.

The change of setting is transformational for all involved, and particularly for Mrs Wilkins – called Lotty, as the women become more intimate. She shares the exuberant love of place that von Arnim had for her German garden. She also has a visionary capacity (like West's later creation, Harriet Hume). She sees people in places, predicting that they will be there, and she leaps from one idea to the next, escaping the logic of Mrs Fisher, who worries that Lotty might be dotty. Lotty is untroubled by the older woman's territoriality, when Mrs Fisher claims several rooms of her own inside the castle. She is equally unperturbed by the self-sequestering of Lady Caroline, who secretes herself in a hidden corner of the garden. Lotty somehow knows that, in this setting, they will change. She explores more widely than the others, going up the hillside, where primroses can be found, and down to the pine trees by the shore. Indeed, von Arnim's landscapes go beyond gardens into forests and vistas – a result, perhaps, of her fondness for hiking. Lotty is also freer than other characters in her expression of affection. She kisses the other women without embarrassment. Class privilege recedes. Lady Caroline, especially, bonds with her, and Mrs Arbuthnot gains healing insight into herself from what Lotty has to say. Mrs Fisher eventually recognises the promise of her friendship, and Lotty is committed to sustaining that need back in England, after the month is over.

While the novel asserts the women's rights to managing money and taking a holiday of their own, it falls short of liberation. Mrs Wilkins remains a Mrs Wilkins, though a happier, more vital one. One of her early visions, once she is in Italy, is of Mr Wilkins and Mr Arbuthnot arriving at the castle, which indeed they do. There is some reassessment by all involved in order for this to go well – most notably in the self-confidence of Mrs Wilkins and her growing capacity not to take her self-serving lawyer husband too seriously. The arrival of a wealthy romantic prospect for Lady Caroline (in the form of the castle's owner) solidifies both privilege and heterosexuality, however.

Mansfield's stories in her early collection, *In a German Pension* (1911), allude to German gardens, attitudes toward the nobility, and perceived differences with the English. A young Anglophone woman observer is the unwilling audience for remarks on the traits of her supposed nationality. In 'Frau Fischer', she turns from a tedious denunciation of the attitudes of the English toward their bodies to 'look out over the garden full of wall flowers and standard rose trees growing stiffly like German bouquets' (p. 700). Attitudes toward nobility and romance are satirised by the same English observer in 'The Sister of the Baroness'. Residents of the pension are in awe of the visitor identified in the 'Baroness' title. A would-be poet's verses compare her to a doe springing in the fields. A Frau Doktor is impressed by the noblewoman's accounts of proposals from young men of exalted birth. These qualify with her as the height of romance, in which 'youth ... is like a wild rose'. It is a delicacy she finds lacking in young Englishwomen, whom she describes humorously 'exposing your legs on cricket fields and breeding dogs in your back garden' (p. 695). Seeking to write love poetry of her own, the Englishwoman takes refuge behind the summer-house in a spot where a 'great bush of purple lilac grew'. Failing with her verses, she comically manipulates the rose metaphor, 'Did my wild rose then already trail in the dust?' (p. 696). From her secluded location, she detects that the sister of the Baroness is also being courted by a young student of no great nobility or romantic style. The final blow to German pretence comes, of course, when the Baroness herself arrives and identifies the woman as the daughter of her dressmaker.

An early prose sketch by Mansfield, 'In the Botanical Gardens', published in an Australian journal in 1907, contrasts the enclosed, linear structure of the formal bedded-out plantings at the entrance to the Wellington Botanical Garden with the native vegetation just over the hill. The first evidence of an alternative to the orthodox banality of the carpet bedding comes in a row of cabbage trees of various heights, glimpsed over a hedge. When young, these endemic trees appear like dark green or purple balls about a foot in diameter on individual sticks; to the observer, a row of them might well resemble the musical notes of a staff – a metaphor that comes naturally to the musical author (a trait she shared with von Arnim). She is lured away from the botanical specimens of rhododendrons and magnolias, leaving behind pansies, forget-me-nots and anemones, into a forest of endemic fern trees. Here she imagines the dancing shadows and lost music of the native, displaced population.

Mansfield's mature, nuanced short story, 'The Garden Party', is keenly sensitive to class, her observations supported by evidence from the garden. The Sheridan home sits high among flowers and lawns, mowed in the early morning by the gardener. The narrator tells us that 'They' (meaning the Sheridans) 'understood that roses are the only flowers that impress people at garden-parties; the only flowers that everybody is certain of knowing', and thankfully hundreds are in bloom (p. 245). While her sisters concern themselves with newly washed hair and frocks, and her mother seems very concerned about bonnets, Laura, being the 'artistic one', is sent outside to determine where a marquee should be erected. In a scene that prepares for Laura's visit to the humble cottage of a carter accidentally killed on the day of the party, she finds herself negotiating her relationship to the workmen. She strives to be business-like while still holding a slice of bread and butter, and wonders if their language is respectful enough. But she follows their advice on where to place the marquee for, as they put it, the greatest 'bang slap in the eye' (p. 247). The lily lawn is rejected. Laura keeps to herself a regret that the chosen location will block the view of the karaka trees – indigenous New Zealand laurels bearing poisonous berries and a Maori name. She is partial to these trees for both aesthetic and imaginative reasons:

> They were so lovely with their broad, gleaming leaves and their clusters of yellow fruit. They were like trees you imagined growing on a desert island, proud, solitary, lifting their leaves and fruit to the sun in a kind of silent splendor. (p. 247)

We might well infer that she identifies with their imagined independence from the cultivated garden. We read another slight reference to the plantings as Laura notices one of the workmen pinch a sprig of lavender, smell the scent, and reach for an envelope to make a sketch. The sensitive gestures separate him from the men and 'silly boys' in her immediate circle, 'all the fault of these absurd class distinctions', she thinks (p. 247).

Back in the house, Laura is consulted on aesthetics once again and she experiences another of the emotional swings in the story. Her mother asks her approval about the placement of an extravagant number of pink canna lilies (cultivars of American tropical origin) that she has ordered from the florist. Laura's reaction to them, like that of other young female characters in Mansfield's writing, is one of sensual merger: '"Oh Sadie!" said Laura, and the sound was like a little moan. She crouched down to warm herself at the blaze of the lilies; she felt they were in her fingers, on her lips, growing in her breast' (p. 249). While Laura gives her mother a mild admonishment over her promise not to interfere in party plans, she is also affectionate: 'She put her arm round her mother's neck and gently, very gently, she bit her mother's ear' (p. 250).

Perceiver and Perceived

Mansfield had mixed feelings about Woolf's taste for abstraction and her tendency to turn into the flower or bird she was evoking, for not seeing things 'humanly'.[33] She did, however, admire Woolf's magnifying focus on a flowerbed at Kew: disregarding the humans present, 'she shows us the flower-bed, growing, expanding in heat and light, filling a whole world'.[34] In her novels, von Arnim might occasionally pause on fruit trees in bloom, or a tall flower, in the course of her panoramas. Mansfield was more apt to linger upon individual plants and flowers, noting the exchange of a carnation between two girls, or connecting the perceiver to the perceived, occasionally merging the two, as she does with Laura and the canna lilies.

In Mansfield's story 'Bliss', Bertha Young is preparing to give a dinner party. She is overcome with a giddy feeling of happiness when she looks at a pear tree in full bloom in her back garden. She also anticipates one of her guests with particular delight. Bertha 'had fallen in love with her as she always did fall in love with beautiful women who had something strange about them' (p. 95). Looking at the 'slender pear tree in fullest and richest bloom', it becomes a 'symbol of her own life' (p. 96). After dinner, both she and that guest, Pearl, look at the pear tree, which seems to quiver and stretch toward a silver moon. It is an expansive, scintillating vision and Bertha senses a common emotion. But, as she so frequently does with relationships, Mansfield brings this one to a crashing fall when Bertha overhears Pearl planning a lovers' meeting with her husband. The end of the story has been variously interpreted, but as Bertha looks once more at the tree, it 'was as lovely as ever and as full of flowers and still' (p. 105). Is it as indifferent to human presence as Woolf's flowers at Kew? Does the tree not stretch sensually upward, and no longer serve as symbolic of her? Or (like gardens in von Arnim's fiction that we have examined), is it a constant, something in nature to stabilise her, particularly compared to the betrayal she has experienced? Here Mansfield challenges us to think how we relate to and make use of the garden.

For both authors, gardens have character and beg to be described. While they may reflect national design, the plants themselves often defy boundaries and are suggestive of other creatures. Gardens exist to the side of the androcentric, male-dominated spaces and expectations. They have the potential to unite women. And they are places of renewing and becoming.

Notes

1. Bonnie Kime Scott, 'Introduction', in *The Gender of Modernism* (Bloomington: Indiana University Press, 1990), p. 10.
2. Virginia Woolf, *A Room of One's Own* (Orlando, FL: Harcourt, 2005), pp. 41–2.
3. When offered as a keynote address to a conference on von Arnim and Mansfield, this essay was presented alongside the great Huntington Garden in Pasadena, California.
4. *Notebooks* 1, p. 20.
5. Virginia Woolf, 'Friendship's Gallery', in *The Essays of Virginia Woolf*, ed. Ellen Hawkes: Vol. 6: *1933–1941*, ed. Stuart N. Clarke (London: Hogarth Press, 2011), p. 526.
6. Bonnie Kime Scott, *In the Hollow of the Wave: Virginia Woolf and Modernist Uses of Nature* (Charlottesville: University of Virginia Press, 2012), pp. 2–3.
7. Bonnie Kime Scott, *Natural Connections: Virginia Woolf and Katherine Mansfield*, Bloomsbury Heritage Series (London: Cecil Woolf, 2015).
8. Patricia Moran, *Word of Mouth: Body Language in Katherine Mansfield and Virginia Woolf* (Charlottesville: University of Virginia Press, 1996), p. 9.
9. Angela Smith, *Katherine Mansfield and Virginia Woolf: A Public of Two* (Oxford: Clarendon Press, 1999), p. 2.
10. Jennifer Walker, *Elizabeth of the German Garden: A Literary Journey: A Biography of Elizabeth von Arnim* (Brighton: Book Guild, 2013), pp. 48–9.
11. Karen Usborne, *'Elizabeth': The Author of Elizabeth and Her German Garden* (London: Bodley Head, 1986), p. 241.
12. Quoted in Usborne, p. 256.
13. Katherine Mansfield, 'Two Novels of Worth', in John Middleton Murry, ed., *Novels and Novelists by Katherine Mansfield* (New York: Knopf, 1930), p. 9.
14. Walker, pp. 48–9.
15. Quoted in Usborne, p. 234.
16. See Isobel Maddison, '"Worms of the Same Family": Elizabeth von Arnim and Katherine Mansfield', in *Elizabeth von Arnim: Beyond the German Garden* (Farnham: Ashgate, 2013), pp. 85–104.
17. Clare Hanson finds the connection obscure. See Hanson, ed., *The Critical Writings of Katherine Mansfield* (Basingstoke: Macmillan, 1987), p. 134, n. 25.
18. *Letters* 2, p. 323.
19. *Letters* 1, p. 327.
20. Anne Olivier Bell and Andrew McNeillie, eds, *The Diary of Virginia Woolf*, 5 vols (San Diego: Harcourt Brace Jovanovich, 1977–84), vol. 2, p. 226.
21. *Letters* 4, p. 287.
22. *Letters* 4, p. 260.
23. *Letters* 4, p. 260.
24. *Letters* 4, p. 267.
25. *Letters* 4, p. 267.
26. *Letters* 4, p. 260.
27. Mansfield, 'Prelude', in *The Collected Short Stories of Katherine Mansfield* (London: Penguin, 1984), p. 239. All further references to Mansfield's stories are to this edition and are cited parenthetically in the text.

28. Elizabeth von Arnim, *Elizabeth and Her German Garden* (London: Virago, 1985), pp. 8–9.
29. Von Arnim, *Elizabeth and Her German Garden*, p. 64.
30. Elizabeth von Arnim, *The Enchanted April* (New York: Penguin, 2015), p. 28.
31. Von Arnim, *The Enchanted April*, p. 1.
32. *Letters* 2, pp. 333–4.
33. Mansfield, 'A Short Story', in Hanson, p. 54.

'Our own little grain of truth'

Angela Smith

When Katherine Mansfield was living in Menton to protect her fragile health from a British winter in November 1920, she was inevitably preoccupied by mortality. She wrote on 4 November to John Middleton Murry, who as editor of the *Athenaeum* had to remain in London:

> If the Last Trump ever *did* sound – would it frighten US? [. . .] (I told poor old L. M. [her companion Ida Baker] yesterday that after I died to PROVE there was no immortality I would send her a coffin worm in a matchbox. She was gravely puzzled).[1]

It is a wonderful paradox, proving that there is no immortality by posthumously sending a matchbox; the pun on 'gravely' is characteristically succinct and dry. Mansfield's capacity to laugh without compromising her awareness of the imminence of death permeates her last stories. She read and admired two newly published, sardonically witty novels about death at the end of her life, both of them manipulating the mobile border between comedy and tragedy – R. O. Prowse's *A Gift of the Dusk*, published in 1920, and her cousin Elizabeth von Arnim's *Vera*, published in 1921.

Throughout her life, we can see Mansfield's reading as a trigger, not to imitate or emulate, but to push her imagination further into uncompromisingly new directions. In the context of her reading firstly *A Gift of the Dusk* and then *Vera*, it is intriguing to see her stories treading similar triangular borderlines between the comic, the Gothic grotesque and the tragic. It is possible to argue that both novels and Mansfield's late stories explore their characters' traumatic experience by extended representation of their minds' dark places, though Prowse is much less fluent in doing so than Mansfield and von Arnim. The novels already mentioned and the stories to be discussed here, 'The Stranger' and

'The Daughters of the Late Colonel', have in common a controlling male figure. In *A Gift of the Dusk* it is generalised as a hotel manager/warder persona; in the others it is an autocratic husband or father. Such physical and psychological control can induce abjection in its object. Julia Kristeva describes it like this:

> There looms, within abjection, one of those violent, dark revolts of being, directed against a threat that seems to emanate from an exorbitant outside or inside, ejected beyond the scope of the possible, the tolerable, the thinkable. It lies there, quite close, but it cannot be assimilated.[2]

That this revolt can be communicated to a reader through comedy intertwined with the grotesque and the tragic is the focus of this essay.

The way in which Mansfield (Fig. 3) uses her reading as a trigger is clear in her response to Prowse's novel, an account of the tubercular protagonist's stay in a Swiss sanatorium. In a letter to Murry written on 1 October 1920, Mansfield asks if he read the book before he sent it to her for review. This is her response to it:

> A simply terrible book – awful – ghastly! And about as good as it could be [...]. One's heart goes out to anyone who has *faced* an experience as he has done [...]. It is, after all, the only treasure heirloom we have to leave – our own little grain of truth.[3]

Murry had not read it; as he writes in his introduction to a later edition of the book published in 1932, he was afraid to read it at the time because 'I knew the *truth* too well.'[4] Reading it after Mansfield's death, he remembers

> how the time came when Katherine Mansfield entered the glass revolving doors of just such another Swiss 'hotel', and as I stood with her on the balcony the look of a trapped animal came into her eyes – bewilderment, anguish, and fear – and we went away. (p. 11)

It is easy to see how she might overrate the novel, as it spoke so directly to her own situation and terror of medical institutions, but, even without the immediate threat of the Grim Reaper at one's shoulder, reading it is a compelling experience.

All we learn about the narrator, Stephen, is that he has worked in an office and lived with his sister in London, but we meet him as he arrives in the Alps at Château d'Or. There is an almost hallucinatory sense of entrapment for the character and the reader in the golden palace; the reiteration of the details of the sanatorium's brightly striped blinds, its balconies, bamboo tables with glass tops and china crachoirs, encodes the situation of its patients, putting a colourful veneer on a terrifying state. The building represents a flourishing post-war business

Fig. 3 Portrait of Katherine Mansfield, 1921. PAColl-6826–1–20–2. John Middleton Murry Collection, Alexander Turnbull Library, Wellington, New Zealand.

opportunity: 'Most of the larger hotels or sanatoriums [...] appear at well-spaced intervals on the mountain-side in a kind of ascending chain [...]. The sanatoriums, all of which face south, stand well back from the road, in grounds that seem unfinished' (p. 35). The narrator's irony pervades his portrayal of the guests, who behave as if they are on holiday but are, in fact, in a strange kind of bondage:

> But we live by appointed hours, and to leave the hotel at a wrong time, or even to be seen wandering in a corridor, may attract unpleasant attention. The surveillance is tactful and not too obtrusive, but a hand that is firm is laid on us, if we transgress too often. We hear of patients who have been sent away. (p. 33)

The hotel has a curious atmosphere; the fear of being sent away is like that of being expelled from boarding school by the invisible headmaster for bad behaviour. The inhabitants become restless, though the narrator reasons with himself:

> The institution makes no pretence to philanthropy, and why shouldn't it be made to pay? If the dividends depend on keeping down the percentage of failures, so much the better for us. What could be less to our interest than to contribute to the company's loss? And yet – and yet.... It's queer to think that tuberculosis is a thing which has money in it. (p. 33)

The plot is minimal. Stephen meets a woman, Mary Rolls, whom he comes to love, though since any physical encounter is likely to provoke a fit of coughing they rarely even touch each other. She is dying while he begins to recover. Life and death follow their course in the sanatorium, but Mary is more astute than Stephen about the business opportunity for entrepreneurs provided by a medical crisis. She realises that mortally ill patients are bundled out just before they die to maintain the sanatorium's profit margins. A patient, Mrs Meakin, is very sick and as Mary says, '"They don't like you to die here"':

> 'They wish to keep down the percentage of failures. It was brought home to me last night. I came to see it very plainly. The statistics are the vital thing. And it's what you would expect, of course. These sanatoriums are commercial speculations, and there is as much competition between them as between ordinary hotels. The syndicate which owns our sanatorium has to compete with the others, and Château d'Or has to compete with hosts of similar places. Switzerland itself has to compete with other parts of the world. The open-air treatment has become an important industry. It has become an important investment. Doctors and all kinds of people have put their money in it, and its ramifications are endless. Any number of persons earn their living by it. This is why it is never properly criticised. Nothing that has much money in it ever is properly criticised.' (pp. 147–8)

'Our own little grain of truth'

The macabre sense that all the patients in the Château d'Or are watching each other, assessing each other's chances and gossiping about them, heightens the weird atmosphere. The narrator's analytical intelligence enables him to pinpoint their plight, commenting that it might be better if they were more ill, as most of them seem like sun-tanned holidaymakers, able to stroll to the town, buy postcards, flirt and maintain a genteel exterior. The truth behind this grotesque masquerade enacted by the inhabitants of the ironically named golden palace is revealed by the narrator:

> Our lot is not quite the lot of the exile, and is not quite the lot of the condemned; it is the lot of the exile, and it is the lot of the condemned, but its distinctive colouring comes from the fact that it is also the lot of the outcast. We are persons who have been put away. (p. 128)

As he sardonically says, it is a little shocking to mention the fact that they do not need a St Lazarus rattle, used as a warning by lepers, but they can pollute others; they are abjects. It is easy to see why Mansfield would engage with the perspicacity of this aspect of the novel, remembering, for instance, her bitter observation about Murry, when she returned from France clearly emaciated by illness but longing to see him. She drafted a letter to him on 5 May 1918, saying, 'you put your handkerchief to your lips & turned away from me [. . .] I have never felt quite the same since.'[5]

What Mansfield most admired about the book is clear in her review of it. Prowse's Stephen, as she expresses it, has realised what it is not to be in the world any more and has attended his own funeral. In the review she writes:

> [Y]ou really won't know, as the last man swings on the box and the horses break into a decent trot, whether it is an adorable wet day – with the sky a waterspout, a soft roaring in the trees, and the first jonquils shaking with flower – or an adorable fine day – when just to walk in the sun and shade is enough. And all your belongings, your cold clothes, all the things you arrange so carefully and love to look at and handle – they will be free once more. Your books . . . the library of the late. . . . Other fingers will rub out the marking under that line.[6]

Poignantly when he wrote his introduction to the 1932 edition of the novel, Murry was looking at passages that Mansfield, herself now dead of tuberculosis, had underlined in Prowse's book. Though Prowse's prosaic language seems leaden in comparison with the sensuous evocation of the weather in Mansfield's review, he certainly invites the reader to grasp that '[a]ll delight in To-day is gone, when you know you have no To-morrow' and makes us recognise the loss of comfort in familiar objects, 'that feeling of severance, of a loss of possession, that constant taking of leave, which has haunted my secret thought' (p. 41; p. 190).

Prowse's Stephen maintains a sceptical distance from the general life of the sanatorium, remarking of a conventional Englishwoman that 'the ending of her days in the promiscuous cosmopolitanism of Château d'Or is a pitiable and malign incongruity' (p. 238). 'Promiscuous cosmopolitanism' is a brilliant phrase – the sanatorium, like smart Swiss hotels, is cosmopolitan because people who can afford it come here from all over Europe, and it is promiscuous not in the sexual sense, as a hotel might be, but because these people are indiscriminately thrown together by the accident of their illness. This dark wit is accompanied by a psychological shift that transforms his ability to live with his disease:

> [The silence] impressed me not only as very real and very near, but as very natural, very friendly, very homelike: I had a conception of it as of some other Self that was waiting to bear me company. I found I could commune with it almost as one communes with a friend. After which I had a conception more intimate still: I had a sense of my oneness with it. I had an intensified sense of living, as if I had entered into mystic relation with that inner permanence and continuity of things. (p. 159)

We are, of course, familiar with the trope of the Secret Self in Mansfield's work, but just at the time that she is reviewing Prowse's novel we find her taking it a step further, in a letter to Murry written on 18 October 1920:

> I have felt very often lately as though the silence had some meaning beyond these signs these intimations [...]. We resist – we are terribly frightened. The little boat enters the dark fearful gulf and our only cry is to escape – 'put me on land again'. But its useless. Nobody listens. The shadowy figure rows on. One ought to sit still and uncover ones eyes.

Part of this revelation is that '[e]verything has its shadow'.[7] The new impetus that uncovering her eyes gives to her writing is the awareness of the shadow in the stories written immediately after she read *A Gift of the Dusk*. She wrote the review of Prowse's novel in mid-October 1920, and finished 'The Stranger' on 2 November and 'The Daughters of the Late Colonel' by 13 December. Both deal with death, with the writer uncovering her eyes to see the shadow, and new ways of rendering it in fiction.

Like the little boat entering the dark, fearful gulf in the letter, 'The Stranger' is permeated by an ominous sense of time and tides: 'But the dusk came slowly, spreading like a slow stain over the water.'[8] The officious and controlling Mr. Hammond is waiting at Auckland harbour for his wife to return from a long visit to their daughter in Europe. He is depicted ironically as bombastic and managing but he is vulnerable. His hands shake with fear as he watches the ship coming into its berth, but he is reassured when he meets his wife; the rhythm of the sentences enacts his ability to breathe normally again after the tension of waiting for her: 'But Hammond didn't see her. He only felt that she was looking at him and that there was no need to worry about anything. She was here to look after things. It was all right. Everything was' (p. 245).

Mr Hammond has been established as a pompous figure of fun and he remains bullying and arrogant, but as the dark places in his mind begin to be revealed, the mood shifts. He longs for a passionate response from his wife when they are finally reunited and alone, but she kisses him 'as she always kissed him, as though the kiss – how could he describe it? – confirmed what they were saying, signed the contract. But that wasn't what he wanted' (p. 248). The inter-penetration of love and death in the story is much more subtle than it is in *A Gift of the Dusk*; in his anguished longing for his wife to respond to his aroused state, he is horrified to discover that he has what he sees as a rival. A young man with a heart condition on board the ship 'died in Janey's arms. She – who'd never – never once in all these years – never on one single solitary occasion –' (p. 249). We are invited to read the relationship through this unfinished sentence; her dutiful but chilly response to his needy sexual ardour contrasts, as he sees it, with a willingness to embrace a dying man. There is a Gothic element in Hammond's momentary collapse:

> Cold crept up his arms. The room was huge, immense, glittering. It filled his whole world. There was the great blind bed, with his coat flung across it like some headless man saying his prayers [. . .]. No; he mustn't think of it. Madness lay in thinking of it. No, he wouldn't face it. (p. 249)

It is for him a glimpse of abjection; he is beside himself, chilled, unable to control himself, with an image of his abjected self, headless, beside him. He thinks he cannot face what has happened to him, but the reader realises that he has faced it. The transferred epithet, 'blind bed', suggests a dawning awareness of his own unwillingness to see and acknowledge his wife's attitude to him. The final line of the story reveals that, for Hammond, the dead man will always be the secret sharer in the marriage, present in their daily lives: 'They would never be alone together again' (p. 249). The stranger of the title is not necessarily the young man who died on board ship. It is also perhaps the abjected self, which will live with Hammond for the rest of his life.

The only comedic element in this story is its dark irony as it mocks Mr Hammond's pomposity, but another story, 'The Daughters of the

Late Colonel', shows Mansfield's extraordinary imagination engaging with death and finding it subversively comic. Our first encounter with the middle-aged daughters finds them in bed, with one of them on the verge of a fit of the giggles. It is girlish, uncontrolled behaviour but it also suggests a suppressed joy that she cannot acknowledge; the old tyrant, the colonel, is no longer there banging his stick and shouting for attention. We only realise this slowly, as the daughters are too dutiful to acknowledge it directly, even to themselves. It is clear in the wonderful scene in which the vicar calls to discuss the funeral and Constantia daydreams of 'a good one that will last' (p. 270). The death of their father means liberation for both sisters, though they cannot yet conceptualise it. As they creep out of its shadow, we see Josephine imagining a small feminist attack on patriarchy when she thinks of sending their father's watch to their brother Benny, a colonial officer who shakes his fist when impatient, as father did:

> She liked the idea of having to make a parcel such a curious shape that no one could possibly guess what it was. She even thought for a moment of hiding the watch in a narrow cardboard corset-box that she'd kept by her for a long time, waiting for it to come in for something. It was such beautiful firm cardboard. But, no, it wouldn't be appropriate for this occasion. It had lettering on it: *Medium Women's 28. Extra Firm Busks.* It would be almost too much of a surprise for Benny to open that and find father's watch inside. (p. 274)

This is the humour of a dawning resistance and reveals poignantly that the sisters, who have been living the lives of abjects, silenced and controlled by their imperious father and his banging stick, have secret selves that could be reasserted:

> Some little sparrows, young sparrows they sounded, chirped on the window-ledge. *Yeep – eyeep – yeep.* But Josephine felt they were not sparrows, not on the window-ledge. It was inside her, that queer little crying noise. *Yeep – eyeep – yeep.* Ah, what was it crying, so weak and forlorn? [. . .] [Constantia] remembered the times she had come in here, crept out of bed in her nightgown when the moon was full, and lain on the floor with her arms outstretched, as though she was crucified. Why? The big, pale moon made her do it [. . .]. What did it all lead to? Now? Now? (pp. 281–2)

The Gothic image of Constantia crucified on the floor by moonlight with dancing figures on a carved screen leering at her, beside a Buddha whose smile 'always gave her such a queer feeling, almost a pain and yet a pleasant pain' (pp. 280–1), hints at suppressed sexual awareness. The tragedy of the story is that both sisters are on the verge of articulating what a new life might be, but they interrupt each other: genteel manners intervene, the sun clouds over and the moment is gone. As Mansfield wrote to William Gerhardi on 23 June 1921, after that window of change 'it seemed to me, they died as truly as Father was dead'.[9]

A Gift of the Dusk and Elizabeth von Arnim's *Vera* can both be read as modernist novels. Unlike 'The Daughters of the Late Colonel', *A Gift of the Dusk* has a conventional chronological structure, but its intense absorption in the consciousness of its narrator, its inconclusive ending, and its heightened focus on certain key objects in the setting, such as the crachoirs, all shift the novel out of the category of what Woolf rebels against in her essay 'Modern Fiction'. She asks whether novels must conform to a generic pattern, in which life escapes in the author's pursuit of painstaking realism; in *A Gift of the Dusk*, realistic details acquire an almost hallucinatory significance as the trapped narrator gazes at his cell, masquerading as a hotel room. Elizabeth von Arnim's *Vera* appears at first to offer the reader a love story like that in her novel *The Enchanted April*, but it turns into a claustrophobic nightmare, shot through with savage humour. Mansfield read and admired the book. Living in the Chalet des Sapins in Montana, Switzerland, and seeing her cousin – who had a chalet nearby – frequently, she writes to her sister Vera in November 1921: 'I think its by far the most brilliant book she has ever written.'[10] Discussing it in letters to Dorothy Brett, she asks on 22 December 1922: 'Wasn't the *end* extraordinarily good. It would have been so easy to miss it; she carried it right through. I admired the end most, I think.'[11]

The dominant modernist element in *Vera* lies in its use of a range of shifting interior monologues, very much like Mansfield's technique in 'The Daughters of the Late Colonel'. In each chapter, though there is a third-person narrator, the narrative perspective changes, enabling the reader to enter disastrously incompatible world views. Rebecca West expressed its idiosyncratic achievement trenchantly in her review in the *New Statesman* when she wrote:

> The author has produced a remarkable novel because she has had the courage to override a tiresome literary convention. She has insisted that there is no real reason why a book should not be just as tragic as it is comic. By the unsentimental justice of its values, by its refusal to make Wemyss less of a comedian because he is murderous or less of a murderer because he is comic, *Vera* achieves a peculiar, poignant effect.[12]

Wemyss has just lost his wife of fifteen years, Vera. He maintains that she carelessly fell out of an upstairs window, though the coroner records an open verdict; press coverage regards her death as suspicious. Wemyss maintains that he was sitting in his library when his wife flashed past the window on her way to being flattened on the flagstones of the verandah. A middle-aged man, he persistently courts young Lucy Entwhistle, whose father has just died suddenly in their rented cottage in Cornwall. Her aunt, her only relative, wants to like Wemyss but finds it difficult as he takes over the space in her little flat during his courtship of Lucy. The prose in this meandering sentence enacts the character as Miss Entwhistle walks reluctantly home:

> But there in that drawing-room would probably still be Mr. Wemyss, no longer now to be Mr. Wemyss for her – would she really have to call him Everard? – or she might meet him on the stairs – narrow stairs; or in the hall – also narrow, which he would fill up; or on her doorstep she might meet him, filling up her doorstep; or, when she turned the corner into her street, there, coming towards her, might be the triumphant trousers. (p. 83)

His trousers are grey and represent to her the reprehensible fact that his clothes do not indicate that he is in mourning for his wife – accurately, as he has sensibly forgotten about her in the excitement of pursuing Lucy. Wemyss overrides all obstacles and marries Lucy less than a year after his wife's death, taking her to his house in the country, The Willows, where Vera died. Lucy wants to think that he will shrink from going there but:

> From the way he looked, the way he spoke, from those tiny indications that one somehow has noticed without knowing that one has noticed and that are so far more revealing and conclusive than any words, she sometimes was sure that he really had forgotten. But this was too incredible. (p. 144)

Wemyss proves to be a self-righteous domestic tyrant like Mr Hammond in 'The Stranger' and the colonel in 'The Daughters'. Mansfield noticed a family likeness and wrote to von Arnim on 23 October 1921, reporting that her sisters had given her father a copy of *Vera*: 'Which makes me gasp. But I expect he will admire Wemyss tremendously and agree with every thought and every feeling and shut the book with an extraordinary sense of satisfaction before climbing the stairs to my stepmother.'[13] The stairs are a significant feature in *Vera*, leading to the marital bedroom. The crisis comes when Lucy sees the photographic portrait of her predecessor on the dining-room wall: '"Vera", he said, in a matter-of-fact tone, as it were introducing them' (p. 162). From then on, Lucy is haunted by Vera's mouth, which 'had a little twist in it as though she were trying not to laugh' (p. 163). After a series of domestic disasters that culminates in Lucy getting soaked by rain and becoming ill, she runs upstairs for refuge to the room from which Vera fell, thinking absurdly: 'Vera would help her [. . .]. If only,

only Vera weren't dead' (p. 190). She huddles close to the fire and takes down a book. Wemyss picks it up when he seeks her out: 'This was one of Vera's, – Vera hadn't taken any care of her books either; she was always reading them [...] *Wuthering Heights.* He hadn't read it, but he fancied he had heard of it as a morbid story' (p. 210). The reader laughs at Wemyss's contempt for books as being anything other than part of the interior décor of the library, like the antlers that were bought by the yard and bristle from the walls of the hall, and at the same time feels terror for the vulnerable and naïve Lucy. If that same reader happens to remember the use of portraits in Brontë's novel, it provides another obliquely sardonic view of Wemyss. Both Edgar Linton and Heathcliff worshipped as an icon the portrait of the dead Catherine, and Heathcliff carried it off from Thrushcross Grange as soon as her husband died, but Wemyss regards the portrait of Vera without emotion, as part of the furniture, lit by glaring, unshaded electric light.

The book's conclusion is tragic, in that it makes clear that Vera's fate prefigures Lucy's. At the same time, it is appallingly comic in that Wemyss's ego is untouched by everything that has happened. Having banished Miss Entwhistle from his house, he:

> felt quite good-humoured again. More than good-humoured, – refreshed and exhilarated, as though he had had a cold bath and a thorough rub down. Now for bed and his little Love. What simple things a man wanted, – only his woman and peace. (p. 318)

The reader longs for him to have an epiphany and realise that books do not exist to be locked up in display cabinets, any more than wives want to be ensnared by their husband's routine. The 'one little grain of truth' in the book is Vera herself, as her name suggests: the truth of a woman trapped by respectable patriarchy, whose only gesture of defiance could be to bring her husband's reputation into question by killing herself. When Miss Entwhistle looks at the books on Vera's shelves, all of them Baedekers and other travel guides and timetables, she understands the message that they are sending her about Vera's life with Wemyss, for Lucy understood the longing for colour and escape in Vera's painting of almond trees in blossom in a warm climate; Wemyss says she was always painting, like her nasty habit of reading.

Isobel Maddison's analysis of the Gothic element in the second half of the book, linking it to *Wuthering Heights,* is very persuasive. She, however, suspects Wemyss of murder: 'Did Vera jump or was she pushed?'[14] For this reader, that is not a valid question, as the self-righteous and respectable Wemyss did not need to push her. He drove her into abjection as he is, by the end of the novel, driving Lucy. She prophesies her own collapse as she recognises her fear of her husband, and of marital scenes:

> And she not only didn't see how they were to be avoided – for no care, no caution would for ever be able to watch what she said, or did, or looked, or equally important, what she didn't say, or didn't do, or didn't look – but she was afraid, afraid with a most dismal foreboding, that some day after one of them, or in the middle of one of them, her nerve would give out and she would collapse. Collapse deplorably; into just something that howled and whimpered. (p. 218)

She is on the verge of what Kristeva calls the dark revolts of being, 'beyond the scope of the possible, the tolerable, the thinkable'.[15] She is beginning to recognise what must happen to her and, unlike Vera, she has no strategies for postponing it. The doctor's image of her conveys her regression: '[On] seeing the small head on the pillow of the treble bed he thought, "Why, he's married a child. What an extraordinary thing"' (p. 278). His comment reflects on Wemyss's perverse delight in jumping Lucy up and down and calling her his little love; although she is twenty-two, she has been infantilised by her father, and Wemyss's domination of her is revealed as a form of child abuse. Lucy takes refuge from him in sleep and illness, but neither offers protection when her aunt is forced to leave. The novel culminates not in an epiphany for Wemyss but in Miss Entwhistle's extraordinary courage in confronting him. Though she is an old woman, as the daughters of the colonel feel themselves to be, she does not collapse and whimper, nor does she take refuge in platitudes:

> 'You don't seem to know anything at all about women, anything at all about human beings. How could you bring a girl like Lucy – any young wife – to this house? [. . .] I tell you that unless you take care, unless you're kinder than you're being at this moment, it won't be anything like fifteen years this time.' (p. 311)

Wemyss turns her out of the house and Lucy is left to her fate. Wemyss's final words are: '"Who's my very own baby?"' (p. 319).

Mansfield's 'own little grain of truth' developed through her capacity to read with insight and appreciation. In a letter to von Arnim dated 23 April 1922 she wrote understanding the vulnerability of the young wife in *Vera*: 'Your Lucy was so lovely, her slender legs as she lay asleep by the fire – her long lashes.'[16] The psychological daring of her last stories, including the grimly Gothic 'A Married Man's Story', is evidence of Mansfield's intellectual energy as it takes her into new fictional territory in the final sustained phase of her writing life. At the same time, her superbly alert senses were registering new sensations as if she were an explorer. It is her glinting wit that adds a sparkle to her grain of truth, like her cousin von Arnim's artistry, the product of what Rebecca West called 'a clear and brilliant head'.[17] As Mansfield reflected in her diary on 17 October 1922, just after her last birthday:

> To be wildly enthusiastic, or deadly serious – both are wrong. Both pass. One must keep ever present a sense of humour. It depends entirely on yourself how much you see or hear or understand. But the sense of humour I have found true of every single occasion of my life.[18]

Notes

1. *Letters* 4, p. 100.
2. Julia Kristeva, *Powers of Horror: An Essay on Subjection*, trans. by Leon S. Roudiez (New York: Columbia University Press, 1982), p. 1.
3. *Letters* 4, p. 57.
4. R. O. Prowse, *A Gift of the Dusk*, introduction by John Middleton Murry, [1920] (Keighley: Pomona, 2006), p. 10. All further references to the novel are to this edition and are cited in parentheses.
5. CW4, p. 248.
6. CW3, p. 681.
7. *Letters* 4, p. 75.
8. CW2, p. 241. All further references to Mansfield's stories are to this volume and are cited in parentheses.
9. *Letters* 4, p. 249.
10. *Letters* 4, p. 309.
11. *Letters* 4, p. 346.
12. Elizabeth von Arnim, *Vera*, [1921] (London: Virago, 1983), p. v. All further references to this novel are to this edition and are cited in parentheses.
13. *Letters* 4, p. 300.
14. Isobel Maddison, *Elizabeth von Arnim: Beyond the German Garden* (Farnham: Ashgate, 2013), p. 116.
15. Kristeva, p. 1.
16. *Letters* 5, p. 154.
17. Von Arnim, p. ix.
18. CW4, pp. 443–4.

Writing Toward a New World: Awakenings in Katherine Mansfield's 'Bliss' and Elizabeth von Arnim's *The Enchanted April*

Noreen O'Connor

> We must search out and counterpose an alternative tradition taken from the neglected works left in the wide margin of the century, a tradition which may address itself not to this by now exploitable because quite inhuman rewriting of the past but, for all our sakes, to a modern future in which community may be imagined again.[1]
>
> Raymond Williams, *The Politics of Modernism: Against the New Conformists* (1996)

Many literary works written in the years during and immediately after the First World War express alienation and hopelessness, a sense of 'disillusionment' with the breakdown of communal understanding. In particular, the future itself becomes a subject of anxiety, of blankness, a space in which previous social norms are dismantled but where no new order can be conceived. In his 1920 preface for *The Theory of the Novel*, literary critic Georg Lukács expresses a strong dissatisfaction with literature of the era, arguing that the modernist novel is a 'symptom' that reflects the alienated nature of the urban bourgeois culture that brought about the war: 'The problems of the novel form are here the mirror-image of a world gone out of joint. This is why the "prose" of life is here only a symptom, among many others, of the fact that reality no longer constitutes a favorable soil for art.'[2] Lukács thus identifies a central problem for artists in the years during and after the First World War that produces the alienated, subjective, bourgeois self-consciousness so commonly found in modernist literature.

Lukács explains that the immediate motive for writing his 1916 work 'was supplied by the outbreak of the First World War. [. . .] [I]t was written in a mood of permanent despair over the state of the world.'[3] Although this was a valid expression of a specific experience in a specific historical moment, it becomes problematic to see it as the singular definition of literary modernism. Raymond Williams argues in *The Politics of Modernism: Against the New Conformists* that, by the late twentieth century, the received idea of literary modernism privileges alienation as a master narrative. Thus, the alienated subject has become canonical, comprising a body of literature that Williams calls 'works of radical estrangement'.[4]

Williams sees this singular understanding of modernism as unsound, and instead urges scholars to look back to recover alternative texts that qualify the notion of a master narrative in order to envision an inclusive, robust community. I argue that by adding to our literary studies the works of those writers not traditionally considered central to modernism or thought to be aesthetically experimental, a clearer picture of the war and its aftermath emerges. Focusing particularly on works by women writers reveals a marked cultural change in the way women imagined – and made narratable to the larger culture through literary forms – their roles in the post-war years. In particular, the changing social roles of women as mothers and marriage partners is reflected in destabilised narratives that differ from many 'alienated' modernist texts.

In this essay, I will address two texts with gently revolutionary narratives, Katherine Mansfield's 1918 short story 'Bliss', and her cousin Elizabeth von Arnim's 1922 novel *The Enchanted April*. These texts each present a specifically female narrative of awakening to consciousness of the alienated, isolated, and spiritually empty nature of their current lives within bourgeois marriage; however, they also open up the possibility for women to reinvent and restructure their lives, allowing the reader to envision possibilities beyond that which seems available to them in the present moment. Both 'Bliss' and *The Enchanted April* feature women struggling to achieve self-awareness and a meaningful engagement with others. *The Enchanted April*, further, in the shape of a double quest narrative,[5] moves beyond the scene of awakening to offer a vision for women of individual self-determination, as well as strategies for imagining and building a supportive, peaceful community based upon mutual understanding, respect and love.

Awakening from Disillusioned Modernisms

For the modernist writer, a desire for a life beyond the conventions of a now-decayed cultural structure must be uncovered, rediscovered and ultimately reinvented. Mansfield's 'Bliss' addresses disillusionment and the struggle to bring a new desire into language, even as it captures the great difficulties that acting on such an awakening presents in the modernist era. 'Bliss' follows the events of a single Spring evening through the perspective of Bertha Young, a married London woman, as she experiences a sudden blooming, an awakening of desire for something she cannot yet express. In the story's first paragraphs, Mansfield's narrator sets up the central problem Bertha will encounter, in the form of questions that the woman asks herself:

> What can you do if you are thirty and, turning the corner of your own street, you are overcome, suddenly, by a feeling of bliss – absolute bliss! [. . .] Oh, is there no way you can express it without being 'drunk and disorderly'? How idiotic civilization is! Why be given a body if you have to keep it shut up in a case like a rare, rare fiddle?[6]

This description of a violent natural emotion, and the cultural prohibition that denies Bertha the opportunity to voice, act upon or even express such emotion, starkly exposes what Lukács calls narrative disillusionment with the 'incongruence of interiority and the conventional world'.[7] However, by calling out these themes, the story itself does narrate awakened desire, and ultimately critiques the strictures of civilised Western culture as epitomised by bourgeois marriage, expressing the possibilities for breaking out by narrating its protagonist's blossoming desire to move beyond the borders of her restricted life.

Bertha comes into focus as a woman who has been living a life severely limited in its access to self-understanding or meaningful connection with others. As Mary Burgan argues, Bertha is typical of 'Mansfield's stories of the childish rich', in which the characters are presented 'through their self-flattering immaturity, back-tracking phrases, [and] exasperation at the failure of language to penetrate to the core'.[8] However, as the story opens, Bertha's interior self is erupting out of control, pushing the limits of the constructed world she inhabits. Culturally trained to think in terms of exteriority, she turns to look into a mirror to 'see' the interior emotion:

> But in her bosom there was still that bright glowing place – that shower of little sparks coming from it. It was almost unbearable. She hardly dared to breathe for fear of fanning it higher, and yet she breathed deeply, deeply. She hardly dared to look into the cold mirror – but she did look, and it gave her back a woman, radiant, with smiling, trembling lips, with big, dark eyes and an air of listening, waiting for something . . . divine to happen . . . that she knew must happen . . . infallibly. (p. 142)

As it is described through the narrator's focalisation of Bertha's thoughts, the bliss is intensely physical and emanating from within. Nevertheless, Bertha feels, passively, that something is happening *to* her, that something is going to happen. Throughout the story, this ambiguous feeling of 'bliss' returns again and again, yet she is rooted in place 'in infantine passivity',[9] waiting for something to occur instead of taking action.

Mansfield's narrator emphasises Bertha's enforced passivity in the domestic sphere, for she is, as Burgan argues, 'kept even further from reality by the intervention of servants'.[10] Upon returning home with flowers and fruit for the dinner party she will hold that evening, Bertha rushes upstairs to visit her baby, Little B. She is greeted with great excitement by the child, who 'looked up when she saw her mother and began to jump', but with far less enthusiasm by the nanny, who greets Bertha by 'setting her lips in a way that Bertha knew, and that meant she had come into the nursery at another wrong moment' (p. 143). However, moved to action by her new sense of bliss, Bertha gently demands that the 'offended' nurse allow her to spend some time with her child. At this moment, she is able to articulate, at least internally, her sense of dissatisfaction with the domestic arrangement: 'How absurd it was. Why have a baby if it has to be kept – not in a case like a rare, rare fiddle – but in another woman's arms?' (p. 143). She takes the baby with delight, and yet her ability to express this emotion in words is muted:

> 'You're nice – you're very nice!' said she, kissing her warm baby. 'I'm fond of you. I like you.'
> And, indeed, she loved Little B so much – her neck as she bent forward, her exquisite toes as they shone transparent in the firelight – that all her feeling of bliss came back again, and again she didn't know how to express it – what to do with it. (p. 143)

The marked difference between Bertha's speech and the narrator's focalised description of her internal feelings – the fact that she can articulate her deep love for the baby only with the muffled words 'nice', 'fond' and 'like' – indicates Bertha's own lack of self-knowledge, for the narrative itself communicates more clearly the multiple desires that Bertha cannot yet speak aloud.

Instead, Bertha's experience of life is oddly detached and empty; she is truly alienated within the bourgeois strictures of her life, unable to connect in a deeply meaningful way with those around her or even with herself. Her 'modern' marriage itself is devoid of connection and desire. Yet, Bertha tries to talk herself out of her dissatisfaction, telling herself that 'Really – really – she had everything', and then inventorying her 'assets' in a list that reveals the depth of her alienation, for it places people – her husband Harry, her 'adorable baby' and 'modern, thrilling friends' – in equal standing with material objects – her house, garden and the 'superb omelettes' (p. 145) made by her new cook. She has been moving in an isolated cloud, her life full of what Lukács would term 'petty and disruptive'[11] elements, unable to take a full part in the life that is going on around her.

Mansfield's narrative links Bertha's bliss to the natural world, the season of Spring and the blossoming of the pear tree in her garden:

> At the far end, against the wall, there was a tall, slender pear tree in fullest, richest bloom; it stood perfect, as though becalmed against the jade-green sky. Bertha couldn't help feeling, even from this distance, that it had not a single bud or faded petal. (p. 145)

The abundantly blooming tree, a startling natural phenomenon in her groomed city garden, mirrors Bertha's bliss both physically and emotionally. Bertha unintentionally dresses for her dinner party in green and white, further mirroring the tree. The luminous detail of this tree stands in stark contrast to the structured and artificial world around it, gesturing toward the fruit that it will bear in a few months. It also contrasts sharply with Bertha's collection of 'modern thrilling friends', whose presence at her party is notable for its lack of meaningful, spiritually sustaining connection. As Polly Dickson argues, the shared meal is a spectacle of empty consumption:

> In a story ostensibly about collective nourishment in the form of a dinner party, food loses all qualities of sustenance and becomes a spectacle of alienation. Eating is ornamental, an act of display [. . .] a precipitator of the hungry lack present in the lines of the domestic sphere.[12]

Though they refer to the 'stodgy' middle class, these people are decidedly superficial themselves. The guests engage in shallow small talk, gossip and inane discussions of literature – a poem about tomato soup, a play called *Love in False Teeth*, and another play idea that none of the guests seem to realise is stolen directly from Henrik Ibsen's *Ghosts*.

Intersubjective Desire

Only one guest seems to share Bertha's Springtime feeling of bliss – her newest friend Pearl Fulton. With Pearl, Bertha feels a deep wordless connection, and – narrated through third-person limited perspective – we learn that she simultaneously, and 'for the first time in her life', realises that she desires her husband Harry, 'ardently! ardently! The word ached in her ardent body! Was this what this feeling of bliss had been leading up to?' (p. 151). In the story, Bertha never expresses her sexual desire to her husband, but it is closely tied to her ongoing feeling – also never voiced – of a communal understanding with her new friend, Pearl. Bonnie Kime Scott argues that 'Mansfield uses [the] pear tree in full bloom to suggest female happiness and connection'.[13] The nature of this connection remains only partially revealed, however; the narrator does not allow access to Pearl's consciousness, but instead depicts the bond between Pearl and Bertha externally and only through Bertha's consciousness. It is, thus, possible that Bertha misrecognises the meaning of this connection, even as it reaches its height when Bertha pulls back her curtains and opens her windows to share her pear tree:

> And the two women stood side by side looking at the slender, flowering tree. [...] How long did they stand there? Both, as it were, caught in that circle of unearthly light, understanding each other perfectly, creatures of another world, and wondering what they were to do in this one with all this blissful treasure that burned in their bosoms and dropped, in silver flowers, from their hair and hands? (p. 149)

This moment is, as Gerri Kimber explains, an example of 'Mansfield's use of Joycean "epiphanies", or to use her own words, the "blazing moment"',[14] which Kimber defines as 'manifestations which go on to produce a profound realisation, perceived by the reader though not necessarily by the characters themselves'.[15] In this brief moment of communion and understanding, Bertha begins to break through her alienated and disillusioned stasis. Seeing herself as part of a larger whole and 'wondering what were they to do', she begins to ponder the possibility that she might act on her newly discovered desires.

Mansfield scholars have debated intensively the meaning of this epiphanic moment and the polymorphous desire it propagates in Bertha. The scene is open to multiple interpretations, as Mansfield deliberately represents it ambiguously; it occurs only within the imaginary realm, for Bertha takes no actual action and fails to voice her desire. In this essay, I argue only that desire is awakened in Bertha, for her strongly sexual desire is unambiguous in the text. Bertha feels totally changed by the experiences of the day and evening, transformed into a new person: '"Good night, good-bye," she cried from the top step, feeling that this self of hers was taking leave of them forever' (p. 151). At this point, the brief connection between Pearl and Bertha has moved us to imagine a woman who may bloom enough to gain some control over her passive, almost internally dead life – she may reinvent her domestic life, more actively mother her child, become a sexually desirous partner in a fulfilled marital partnership with Harry, form deeper friendships or, more radically, leave it all to pursue a romance with Pearl.

Yet the story's ending, in which Bertha observes her husband Harry and Pearl in an intimate moment as they say goodbye at the door, changes the text's direction. The pair are – the reader realises alongside

Bertha – having an affair. This changes the meaning of the domestic arrangement for Bertha and the narrative as a whole. Bertha is not only awakened to her own desire, but also awakened to the essentially intersubjective nature of human desire. As René Girard explains, desire appears to be a simple straight line between desiring subject and desired object, but it is often triangular: 'The mediator is there, above that line, radiating toward both the subject and the object. The spatial metaphor which expresses this triple relationship is obviously the triangle. The object changes with each adventure but the triangle remains.'[16] Girard's work on the literary structures of desire assists us in understanding what is happening in the narrative of 'Bliss', which moves Bertha from undesiring alienation to a position of participation in the economies of desire, into 'the mystery, transparent yet opaque, of human relation'.[17] The triangular structure that Mansfield establishes by the end of 'Bliss' draws Bertha, Harry and Pearl into an unstable, still-developing narrative of intersubjective desire, each character simultaneously shifting between the subject, object and rival narrative position.

This change is also reflected in the narrative distance of the final paragraphs, which draws back from Bertha's interior thoughts. Throughout the story, Mansfield's third-person limited style of narration has provided an internal commentary that shows the disjunction between what Bertha expresses verbally and what she is feeling but not expressing. Bertha's awakening to the truth of her marriage – and to the overall structure of her life – is undoubtedly profoundly painful, but we are privy to no interior commentary on these emotions. The scene she witnesses completes Bertha's transformation and brings her fully into language; she simply says goodbye to Pearl out loud, expressing fully, for the first time in the story, exactly what she is thinking. And, tellingly, Bertha asks the final question of the story – 'Oh, what is going to happen now?' (p. 152) – aloud for the world to hear and answer. The dramatic transformation in Bertha takes her fully into language and roots her instead in lived reality. Bertha, like the pear tree – a trace of a deeper natural rhythm contained in an artificial private city garden – remains in the final sentence of the story 'as lovely as ever and as full of flower and as still' (p. 152). And like the blossoming tree, Bertha is undergoing a dramatic internal process that will allow her to bear fruit. By asking the question out loud, however, Bertha voices her recognition of the constructedness and aridity of the world that is binding her and a now-spoken desire for a life that is lived beyond these strictures. Bertha remains, at the end of the story, vibrantly alive and desirous, perhaps for the first time in her life. Thus, we are led to imagine that Bertha's quiet transformation will bring forth something new and fruitful. Though she has not yet identified the object of her new desire, this blooming, desiring woman, awakened to the possibilities of self-definition and action, is now equipped to go on past the margins of this tale to speak, act and ultimately reinvent her life.

From Hampstead to Heaven: Visions and Quests

In the years following the end of the First World War, Mansfield formed an important writerly friendship with her cousin, Elizabeth von Arnim.[18] The cousins became close during 1921 and 1922, when Mansfield moved to the mountains of Switzerland, a short funicular ride from von Arnim's own chalet. Despite the ravages of Mansfield's progressing tuberculosis, these years were 'the most fruitful period of her life'.[19] It was also during this period that von Arnim wrote and published her novel, *The Enchanted April*.[20] Written in the form of a double quest narrative grounded both in the material realities of women's lives after the war and in the utopian ideas of post-war peace-building, *The Enchanted April* not only offers a sharp criticism of post-war patriarchal and cultural structures, but also gently suggests a vision for a new world.

Von Arnim's novel can be read as a healing narrative that stands in fascinating contrast to Mansfield's 'Bliss'. While sharing some key themes and concerns with her cousin's story, *The Enchanted April* is focused more fully from the start on the nature of human relations, narrated in a style that is, in Isobel Maddison's words, 'uniquely Arnimesque': 'Her virile satire and original style belie a seriousness borne of a shrewd understanding of human psychology as it is lived through the complexities of personal and social relationships.'[21] In particular, Maddison notes von Arnim's 'seamless use of shifting narrative perspectives',[22] her own brand of free indirect discourse that emphasises the place of the individual within her society and the intersubjective nature of desire.

The narrative of *The Enchanted April* is set in motion and guided throughout by the visions of an unlikely heroine, Lotty Wilkins. Lotty is described as 'negligible' at the novel's beginning: '[h]er clothes, infested by thrift, made her practically invisible; her face was non-arresting; her conversation was reluctant; she was shy'.[23] But she emerges within the narrative as a passionate and inspiring leader of a double quest, first achieving her own desire for freedom and self-determination, and then creating a loving, supportive community at peace with itself.

Lotty's transformation begins 'in a woman's club in London on a February afternoon – an uncomfortable club, and a miserable afternoon', through the medium of an item in the 'Agony Column' of *The Times*: 'To those who appreciate Wisteria and Sunshine. Small medieval

Italian Castle on the shores of the Mediterranean to be let furnished for the month of April' (p. 1). Like Bertha's pear tree blooming in the confines of a walled London garden, the advertisement, planted within a mass-produced newspaper, gestures beyond the confines of the life that Lotty knows, sowing a seed of desire in a way von Arnim's narrator likens to an impregnation: 'That was its conception; yet, as in the case of many other, the conceiver was unaware of it at the moment' (p. 1).

The true centre of this novel is female friendship, beginning with a partnership that reawakens desire deadened by years of alienated married life. Moved by her vision of a month in Italy, shy, invisible Lotty reaches out for the first time to Rose Arbuthnot, a Hampstead neighbour with whom she has never spoken. Lotty is hesitant to speak to her neighbour, but her need to make a connection with the other woman overwhelms her reluctance. As she looks across the room, she sees Rose holding a copy of *The Times*:

> And she could not help thinking that Mrs. Arbuthnot, too, was reading that very same advertisement. Her eyes were on the very part of the paper. Was she, too, picturing what it would be like – the colour, the fragrance, the light, the soft lapping of the sea among little hot rocks? (p. 7)

Von Arnim's omniscient narrator moves between the thoughts of the two women, revealing that the advertisement has created an as yet unspoken but wholly intersubjective vision. Rose is dreaming of the same thing in the exact same language: 'of light, of colour, of fragrance, of the soft lapping of the sea among little hot rocks' (p. 7). Thus, Lotty and Rose – like Bertha and Pearl standing before the pear tree in 'Bliss' – share a wordless moment of communion and understanding. Von Arnim's narrative here echoes that of Mansfield's, emphasising the flawed bourgeois social conventions that constrain these women from acting upon their desires. However, the narrative also emphasises the truly shared nature of the women's experience, and quickly pushes past the isolated alienation that Mansfield's Bertha experiences. Lotty, instead of silently 'wondering what they were to do' (p. 149) as Bertha does, speaks her desire aloud. By stumblingly voicing her desire to share the real castle with Rose, Lotty quickly moves this desire from the imaginary to the symbolic realm, 'infecting' Rose with desire to begin their first quest, a heroic journey toward self-definition and independence.

While in *The Enchanted April* a light-hearted narrative voice often bars the reader from entering into a deeply sympathetic relationship with the characters' unhappiness, the novel nevertheless exposes the problems of women's subjectivity within patriarchy. In speaking and connecting, Lotty begins her quest, but she must first struggle to free herself from the bourgeois cultural restrictions on her life. As Claudia Tate observes, early twentieth-century bourgeois marriage is 'most often a form of socially sanctioned brokerage in which women serve as currency in masculine but not feminine fulfillment, [. . .] a socially regulated and reductive form of desire in which female identity is sacrificed to selflessness'.[24] The unequal power relations between Lotty and her husband Mellersh closely follow this pattern; Mellersh, a pragmatic and unemotional lawyer, treats his wife chiefly as a prop to show potential clients that he is a stable family man. Lotty herself describes her marriage as entirely without recognition or love, likening it to 'a bitter wind' that blows 'colder and colder till at last you die of it' (p. 159). Silenced and cowed, Lotty has had little chance for self-definition or agency within the confines of her marriage.

Despite the humour with which von Arnim tempers her narration of the marital and financial issues the women face, it is a difficult process for these women to escape the patriarchal bourgeois values within which they have been formed. In planning their journey, both Lotty and Rose are gradually moved to think differently about their lives. Rose is 'stirred out of sleep' (p. 14) by Lotty's proposal, and for the first time in years, she allows herself to be moved 'off and away from her compass points of God, Husband, Home, and Duty' (p. 15). However, each woman initially sees this quest as transgressive, requiring secrecy, silence, careful planning and occasional mendacity. The difficulty each woman feels as she imagines her escape is a symptom of the struggle to understand and act upon a new narrative desire. But it is at first framed in more familiar bourgeois terms as a secret romance, complete with confused emotions of euphoria and guilt. As she begins planning the trip with Lotty, Rose finds 'she felt happy, and she felt guilty, and she felt afraid, and she had had all the feelings, though this she did not know, of a woman who has come away from a secret meeting with her lover' (p. 25).

The narrative frames the journey to San Salvatore itself as the most spiritually and ideologically transformative element of the women's quest. When Lotty and Rose begin their trip on 30 March, the weight of their perceived transgression causes them to feel 'no exhilaration about the departure, no holiday feeling at all' (p. 50). But when Lotty awakens on the first of April in San Salvatore, she is flooded with a feeling of 'sheer bliss' (p. 66), an emotion that mirrors that of the heroine in Mansfield's 'Bliss'. However, Lotty's emotion has a clearer antecedent than that of Bertha, for her friendship with Rose, cemented by their shared journey, has become a deeper love. The journey has certainly transformed the women's relationship, for within a day they no longer feel guilt or anxiety: 'Their husbands would not have known them. They left off talking. They ceased to mention heaven. They were just cups of acceptance' (p. 99). The first of many kisses shared in the place is between Lotty and Rose, and it is clear in this moment that their loving friendship will continue to blossom.

Additionally, Lotty's bliss stems from her successful pursuit for self-determination. On her first morning in San Salvatore, Lotty luxuriates in the 'fruit' of her own quest:

> her room bought with her own savings, the fruit of her careful denials, whose door she could bolt if she wanted to, and nobody had the right to come in. [. . .] 'And the name of the chamber', she thought, quoting and smiling round at it, "was Peace"' (p. 67)

By freeing herself and awakening to her own agency to define and achieve her desires, she has transformed herself fully from the shy and insignificant woman she had been in London. At San Salvatore, Lotty almost immediately becomes a beautiful, confident, outgoing – even sometimes 'excessively friendly' (p. 167) – woman who speaks her mind and makes things happen.

The Second Quest

About halfway through the novel, the narrative takes a startling turn. Lotty, 'turning into something surprisingly like a saint' (p. 145), embarks on a second quest: a heroic journey to transform everyone around her through love, forgiveness and reconciliation. Most surprisingly, the initial object of her effort is her own husband. On her very first afternoon in San Salvatore, led by another vision, Lotty writes a letter to Mellersh inviting him to join her. When she tells Rose what she has done, her friend is 'astonished' (p. 145) and once again thrown off balance, thinking, 'Mellersh at San Salvatore? Mellersh, from whom Lotty had taken such pains so recently to escape?' (p. 147). Through the voice of Rose, von Arnim's text itself comments upon this strange reversal:

> 'You're so quick,' said Rose. 'I can't follow your developments. I can't keep touch.' [. . .] 'The whole idea of our coming here', she went on again, as Lotty didn't seem to have noticed, 'was to get away, wasn't it? Well, we've got away.' (pp. 147–8)

Lotty admits that her decision is 'idiotically illogical' (p. 148), but she explains that the place of San Salvatore has had a transformative effect: 'I'm so happy, I'm so well, I feel so fearfully wholesome. This place – why, it makes me feel *flooded* with love' (p. 148). She has developed an unearthly faith in her visions, and proceeds confidently on the path of her second quest.

Lotty's character often has a destabilising role within the narrative; however, her second quest seems at first to be irreconcilable with the motion and structure of the plot. To untangle this narrative shift, it is helpful to consider the ways in which Lotty's turn toward the goals of universal love, unity and community is accompanied by a marked change in her language. Rose notes that 'one odd effect of San Salvatore on her rapidly developing friend was her sudden and free use of robust words. She had not used them in Hampstead. [...] In words, too, Lotty had come unchained' (p. 149). Throughout the second half of the novel, Lotty speaks of love often; she explains that '[t]he great thing is to have lots of love *about*' (p. 148) without expecting reciprocation:

> 'I don't see here, though I did at home, that it matters who loves as long as somebody does. I was a stingy beast at home, and used to measure and count. I had a queer obsession about justice. As though justice mattered. As though justice can really be distinguished from vengeance. It's only love that's any good. At home I wouldn't love Mellersh unless he loved me back, exactly as much, absolute fairness. Did you ever. And as he didn't, neither did I, and the *aridity* of that house! The *aridity*....' (pp. 148–9)

The love that Lotty invokes here is neither precisely friendship (*philia*) nor sexual/romantic love (*eros*), which are based upon mutual recognition and exchange, but universal love, the type of love also called *agape*, in which the person giving love expects nothing in return. This idea is also articulated by Caroline Dester, who realises that Lotty 'never wanted anything of anybody, but was complete in herself and respected other people's completeness [...]. With her one was free, and yet befriended' (p. 270). While we are accustomed to novels that focus on romantic love, a novel with a female hero who articulates a quest for a polymorphous and universal love is quite rare.

Through Lotty's second quest, von Arnim inscribes within the domestic sphere the kind of vision for human interaction more often articulated in the work of philosophical and political writers, including the writings of her brother-in-law, Bertrand Russell. The direct influence of Russell's ideas is certainly present in Lotty's quest for love and reconciliation; in particular, the language Russell employs in his article 'The Essence of Religion' is echoed directly in Lotty's own words in the second part of the novel. For example, Russell discusses 'universal love' as a force that brings communities together:

> More than anything else, divine love frees the soul from its prison and breaks down the walls of self that prevent its union with the world. [...]

> The loves of the natural life survive, but harmonized with universal love, and no longer setting up walls of division between the loved and the unloved. And above all, through the bond of universal love the soul escapes from the separate loneliness in which it is born, and from which no permanent deliverance is possible while it remains within the walls of its prison.[25]

Von Arnim was well acquainted with Russell's thinking; as her biographer Jennifer Walker explains, von Arnim attended Russell's lectures and met with his intellectual friends at the Russell home in Gordon Square, London. When Russell was imprisoned in 1918 for his pacifist activism, von Arnim 'often visited him there, sometimes in the company of Ottoline Morrell, taking in books and smuggling out letters'.[26] Von Arnim even gently pokes fun at Russell's ideas about universal love when Lotty learns that she and Mellersh will be sharing her hard-won bedroom when he arrives at San Salvatore. Lotty meditates on the limitations of universal love in the context of marriage:

> Love, even universal love, the kind of love with which she felt herself flooded, should not be tried. [. . .] Her happiness, she felt, and her ability to be friends with everybody, was the result of her sudden new freedom and its peace. Would there be that sense of freedom, that peace, after a night shut up with Mellersh? (p. 163)

In these terms, we can understand that Lotty's invitation to Mellersh is an act of selfless giving, part of her overall quest to make peace with him and to integrate him into a healthier community, rather than a spontaneous blossoming of romantic love within their heretofore loveless marriage.

Questing Beyond the Ending

Juliane Römhild argues that in von Arnim's final three books – *The Jasmine Farm, All the Dogs of My Life* and *Mr. Skeffington* – her 'writing gains a new level of insight when she describes women whose inner freedom and happiness are affected not by their relationship with men but rather by conflicts within themselves'.[27] *The Enchanted April* also focuses strongly on its women characters' need to resolve their internal conflicts and search for self-knowledge. While Lotty's transformation is mysterious and sudden, the three women who accompany her to San Salvatore must achieve self-discovery through hard and conscious work. Scott notes that '[m]ature women [writers] recovering from trauma make their own decisions about assembling complex natural images' in their texts.[28] Von Arnim employs lush descriptive passages throughout her novel to evoke a liminal space of healing and harmony. The peace of San Salvatore, in close contact with the natural world, allows each woman the space to retreat within herself and, for once, to engage in contemplative and self-critical thought. In San Salvatore, Rose, Scrap and Mrs Fisher each begin to narrate to themselves their own dissatisfaction with the lives they have been living and to think out new possibilities for the future.

Within the second half of the novel, each woman achieves a measure of self-acceptance through her contemplative journey, and each then turns toward the universal love and the vision of community that Lotty has offered. With her confident vision and an empathetic ability to see into others and understand them, Lotty becomes the centre toward which each of the women eventually gravitates. Ultimately, von Arnim's novel focuses upon these female friendships, and these are the most vibrant and important relationships of the narrative. In contrast, Lotty's husband Mellersh does not achieve comparable self-knowledge within the boundaries of the novel. Instead, Lotty's own change, which has garnered her meaningful friendships with three women whom he respects, reshapes his regard for her. We might say Mellersh begins to 'value' his wife imitatively through triangular intersubjectivity: 'endorsed by the affection and even admiration Lady Caroline showed for her', he concludes, 'Lotty was evidently, then [. . .] valuable' (pp. 231–2). This profoundly limited view of Lotty seems to be all that Mellersh is capable of, even in the heavenly and healing space of San Salvatore. Yet his imitative desire for Lotty – together with Lotty's own universal love – produces positive change in their relationship:

> [T]he more he treated her as though she were really very nice, the more Lotty expanded and became really very nice, and the more he, affected in his turn, became really very nice himself; so that they went round and round, not in a vicious but in a highly virtuous circle. (p. 219)

The marital triangle von Arnim introduces here echoes that of Mansfield's 'Bliss', but with an important difference, for the Wilkins marriage seems, at least, to have broken out of its previous pattern and moved into a forward-looking, hopeful phase marked by mutual respect and growth.

Both Mansfield's 'Bliss' and von Arnim's *The Enchanted April* mourn and critique their historical period; however, they also ask, in the words of Bertha in 'Bliss', 'What is going to happen now?' (p. 152). Mansfield's Bertha, at the end of her story, is ready to set out to find an answer to this question. In von Arnim's novel, the narrative undertakes a double quest to discover what might happen if the now-broken patriarchal marriage plot of the bourgeois novel is restructured. To escape the hold of this well-established narrative, women 'run away' from marriage and cultural restrictions in these stories, for the old social structure that binds the women must be broken. Within the quest, the narrative itself moves from realism into a liminal realm of the imagination, for San Salvatore is an imaginative space where the female characters can discover and find the selves they might be if they were not defined so strongly within patriarchy.

These narratives revise the traditional marriage plot and reimagine women's roles beyond the strongly binary power structure of patriarchy. In the closing pages of *The Enchanted April*, Lotty also envisions renewed and new marriages for Rose, Frederick, Scrap and Mr Briggs. For a narrative that opens upon such clear-eyed criticism of the inequalities within marriage, such a conventional ending is unsatisfying. However, even as it returns to the narrative structure of the marriage plot, with marriage or marriage-like relationships realised at its ending, the novel does not succumb to the previous forms of culture and of narrative. As Frederic Jameson observes, it is typical to find that, within utopian texts, 'dangerous or protopolitical impulses are "managed" and "defused"' by the ending of the narrative'.[29] However, he argues, the truly utopian aspect of these texts lies in the fact that these impulses are raised as serious subjects of inquiry within the narrative. Through Lotty's two quests, the community the women form in the novel becomes a new narrative strand that is not easily organisable into either the pre-war narrative forms or the alienated individuality we have come to expect from modernist works. This is finally a narrative of created communities that will last, bringing people toward Raymond Williams's vision of a '[m]odern future where community can be imagined again'.[30]

Notes

1. Raymond Williams, *The Politics of Modernism: Against the New Conformists* (London: Verso, 1996), p. 35.
2. Georg Lukács, *The Theory of the Novel: A Historico-Philosphical Essay on the Forms of Great Epic Literature* (Cambridge, MA: MIT Press, 1971), p. 17.
3. Lukács, p. 12.
4. Williams, p. 35.
5. I am grateful to Claudia Tate for suggesting this strategy for understanding the narrative structure of *The Enchanted April*.
6. CW2, p. 142. Hereafter, page references to this story are placed parenthetically in the text.
7. Lukács, p. 144.
8. Mary Burgan, *Illness, Gender, and Writing: The Case of Katherine Mansfield* (Baltimore: Johns Hopkins University Press, 1994), p. 62.
9. Burgan, p. 63.

10. Burgan, p. 63.
11. Lukács, p. 146.
12. Polly Dickson, 'Interior Matters: Secrecy and Hunger in Katherine Mansfield's "Bliss"', in Clare Hanson, Gerri Kimber and Todd Martin, eds, *Katherine Mansfield and Psychology* (Edinburgh: Edinburgh University Press, 2016), pp. 11–22 (p. 13).
13. Bonnie Kime Scott, *In the Hollow of the Wave: Virginia Woolf and Modernist Uses of Nature* (Charlottesville: University of Virginia Press, 2012), p. 30.
14. Gerri Kimber, *Katherine Mansfield and the Art of the Short Story* (New York: Palgrave Macmillan, 2015), p. 22.
15. Kimber, p. 24.
16. René Girard, *Deceit, Desire and the Novel: Self and Other in Literary Structure* (Baltimore: Johns Hopkins University Press, 1961), p. 2.
17. Girard, p. 3.
18. Jennifer Walker details the years of the cousin's friendship in her biography, *Elizabeth of the German Garden: A Literary Journey* (Brighton: Book Guild, 2013).
19. 'Publisher's Note', *The Montana Stories by Katherine Mansfield* (London: Persephone Books, 2001), p. v.
20. Leslie de Charms's biography, *Elizabeth of the German Garden* (New York: Doubleday, 1959), notes that von Arnim's diary entries and letters during her Spring 1921 stay at a 'poetic Castello' in Portofino show she had begun the novel, and even had its title, by 3 April 1921. The book was published on 31 October 1922.
21. Isobel Maddison, *Elizabeth von Arnim: Beyond the German Garden* (Farnham: Ashgate, 2013), p. 187.
22. Maddison, p. 187.
23. Elizabeth von Arnim, *The Enchanted April* (New York: Doubleday, 1923), p. 4. Hereafter, page references to this story are placed parenthetically in the text.
24. Claudia Tate, *Domestic Allegories of Political Desire: The Black Heroine's Text at the Turn of the Century* (Oxford: Oxford University Press, 1992), p. 73.
25. Bertrand Russell, 'The Essence of Religion', *Hibbert Journal* (October 1912), pp. 46–62 (pp. 58–9, 60).
26. Walker, p. 208.
27. Juliane Römhild, *Femininity and Authorship in the Novels of Elizabeth von Arnim: At Her Most Radiant Moment* (Madison, NJ: Fairleigh Dickinson University Press, 2014), p. 160.
28. Scott, p. 40.
29. Fredrick Jameson, *The Political Unconscious: Narrative as a Socially Symbolic Act* (Ithaca, NY: Cornell University Press, 1981), p. 287.
30. Williams, p. 35.

'*Ces femmes avec ces fleurs!*': Flowers, Gender and Relationships in the Work of Elizabeth von Arnim and Katherine Mansfield

Karina Jakubowicz

When Katherine Mansfield was staying in Italy in 1919, she recorded an episode that epitomises a common assumption about women and flowers:

> Up to our steps came Caterina with a gardener in tow [...] I asked for violets & he said he would bring them, both savage and mild. [...] He will also bring roses – but when he asked me if I wouldnt like some little palms I said 'no' I loved plants with flowers – I saw by his shrug & his 'moue' that he despised me – 'Ah – ces femmes avec ces fleurs!' was what I felt.[1]

Mansfield is shown expressing her preference for flowers, and she imagines that the gardener 'despises' this partiality and that he sees women as having a particular (and irritating) obsession with flowers, one that even he, as a gardener, cannot share. The vignette is useful for demonstrating Mansfield's assumptions concerning *his* assumptions. She feels that he, by virtue of being male, reads her appreciation of flowers as merely indicative of her womanliness. This scene provides one example of how the association between women and flowers was a common one. Mansfield and her cousin, Elizabeth von Arnim, both had a particular affinity with flowers and were often in dialogue with this cultural concept, frequently presenting their passion for these plants alongside explorations of femininity and feminism. By exploring their understanding of flowers, it is possible to see that both writers utilise this subject as a 'language' to describe relationships, desire, gender and sex.

I.

July 1921 to January 1922 marks the period when Mansfield and von Arnim were at their closest. Mansfield was staying in Crans-Montana,

Switzerland, a short walking distance away from her cousin's chalet. The two women visited each other often, and Mansfield became increasingly impressed by von Arnim's appearance and personality. In a letter to Dorothy Brett, Mansfield describes her as 'my ravishing cousin', who is 'lovely to look upon as well as to hear', and adds that they 'exchange books and flowers and fruits'.[2] Just over a year previously, Mansfield had referred to von Arnim as 'a little bundle of artificialities' that she could hardly bear to have tea with,[3] but in Switzerland, von Arnim was 'fascinating [. . .] a real enchantress'.[4] This new-found enthusiasm was partly aided and expressed through their mutual love of flowers.

Flowers feature in every account that Mansfield gives of von Arnim during this period and constitute a common interest that facilitates a genuine bond.[5] Towards the end of her stay in Switzerland, Mansfield records:

> Elizabeth was here yesterday and we lay in my room talking about flowers until we were really quite drunk – or I was. She – describing – 'a certain very exquisite *rose*, single, pale yellow with coral tipped petals' and so on. I kept thinking of little curly blue hyacinths and *white* violets and the bird cherry.[6]

In another letter to Brett she notes:

> Her love of flowers is her greatest charm. Not that she says very much, but every word *tells*. A man would never discover it in her – he wouldn't realise how deep it is. For no man loves flowers as women *can*. Elizabeth looks cooly at the exquisite petunias and says in a small faraway voice: 'They have a very perfect scent.' And I can hear oceans of love breaking in her heart for petunias and nasturtiums and snapdragons.[7]

Even though von Arnim does not say 'very much', her brief praise of the petunias is enough to convince Mansfield that there are 'oceans of love' behind her words. Mansfield interprets her cousin's appreciation of flowers as a sign of emotional depth, a quality that may not have been easy to discern otherwise if, as Mansfield suggests, von Arnim was a woman of few words. Not only does this common interest spark an affinity between the cousins, but for Mansfield it indicates a particularly gendered connection. She argues that men can neither notice the love of flowers in women, nor be capable of such love themselves. Flowers are a key element of what is framed as an emphatically female, homosocial relationship, and their discussion constitutes part of an intimate exchange that reinforces this bond.

Mansfield's and von Arnim's passion for flowers, as well as the gendered dynamics of this passion, were undoubtedly affected and encouraged by recent and contemporary trends. Flowers had been a defining element of horticultural design throughout the Victorian and Edwardian periods and formed an intrinsic part of social, scientific, religious and romantic spheres.[8] This was aided by the popularity of nature poetry and sentimental flower books, particularly texts concerning the language of flowers, such as Frederic Schoberl's *The Language of Flowers: With Illustrative Poetry* (1834), Thomas Miller's *Poetical Language of Flowers* (1847) and Kate Greenaway's *The Language of Flowers* (1884).[9] In these books, flowers are presented as vehicles for communication and are seen as poetic and symbolic subjects that could have moral and religious dimensions. Such works rarely figured flowers in their botanical or horticultural context, focusing instead on their use in maintaining social relationships. Greenaway's, for instance, provided women with a floral code that enabled them to communicate meanings subtly to friends and lovers. The language of flowers thus occupied a position between the said and unsaid, being both silent and covert while also sustaining a dialogue. Used in this way, flowers served to maintain a feminine exterior (preserving traits such as timidity and subtlety) while also providing a means to express intimacy and desire.

There is evidence to suggest that flowers had both feminine and feminist dimensions in the late Victorian and Edwardian periods. Beverly Seaton argues that flowers were 'talismans of gentility and femininity' in the nineteenth century and that 'the Victorian woman was clearly aware that her society believed the floral kingdom to be essentially the domain of Woman'.[10] She explains that flowers 'were seen as the most suitable aspect of nature to represent women, or to interact with them, reflecting as they do certain stereotypical qualities of the female being: smallness of stature, fragility of mind and body, and impermanence of beauty'.[11] As Seaton highlights, the association between femininity and flowers could reinforce gender stereotypes to the detriment of women, yet in the hands of some female writers this relationship was repurposed in subversive ways. Fabienne Moine explains how 'Victorian women poets cultivated the defence and celebration of their natural affinity with flowers because it offered a means to carve out a distinctive natural and literary territory of their own, without upsetting gendered understandings of nature.'[12] She points out that while some women poets used this literary 'territory' to bolster societal norms, others 'chose to concentrate on flower poetry because it empowered them to construct their own discourse on decency and to discuss gender-related issues, partially hiding themselves behind the veil of gentility'.[13] This trend extended into the Edwardian period, with writers such as Mary Webb writing proto-ecofeminist novels that positioned nature in opposition to the dictates and expectations of a patriarchal society.

The role of the natural world in feminist discourse is particularly evident in numerous gardening books written for women during the Victorian and Edwardian periods. These texts were frequently written for women by women and ranged from giving practical advice on growing and landscaping to more informal accounts of domestic life.[14] These books used the garden as a means to discuss power and authority, while also providing practical advice on how to gain a degree of independence. As Dianne Harris explains, many of these texts encouraged 'women to question and resist societal norms and to empower themselves through domestic gardening activity',[15] and Lynne Hapgood goes as far as to call them 'stories of female empowerment and progress'.[16] Works such as *Miss Tiller's Vegetable Garden and the Money She Made By It* (1872) by Anna Warner advocate the practical benefits of a garden and explain how one can be used to bolster financial independence. This genre facilitated a discourse between women and created a space where gender roles could be discussed away from the eyes of male readers. It was a genre that excluded men in more ways than one. As Harris points out, men are frequently maligned and stereotyped in these texts, depicted as necessary evils that interrupt the synthesis between women and the garden space.[17] An example is Marion Cran's *The Garden of Ignorance: The Experiences of a Woman in the Garden* (1918), where she alludes to her husband as 'the Master', thus highlighting the inequality that underpinned the need for a garden of her own in the first place.

Cran's depiction of her marriage followed in the tradition of one of the great writers of women's gardening literature: Elizabeth von Arnim. Von Arnim had referred to her first husband, Count Henning von Arnim, as 'The Man of Wrath' in her book, *Elizabeth and Her German Garden* (1898), which served as a commentary on social expectations as well gardening. This text was key to the genre of women's garden writing and was indicative of a new phase in its development, one that steered away from the style of the practical handbook. Indeed, it was so popular that it had to be reprinted eleven times in its first year of publication. By virtue of their association with this one text, both von Arnim and Mansfield would be permanently linked to a significant moment in the development of both garden writing and feminism.

II.

Von Arnim embraced the form of the garden book as a way to explore and express aspects of her personal life, not least of all her strained relationship with her husband.[18] She frames the garden as a liberating space that is placed in opposition to the house and her domestic duties.

She writes that 'the garden is the place I go to for refuge and not the house'[19]:

> [In the garden] I feel protected and at home, and every flower and weed is a friend and every tree a lover. When I have been vexed I run out to them for comfort, and when I have been angry without just cause, it is there that I find absolution. Did ever a woman have so many friends? And always the same, always ready to welcome me and fill me with cheerful thoughts. (p. 33)

The garden is more than just a refuge; it is a substitute for close relationships. An alternative to the coldness of her husband, it acts as a 'friend' and 'lover' that provides 'comfort'. While von Arnim presents this as positive, suggesting that the number of plants means that she has 'many' friends, it is clear that a certain loneliness underpins her need for this companionship.

Rachel O'Connell sees the theme of enforced isolation as intrinsic to von Arnim's feminism: her preference for the garden over the house constitutes a 'politics [. . .] of refusal and retreat' that ultimately serves to reject the social pressures that have been placed on her.[20] While Elizabeth seeks escape through her garden, this space never truly affords her freedom from her social and familial responsibilities, leading O'Connell to conclude that the 'book presents a protest against the inaccessibility of retreat for women'.[21] The use of plants and flowers in the text can be seen as an extension of this desire for solitude. Indeed, her isolation is exacerbated by the fact that her husband, servants and neighbours do not understand why she is so fond of plants. When she fills the house with lilac flowers, the servants 'wonder why the house should be filled with flowers for one woman by herself', and she 'long[s] more and more for a kindred spirit' (p. 42). Her interest in flowers thus emphasises her difference from her peers, and marks out her particular eccentricity. Her flowers are consequently a source of comfort, while also being a reminder of why this comfort is necessary.

As was typical of garden books, von Arnim dedicates long passages to the description of flowers. O'Connell argues that many of these passages constitute a part of von Arnim's 'discourse of withdrawal'.[22] She explains that these descriptions often employ 'repetitive, inaccessible, even somewhat boring textual material' that keeps the reader at a distance.[23] Yet, in many cases, these accounts constitute a direct engagement with the oppression of women rather than a retreat from its effects. She frequently uses flowers as a medium through which to dramatise her struggle for autonomy. For example, she advocates planting schemes that create a 'natural effect by allowing weeds to grow', and particularly dislikes placing flowers in neat rows (p. 24). She also refuses to relegate flowers to greenhouses, a practice she describes as 'imprisoning them for life, and depriving them forever of the breath of God' (p. 21). Her treatment of plants thus replicates the freedom that her garden represents.

The correlation between her attitude to plants and her feelings about the treatment of women is particularly clear when she states a preference for hardy over tender plants: 'Give me a garden full of strong, healthy creatures, able to stand roughness and cold without dismally giving in and dying. I could never see that delicacy of constitution is pretty, either in plants or in women' (p. 70). Her disparagement of delicate plants and delicate women succeeds in snubbing both the landscaping and feminine ideals of the Victorian period in one blow. Although von Arnim's celebration of flowers may appear to support a traditional feminine stereotype, her attitude towards them reveals sentiments that were ultimately progressive.

Men are frequently presented as outsiders to von Arnim's garden; they either sabotage it or do not see its importance.[24] This includes her gardeners, all of whom are male and whom she suggests are incompetent and inconstant. One 'went mad', and another fell in love with the cook and left shortly afterwards (p. 52). Von Arnim wishes that she 'were a man' so that she 'should have the delight of doing everything for [her] flowers with [her] own hands' and not have to explain herself to someone else (pp. 97–8). She occasionally personifies the flowers as female, making the garden an even more decidedly feminine space. In one case, some tulips next to a hyacinth 'look like a wholesome, freshly tubbed young girl beside a stout lady whose every movement weighs down the air with patchouli' (p. 72). The only flower that is personified as a man is a rose named Dr Grill. That the rose is a doctor suggests an archetypal, masculine authority, and indeed, the rose refuses to bend to von Arnim's will, resulting in a horticultural battle of the sexes. Although she had high expectations for the plant, it 'stood in a row and simply sulked' (p. 99). Even with coaxing, it still did not respond, and she became 'disgusted with Dr Grill', complaining that 'he had the best place in the garden [. . .] and he refused to do anything but look black and shrivel' (p. 100).

Dr Grill shares many features in common with 'The Man of Wrath' – her husband – who is continually placed in opposition to the garden and von Arnim's more progressive political views. What she calls his 'indifference' to gardens is not merely a matter of taste, but an expression of selfishness (p. 156). Von Arnim writes that he 'has no eye for nature' and 'is simply bored by a long drive through a forest that does not belong to him'. She jokes that 'a single turnip on his own place is more admirable in his eyes than the tallest, pinkest straightest pine'. 'Now observe the superiority of woman', she adds, 'who sees that both are good' (p. 178). Von Arnim swiftly turns a personal comment about her husband into one about gender and property. She avoids seeming catty or indiscreet by keeping the tone light, yet she succeeds in demonstrating how patriarchal attitudes to ownership limit an individual's appreciation of the natural world. A similar dynamic is evident in von Arnim's 1921 novel *Vera*, which describes the suffocating relationship between a young woman named Lucy and her domineering husband, Wemyss. Wemyss's selfishness is epitomised in a tradition that he has created for himself, whereby he expects a 'certain yellow flower' to bloom on his birthday every year: 'If these flowers came out before his birthday he took no notice of them, treating them as non-existent, nor did he ever notice them afterwards, for he did not easily notice flowers.'[25] The yellow flowers are interesting to Wemyss only in so far as they exist to mark his birthday, and if they appear beforehand then he ignores them completely. For both Wemyss and 'The Man of Wrath', flowers, like women, have little significance beyond their relationship to men. Elizabeth's attempt at reclaiming nature for herself serves as a challenge to these accepted modes of thinking.

As with the Victorian language of flowers, von Arnim's use of flowers reinforces traditional conceptions of femininity, while also acting as an instrument of feminism. While the language of flowers is feminist only in so far as it provides a way of speaking and being heard, von Arnim goes further by using flowers to convey the experiences and frustrations of women. She consequently toes the line between hyperfemininity and feminism, appearing both coy and politically subversive.[26]

III.

The extent to which Mansfield was affected by von Arnim's writing is subject to debate. Kathleen Jones goes as far as to claim that her influence was a vital part of Mansfield's decision to become a writer and that the acceptance of this decision by her family was partly because of her cousin's success.[27] *Elizabeth and Her German Garden* was published when Mansfield was still a child, and it was some time before she could judge her cousin's work from the perspective of a fellow accomplished writer. Her opinion of von Arnim's writing tended to vary in accordance with her opinions of her cousin's character more generally. One of the books that Mansfield enjoyed was *Vera* (1921), which she read after having kindled a rapport with its author in Switzerland. She tells

Brett that the book is 'amazingly good!' She goes on to ask, 'have you ever known a Wemyss? Oh my dear they are *very* plentiful! Few men are without a touch.'[28]

As an upper middle-class woman, Mansfield was also deeply embedded in the cultures around flowers and gardening. It is difficult, however, to judge to what extent her enthusiasm may have been cultivated or exaggerated in response to literary and social trends. For her part, Mansfield was convinced that her enthusiasm for flowers stemmed from a deep and long-held devotion, one that went beyond the fashionable norm. She explained, 'I had so many flowers when I was little, I got to know them so well that they are simply the breath of life to me,' adding that this feeling is 'no ordinary love; it is a passion'.[29] This tension between 'ordinary' and passionate love is also at the heart of her note about that presumptuous Italian gardener mentioned at the beginning of this essay, where her personal preference for flowers enters into dialogue with a wider cultural trend concerning '*ces femmes*'.

Mansfield's instinctive appreciation of flowers was undoubtedly encouraged by their social and cultural importance in the early twentieth century. In one of her earliest published letters to her sister Vera from 1908, she notes that 'All the florists windows are full of the blue light of violets. And I can't resist them – tight posies tied with yellow flax – *Do* you feel flowers like this – a sense of complete magic – I am spell bound – entranced.'[30] The florist's windows were filled with violets because of the fad for 'violet teas', where the flowers, decorations and even the sweets were violet. Mansfield herself attended one such afternoon tea – a farewell party before her departure for England – on 19 June 1908, and wrote a short verse about violets to read to the guests.[31] These teas were a transnational trend, and Alice Muriel Williamson describes an elaborate American version in her 1906 novel, *Lady Betty Across the Water*.[32] The 'violet tea' is an example of flowers featuring at the heart of a female community, acting as a unifying theme or fashion that successfully bonds individuals of a certain gender and class.[33] The adoration of flowers that Mansfield shows in her letter to her sister is therefore very much in keeping with the then contemporary trends for fashionable women, but it is also clear that this appreciation goes far beyond the norm. Her being 'spell bound' and 'entranced' by the 'complete magic' of flowers suggests a far deeper connection, one that is not being performed but is instead genuine and heartfelt.

Throughout Mansfield's writing, flowers are frequently associated with the themes of love and longing. This is noticeable in the number of letters where she describes not having flowers but intensely wanting them. Writing to von Arnim in 1921, Mansfield recalls the flowers they had shared in Switzerland: 'The petunias, asters, nasturtiums, sweet peas – oh how glorious they were! – flash upon my inward eye very often. But only to mention them is to remember how one loves flowers and longs for them.'[34] The 'loving' and 'longing' for flowers are bound up together, with each feeding the other. This is repeated several days later when she writes in a similar vein to Brett:

> I read of primroses in the paper. Primroses! Oh, what wouldn't I give for some flowers. Oh Brett – this longing for flowers. I *crave* them. I think of them – of the feeling of tulips stems and petals, of the touch of violets and the light on marigolds & the smell of wall flowers. No, it does not bear writing about. I could kiss the earth that bears flowers. Alas, I love them far TOO much![35]

Again, the phrases 'longing' and 'love' are used, as is the stronger term 'crave'. In this letter, Mansfield is keen to emphasise the extent of her feelings and to explain that they go beyond the ordinary love that many people feel for plants. She describes being *too* affected by flowers and of having an unusual, even alarming, attachment to them.

Mansfield's attraction to flowers was so strong that she was even moved by photographs of them. After reading copies of *Country Life* magazine in the Spring of 1920, she wrote to John Middleton Murry stating that the pictures alone were so beautiful they made her feel faint:

> Country Life has come. It has some flower pictures in it. Do you know Bogey (this is literally true) flower pictures affect me so much that I feel an instant tremendous excitement and delight. I mean as strong as if a great band played suddenly. [. . .] Boge I REALLY nearly fainted. I had to lie down.[36]

This was despite the fact that she was staying in Menton, France, and had what she calls 'gentleman's buttonholes' 'in every conceivable colour [. . .] massed together' in the garden. These flowers affect her almost as much as the image in *Country Life*, but even though she has these in abundance, her adoration of the buttonholes is still accompanied by a powerful yearning:

> We *must* remember to grow them so in our garden a round bed. Country Life of course, makes it almost impossible to wait for a garden [. . .] I think I shall become a very violent gardener. I shall have shelves of tomes & walk about the house whispering the names of flowers.[37]

Much like von Arnim, Mansfield craves flowers and a garden of her own, and as for her cousin, this earthly paradise is never completely realised. Instead, it constitutes a space that is tantalisingly close and yet ultimately out of reach.

When it came to sharing her affinity with flowers, Mansfield chiefly chose women as her confidantes. All of the letters quoted above were, with the exception of Murry, written to female friends. Like von Arnim, she also associated flowers and floral imagery with women. When writing to her sister Chaddie's new husband to congratulate him on their marriage in 1913, Mansfield uses flowers to express her deep affection for her sister. She explains their childhood relationship as 'very close [. . .] and whole pieces of my memory are planted with her sweet and charming flowers'. She adds, 'whenever I think of my sister I see her walking in our garden with a little smile on her lips and a great posy in her arms. I am sure that is how she walks over the world.'[38] The letter serves as yet another example of flowers entering into an emotional discourse: it is part of Mansfield's attempt to describe the childhood intimacy that she and Chaddie shared and which has been supplanted (in part) by her marriage. In this account, the scene of their closeness is conflated with Chaddie's character, until she seems to carry a part of the garden with her as she 'walks over the world'. Mansfield's memories of her sister are so tied up with this image that they are 'planted' like the garden in her mind. Mansfield gives an account of von Arnim in 1921 that is not dissimilar to the one she gives of her sister. It describes her as 'a garden walking':

> [Elizabeth] appeared today behind a bouquet – never a smaller woman carried bigger bouquets. She looks like a garden walking – of asters, late sweet peas, stocks and always petunias. [. . .] I have gathered Elizabeths frocks to my bosom as if they were a part of her flowers.[39]

In this account, a whole collection of flowers come together to turn von Arnim into a walking landscape. Mansfield is then inclined to gather her cousin's clothes to her bosom, to draw her (like the flowers) into herself.

The tendency to associate female friends with the production or appearance of flowers extends back to Mansfield's adolescent friendships. In 1908, she was particularly fond of a girl in Wellington who was nicknamed 'Trix'. 'Trix', Mansfield enthuses, 'is one of the best'; she 'puts cushions at my back – and flowers in my soul'. She continues:

> I do verily think that a woman is one of the most delightful creations possible – I feel – here is a breath of my own life – The voice of the chrysanthemum is heard in the land. Two blossoms – so full of colour that I feel they are lighting the dead summer on her journey – greet you from my table.[40]

The phrase 'here is a breath of my own life' is echoed in the letter to Brett in 1922, where she states that 'flowers are the breath of life to me', having referred to a lively conversation with von Arnim about the subject. In both cases, Mansfield uses the metaphor after having praised a female friend and highlighted their connection with flowers.

In the rare cases when Mansfield brought floral imagery into her accounts of relationships with men, the connection is typically romantic. This is the case in an account she gives of music played by Tom Trowell:

> Flowers like Tom's music seem to create in me a divine unrest – They revive strangely – dream memories – I know not what – they show me strange mystic paths – where perhaps I shall one day walk – To lean over a flower – as to hear any of his music is to suddenly [have] every veil torn aside – to communicate soul with soul.[41]

Mansfield was as fond of music as she was of flowers (as, indeed, was von Arnim), and Tom's music had a particular effect since she had fallen in love with him. By connecting her passion for music, flowers and Tom, she creates an emotional description that is steeped in pathos. As in her accounts of Trix and von Arnim, the emphasis is on the ability to 'communicate soul with soul'. When she transferred her affection for Tom to his brother, Garnet, she continued making this association between flowers and romantic love, commenting that her love for Garnet 'grows like a magic flower'.[42] Several days later, she elaborated, 'each day, it seems, do I take the blossoms from the tree of Love, and each day new and more wonderful flowers burst into bloom in their place'.[43]

The range of themes and emotions that Mansfield demonstrated towards flowers in her correspondence is reflected in her use of this motif in her fiction. She frequently uses them to explore homosocial and erotic love, and often invokes the impermanence of flowers in order to show that these relationships are fragile and fleeting. As her perspectives on romantic relationships changed throughout the course of her life, and as she matured in her writing style, it is possible to see flowers occupying a subtler and more sophisticated place in her work.

One of her earliest short stories, 'My Potplants' (1906), prefigures her later work in its use of flowers as a symbol for lost innocence, loneliness and death. The story concerns a woman who has bought 'great bunches' of primroses[44] and is thus prompted to recall her isolated childhood when she 'lived surrounded by a luxurious quantity of flowers'.[45] However, these were her 'only companions', since her mother had died and she has no siblings.[46] She remembers an occasion when she found a tall lily and began speaking to it, at which point a woman appeared with roses in her hands, 'dressed all in a white soft gown'.[47] She plays with the woman every day until Summer ends and the woman leaves, promising to return next year. At the end of the story the woman does not return, and the child walks a very long way to find her, only to see that she is weak. The protagonist is then roused from her reverie to find that her primroses have wilted. Mansfield's presentation of women and flowers in this piece presents a complex interplay between the feminist and the feminine. On the one hand, the story concerns an expression of female desire, yet the desire is for an angelic mother figure that reinforces the traditional female archetype. The flowers in the text would initially seem to bolster these archetypal qualities, with the character manifesting from a white lily, a flower associated with the Virgin Mary. However, it is the symbolism of flowers that undermines the permanence and authority of this figure; like the primroses that bookend the tale, her lifespan is painfully short. Mansfield suggests that femininity, while beautiful and desirable to some, has the ephemeral quality of a cut flower.

As Mansfield began to embark on her early romantic relationships, flowers begin to feature more prominently in narratives about love. 'The Yellow Chrysanthemum' (1908) is a work that coincided with the period when Trix was being hailed as 'the voice of the chrysanthemum'. In this Wildean text, a pair of lovers sit in a circular room. The woman, Radiana, is shaking chrysanthemum petals over her hair when she realises that 'the body of Summer is lying dead in the room'.[48] Her lover, Guido, then describes her in relation to the natural world: she is 'golden and white like the heart of a water lily', her 'face in the depths of her hair is like a pale flower in a deep forest'. 'One cannot possess so much beauty and yet live,'[49] he states with dramatic irony and, of course, since Radiana is an embodiment of Summer, she dies. The play ends with Guido flinging the purple curtains over Radiana's dead body, as though to draw them over the scene of Summer ending outside the window. The story has much in common with the somewhat melodramatic 'Study: The Death of a Rose' (1908), written in the same year, which compares the death of roses with the death of people, contrasting the 'tedious sobbing and gasping' of humans with the 'dainty delicate' demise of the flowers.[50] As in 'My Potplants', there is a correlation between the desired woman and the transience of flowers, and it is through the symbolism of flowers that Mansfield is able to depict a femininity that is both appealing and unsustainable.

When Mansfield wrote 'Carnation' in 1917, her narrative style and use of symbolist tropes were far more sophisticated. Whereas her earlier uses of flowers had more in common with von Arnim's approach to the subject, this story shows a departure from the tendency to dichotomise men and women by aligning the former with culture and the latter with nature. Instead, nature is used by both sexes as a way to explore sexuality and power. The story concerns two schoolgirls, Eve and Katie, who attend a French class on a hot summer's day. Eve is introduced as a girl who 'always carried a flower' and ended the school day by 'pulling it to pieces and eating it, petal by petal'.[51] Of the two girls, Eve is the more sensuous, confident and decidedly 'curious'; Katie is less sure of herself. This even extends to their command of French; Eve understands this R/romantic language fairly well, but Katie struggles with the vocabulary. Eve takes on the dominant role of educating Katie about the way that different flowers taste, encouraging Katie to 'taste' and eat, like the biblical Eve. Katie even perceives a danger and cruelty in Eve and imagines that her laugh had a 'long sharp beak and claws'.[52] While Eve is satisfied to hold the carnation in her cupped hands, Katie is occasionally overwhelmed by its scent, feeling that 'it was too much'.[53]

The two girls represent different stages of maturity and sexual confidence, and this is tested when M. Hugo, the teacher, reads them a long French poem. His manner of reading is highly sexual, oppressing his young, female listeners and building up to a crescendo of intensity that Gerri Kimber notes is orgasmic.[54] Although M. Hugo forces his sensuality and sentiments on to the class, his sexual potency is undermined by his 'pleading and imploring and entreating' tone and his silk bookmarker, which is 'embroidered in forget-me-nots'.[55] The name of this flower, with its entreaty to 'forget me not', matches Hugo's 'pleading' voice. His is a sentimental, delicate flower, but Eve's is more luxurious, being a deep red carnation 'that looked as if it had been dipped in wine and left in the dark to dry'.[56] The red wine colour corresponds with the carnation's intoxicating scent and adds to its heady, passionate associations. Kimber explains that carnations were religious symbols linked to the concept of reincarnation, and underlines their role in contemporary homosexual culture.[57] Their link with Eve's passionate nature is deepened in light of the fact that they were also a deeply romantic flower, often representative of true love.[58] The name of the flower also has slightly sexual undertones, having an aural link with the word 'carnal'. The sexual and romantic meanings of the carnation are apt in light of the end of the story, when, instead of eating the flower, Eve gives it to Katie as a '*Souvenir tendre*', dropping it 'down the front of Katie's blouse'.[59] In this story, the flower functions as a sophisticated representation of innocence and knowledge, signifying romantic courtship while indicating its more sinister and sexual undertones.

Over the course of both of their literary careers, Mansfield's and von Arnim's use of flowers demonstrates different approaches to nature, gender and sex. Their work represents an evolution in style that stretches from the height of Victorian garden writing to the modernist short story, and the representation of flowers in their work is indicative of the disparities between these two literary moments. Von Arnim's use of flowers is very much in keeping with the discussions in the earlier period and added significance at a time when gardening was becoming available to women as a profession. She uses the subjects of flowers and gardening as a way to explore woman's position in a patriarchal society, which results in a proto-ecofeminist exploration of women's relationship with the natural world and their interaction with a culture dominated by men. Mansfield similarly integrates flowers into her depiction of women and female relationships. This is evident in her personal life, where flowers served as a metaphor for intimacy between herself and other women, not least of all for her rapport with von Arnim. As her career progressed, however, her depiction of flowers changed in response to her more modernist approach, and she frequently subverted or inverted their cultural associations in order to create metaphors that were both surprising and multi-faceted. Ultimately, von Arnim's and Mansfield's passion for flowers reveal an intertextual dialogue that provides a window not only into the relationship between their work, but into their wider cultural and literary *milieu*.

Notes
1. *Letters* 3, p. 30.
2. *Letters* 4, p. 253.
3. *Letters* 3, p. 13.
4. *Letters* 4, p. 253.
5. That von Arnim was fond of flowers would not have been a new discovery, but it is possible that they had not spoken about this subject at length before, or that they were not in the right frame of mind to connect over it.
6. *Letters* 5, p. 23.
7. *Letters* 4, p. 260.
8. This is outlined by Jane Brown in her work *The Pursuit of Paradise: A Social History of Gardens and Gardening* (London: HarperCollins, 1999).
9. Greenaway's is perhaps the most famous of the flower language books, and Mansfield and von Arnim would certainly have been aware of it, not least because Greenaway would later illustrate von Arnim's book, *The April Baby's Book of Tunes* (1900). Greenaway also provided the illustrations for a section of *Elizabeth and Her German Garden* that was edited out from the first edition and published separately in Boston as *A Pious Pilgrimage* in 1901.
10. Beverly Seaton, *The Language of Flowers: A History* (Charlottesville: University Press of Virginia, 1995), p. 35.
11. Seaton, p. 17.
12. Fabienne Moine, *Women Poets in the Victorian Era: Cultural Practices and Nature Poetry* (Farnham: Ashgate, 2015), pp. 55–6.

13. Moine, pp. 53–4.
14. This range is described in Sarah Bilston's 'Queens of the Garden: Victorian Women Gardeners and the Rise of the Gardening Advice Text', *Victorian Literature and Culture*, 36:1 (2008), pp. 1–19 (p. 36).
15. Dianne Harris, 'Cultivating Power: The Language of Feminism in Women's Garden Literature, 1870–1920', *Landscape Journal*, 13:2 (1994), pp. 113–23 (p. 113).
16. Lynne Hapgood, *Margins of Desire: The Suburbs in Fiction and Culture, 1880–1925*, (Manchester: Manchester University Press, 2009), p. 93.
17. Harris, p. 120.
18. Talia Schaffer goes as far as to read the whole text as a veiled description of von Arnim's marriage. See *The Forgotten Female Aesthetes: Literary Culture in Late Victorian England* (London: University Press of Virginia, 2000).
19. Elizabeth von Arnim, *Elizabeth and Her German Garden* (London: Virago Press, 1985), p. 33. All further references are to this edition and are placed in parentheses in the text.
20. Rachel O'Connell, 'Love Scenes and Garden Plots: Form and Femininity in Elizabeth von Arnim's *Elizabeth and Her German Garden*', *Women: A Cultural Review*, 28:1–2 (2017), pp. 22–39 (p. 32).
21. O'Connell, p. 28. This motif of isolation is reinforced in *The Solitary Summer* (1899), the sequel to *Elizabeth and Her German Garden*, where Elizabeth yearns to have the garden to herself for the duration of one season.
22. O'Connell, p. 31.
23. O'Connell, p. 32.
24. The one exception is a male visitor who 'knows a great deal about gardening' and approves of all the work that she has done. Von Arnim, *Elizabeth and Her German Garden*, pp. 66–7.
25. Elizabeth von Arnim, *Vera* (London: Macmillan, 1921), p. 130.
26. It is this oscillation between hyperfemininity and feminism in von Arnim's work that Juliane Römhild identifies in her book, *Femininity and Authorship in the Novels of Elizabeth von Arnim: At Her Most Radiant Moment* (Madison, NJ: Fairleigh Dickinson University Press, 2014).
27. Kathleen Jones, *Katherine Mansfield: The Story-Teller* (Edinburgh: Edinburgh University Press, 2010), p. 60. See also Isobel Maddison, '"Worms of the Same Family": Elizabeth von Arnim and Katherine Mansfield', in *Elizabeth von Arnim: Beyond the German Garden* (Farnham: Ashgate, 2013), pp. 85–103.
28. *Letters* 4, p. 287.
29. *Letters* 5, p. 23.
30. *Letters* 1, p. 48.
31. She won a prize for the poem, which was published with details of the party in the *New Zealand Free Lance*, 27 June 1908. *Letters* 1, p. 49, n. 7.
32. 'One room, where tea was to be served, was entirely draped with violet silk, from the palest to the darkest shades [...]. All the furniture was taken away, and instead, along the walls, were placed banks of artificial moss and violets.' Alice Muriel Williamson, *Lady Betty Across the Water* (London: McClure, Phillips, 1906), p. 78.
33. This may be reflected in the symbolism of the flower, which, in addition to meaning 'modesty, prudery, candour', was also representative of 'reciprocal friendship'. Seaton, p. 196.
34. *Letters* 4, p. 340.
35. *Letters* 4, pp. 346–7.

36. *Letters* 3, p. 263.
37. *Letters* 3, p. 223.
38. *Letters* 1, p. 121.
39. *Letters* 4, p. 287.
40. *Letters* 1, p. 43.
41. *Letters* 1, p. 43.
42. *Letters* 1, p. 71.
43. *Letters* 1, p. 76. She sent him a poem titled 'The Lilac Tree', which she asks him to set to music.
44. CW1, p. 32.
45. CW1, p. 33.
46. CW1, p. 33.
47. CW1, p. 33.
48. CW1, p. 117.
49. CW1, p. 117.
50. CW1, pp. 138–9.
51. CW2, p. 160.
52. CW2, p. 160.
53. CW2, p. 162.
54. Gerri Kimber, *Katherine Mansfield: The View from France* (Oxford: Peter Lang, 2008), p. 107. Kimber considers this one of Mansfield's most 'sexually charged stories' and argues that it is loosely based on Baudelaire's poem 'Parfum exotique', from *Les Fleurs du mal*. See Kimber, p. 105.
55. CW2, p. 163.
56. CW1, p. 160.
57. Kimber, p. 107.
58. Seaton, p. 146.
59. CW1, p. 162.

Strange Monsters: The Struggle for Women's Validity as Artists in the Writings of Elizabeth von Arnim and Katherine Mansfield

Richard Cappuccio

> And now we who are writing women and strange monsters
> Still search our hearts to find the difficult answers
> Still hope that we may learn to lay our hands
> More gently and more subtly on the burning sands.[1]
>   May Sarton, 'My Sisters, O My Sisters'

The success of Elizabeth von Arnim's novel *Elizabeth and Her German Garden* (1898) with both English and German audiences loomed large for the young Katherine Mansfield. As early as 1937, Guy H. Scholefield acknowledged von Arnim's influence on Mansfield's writing:

> [Von Arnim's] success [...] fired [Mansfield's] imagination and formulated in her mind the possibilities which until then had been mere dreams, and something childish at that. All through life the younger girl admired with increasing enthusiasm the personality and the talent of her elder cousin.[2]

With an increased acknowledgment of Mansfield's impact on modernism, there has, too, been a more receptive attitude towards von Arnim's influence on her young cousin, especially when considering those stories collected as *In a German Pension* (1911). Isobel Maddison, for instance, reminds readers that the older cousin's 'skill as an author seeped into Mansfield's [...] early work'.[3] This essay examines those influences through the strength of the narrator in the form of the fictional diary in *Elizabeth and Her German Garden* and through the use of the arts as a subtext for the emerging position of the woman writer. Traditionally, women's diaries were surrounded by the myth that they were '"private, domestic, and psychological [and] thought to conform to the [...] banal elements" of a woman's life'.[4] Elizabeth's diary, however, is more than the quotidian details of domesticity; von Arnim's narrator exposes the cultural attitude that artistic women battled against. In the foreground, Elizabeth embraces the womanly arts; she is the gardener who fills beds with 'pansies, [. . .] dwarf mignonette' and roses. More importantly, the narrator stands out as a diarist, a stronger identity than gardener, wife, or mother.[5] Furthermore, she recognises that having her creative instincts limited by another is cruel; she 'shall never pander to the Man of Wrath's wishes again' (p. 26). In her garden, Elizabeth finds expression that stimulates a major literary achievement, which, much like Mansfield's actual diaries, allows her to be 'a mimic, ingénue, prima donna, tragedian, and comedian', able to confront the 'cultural expectations of marriage'.[6]

The original publication in *The New Age* of Mansfield's story 'Germans at Meat' (1910) included a main character, an Englishwoman named Kathleen, indicating that she was using her personal experience at the Pension Müller in Bad Wörishofen.[7] Maddison offers the suggestion that Mansfield's revision of the original third-person perspective to the first person for book publication was 'probably made to create greater coherence across those "Pension Sketches"'.[8] Consistent voice and tone in several of the sketches also lend the impression that the stories are diary entries.[9]

Both von Arnim and Mansfield employ Anglophone narrators on foreign soil, but the male hegemonic culture is not limited to its German boundaries. In her travels, Mansfield recognised an 'impertinent, arrogant and slightly amused attitude towards a woman who traveled alone'.[10] Von Arnim similarly wrote, 'It's no fun travelling alone [. . .] if you're a woman.'[11] But the works set around a German garden and in a German pension discussed here are not travel narratives; instead, the foreign setting generates an understanding of, and empathy for, the narrators as female artists who are not accepted within the cultural norm. The female artist's criticism of traditional roles is more clearly spotlighted in a foreign setting and would have been more palatable to contemporary English audiences willing to take the side of an English character. Present-day readers of Mansfield and von Arnim, especially the latter's novel *Christine* (1917), may be distracted by the unfavourable portrayal of German characters that would have been more acceptable at the time of publication. Both Todd Martin and Maddison, however, offer correctives: Martin notes the difference in attitude at the time in New Zealand and Great Britain towards Germany and finds that Mansfield 'demonstrates some empathy with the Germans and, even when she criticises them, her critiques have less to do with racial stereotypes and more to do with human weaknesses'.[12] Maddison's assessment of *Elizabeth and Her German Garden* and its sequel, *The Solitary*

Summer (1899), is that they 'include an indirect, irreverent critique of a nation and its people, though neither is without affection for individual Germans'.[13] While readers must inevitably confront the ridicule of German characters at a time of Anglo-German tensions when reading these texts by Mansfield and von Arnim, this is also a mirror of the artist's struggle.

While some critics have neglected von Arnim's work, her writing anticipates a modernist vision for female autonomy. In particular, Elizabeth visualises the writer's need for private space:

> The Hirschwald is a little open wood of silver birches and springy turf starred with flowers, and there is a tiny stream meandering amiably about it and decking itself in June with yellow flags. I have dreams of having a little cottage built there, with the daisies up to the door, and no path of any sort [. . .]. (p. 30)

Despite the cultural limits she encounters, the female artist envisions agency, overseeing conditions for the writer's private space. Her cottage should, she states,

> Just [be] big enough to hold myself and one baby inside [. . .]. Sometimes, when in the mood for society, we would invite the remaining babies to tea [. . .] but no one less innocent and easily pleased than a baby would be permitted to darken the effulgence of our sunny cottage [. . .]. (p. 30)

By necessity or choice, Elizabeth allows the youngest child entrance, but she also controls the situation to avoid the intrusion of 'Handfuls of babies' that residents of Mansfield's German pension see as every woman's future.[14] In Mansfield's story 'Frau Fischer', for example, the Frau accepts the captivity that comes with her motherhood, a '"father of a family [who] cannot leave you. Think of the delight and excitement when he [sees] you!"' (p. 198). Rather than this worrying picture of domestic captivity, Elizabeth articulates the necessity for a space that is free from the presence of a husband, a place with no path for others to find her. She envisions further control over her space by embracing the empty bed: 'I am quite happy [alone]' (p. 31). But she must also explain her sense of freedom against the protestations from women who accept their roles:

> 'But I am quite happy,' I began, as soon as I could put in a word.
> 'Ah, a good little wife, making the best of it,' and the female potentate patted my hand, but continued to gloomily shake her head.
> 'You cannot possibly be happy [. . .],' asserted another lady, the wife of a high military authority and not accustomed to be contradicted. (pp. 31–2)

Elizabeth ironically describes these women who live within the confines of assigned roles with titles and associations that accentuate their false sense of authority. Despite their self-perceived status and power, they cannot believe that a woman could find anything satisfying about her independence, believing such unconventionality is unnatural.[15] Elizabeth interrupts herself when she realises that she cannot convince them otherwise:

> 'I am not solitary. [...] I sleighed and skated, and then there were the children, and shelves and shelves full of ——' I was going to say books, but stopped. Reading is an occupation for men; for women it is a reprehensible waste of time. And how could I talk to them of the happiness I felt when the sun shone on the snow, or of the deep delight of hoar-frost days? (pp. 32–3)

Elizabeth's idea of the empty bed includes many desirable elements: seclusion, children in their place, and her garden, suggesting a poetic sensitivity to nature and a rich intellectual life of reading. There is a telling entry when she records, 'he sang true who sang – Two paradises 'twere in one to live in Paradise alone' (p. 28). With this reference to Andrew Marvell's 'The Garden', von Arnim portrays Elizabeth's pleasure in solitude by regendering the creation story. In his lines leading to the quotation, Marvell celebrates the peace Adam knew before Eve:

> Such was that happy garden-state,
> While man there walk'd without a mate;
> After a place so pure and sweet,
> What other help could yet be meet!
> But 'twas beyond a mortal's share
> To wander solitary there:
> Two paradises 'twere in one
> To live in paradise alone.[16]

Elizabeth turns her back on the 'rude' world that views her as '*sehr anspruchslos* [very undemanding]' and concludes, 'I can entertain myself quite well for weeks together, hardly aware, except for the pervading peace, that I have been alone at all'; if someone is to share her company, it must be as an equal, 'to enjoy the beauty with me. [...] the whole garden [...] singing – not the untiring birds only, but the vigorous plants, the happy grass and trees, the lilac bushes – oh, those lilac bushes!' (p. 35). The inclusion of the interjection 'oh' before the repetition of 'lilac bushes' has the depth of Hopkins's 'ah' in 'God's Grandeur'.[17] Elizabeth's is not a garden for a hobbyist; instead, it is a garden where feeling inspires self-awareness.

Like Mansfield and Virginia Woolf in their later diaries, von Arnim elevates the diary from a record of the mundane to an exploration of the mind. To differentiate Elizabeth's voice from that of other women, von Arnim contrasts her narrator with Minora, the 'ambitious and hardworking' student whom Elizabeth befriends and lets visit at Christmas (p. 87). The self-absorbed Minora, as her name suggests, is a lesser writer, and more an invader than an expatriate. The April baby mistakes Minora's name for that of a distant island; Elizabeth and another guest, Irais, are cautious around her: '"My dear," I said breathlessly to Irais [...] "she writes books!"' (pp. 92–3). Irais is shocked: '"How dreadful! [...] I never met a young girl who did that before"' (pp. 92–3). Von Arnim's criticism is not, however, of a woman writer, but about a writer without her own voice, a parrot rather than a poet. Minora looks to others for 'copy', writing in her notebook what others say: '"If you jot down all we say and then publish it, will it still be your book?" asked Irais. But Minora was so busy scribbling that she did not hear' (p. 95). When Elizabeth hears Minora speaking in an 'unknown tongue', it turns out to be an over-confident attempt at speaking German. Minora's language skills, like her musical ones, are out of practice, and, as Elizabeth observes, she knows 'what *that*' sounds like (p. 96).

This criticism of Minora demands more of women writers and reflects a standard that breaks with the culture's denial of women's voices. As Scholefield notes:

> You must remember that when the twentieth century opened, the saying of Queen Victoria 'We are not amused' was still the keynote of social convention in England, and no less in New Zealand. Women authors, few and far between, still wrote under *noms de plume* [...] for the old reason that it was considered not quite the thing for a woman to write at all.[18]

In 'The Advanced Lady', Mansfield comments on the status of women by denying both writers, one German and one English, their given names. Another character, Fräulein Elsa, sees the creative spirit as a sign that a woman is lost: she 'cannot help feeling convinced that [the advanced lady] has some secret sorrow [because] she remains hours and hours by herself, writing' (p. 235). In 'Frau Fischer', the narrator is a secretive writer, admitting only to writing letters, traditionally 'the form of writing most accessible to and acceptable for women'.[19] Positioning the authorship of the sketch in the background reinforces the status quo, a culture in which men are the ones expected to write books. Frau Fischer laments that the guest, Herr Rat, has not yet gathered his tales for publication; as the German word *Rat* [advice] suggests, readers turn to men for guidance. Herr Rat, however, is unproductive, a situation he blames on the difficulty of his task: '"Time – time. I am getting a few notes together"' (p. 196). The narrator also requires time and solitude to write; she removes herself to 'write some letters', a cover that allows her to record the tale. She mentions the popular hagiographies she reads, distracting the reader from her primary task, a meticulous record of her observations about the pension guests who are certainly not portrayed as saints.

Frau Fischer is the busybody who knocks on the door, invading the narrator's privacy and demanding a background story: '"Now, tell me something really interesting about your life. When I meet new people I squeeze them dry like a sponge"' (p. 196). Frau Fischer, who has spent many years around residents of the pension, anticipates a fiction: '"To begin with – you are married"' (p. 196). The narrator complies with a first draft about her fictional husband to explain her stay and quickly revises it with a romantic scenario: her husband is 'a sea-captain on a long and perilous voyage' (p. 196). Frau Fischer suggests her own changes to this plot:

> 'Admit, now, that you keep your journeys secret from him. For what man would think of allowing a woman with such a wealth of hair to go wandering in foreign countries? Now, supposing that you lost your purse at midnight in a snowbound train in Russia?' (p. 196)

Such a demanding editorial recommendation raises the spectre of her unattached status.

Jenny McDonnell argues that Frau Fischer is a stand-in for Beatrice Hastings, who was 'invested with the authority of reshaping Mansfield's own writing for the *New Age*'.[20] The narrator, McDonnell argues, 'gives a conventional (and melodramatic) shape to her fiction. [... H]er violent and abrupt conclusion [. . .] proves to be an act of self-silencing [. . .] that ultimately indicates her realization that Frau Fischer wields the power to shape her narrative.'[21] The narrator, rather than 'awaiting that phantom ship for which all women love to suppose they hunger', the conventional role satirised in the German pension stories, instead decides to 'send [her fictional husband] down somewhere off Cape Horn' (p. 198). Rather than being led into a plot of resigned motherhood, the narrator kills off the imaginary husband, keeping the final revision to herself, and reveals the writer fighting for her authorial voice.

Mansfield further explores this struggle for an independent voice in 'The Modern Soul'. Fräulein Sonia possesses some characteristics of the modern woman: she recognises a woman's need for self-expression, telling the narrator, 'when I act I *am*' (p. 218). However, if the men in *In a German Pension* have gluttonous appetites in their need to devour the women, the woman artist suffers a starvation with a misplaced alliance to other women, especially the dominant mother. About that relationship Sonia admits, 'Living with her I live with the coffin of my unborn aspirations' (p. 219). Such maternal dominance undermines women's self-expression: '"There is so little magic. [. . .] There is none of that mysterious perfume which floats almost as a visible thing from the souls of the Viennese audiences. My spirit starves for want of that. . . . Starves," she repeated' (pp. 218–19).

Conversely, there is no such self-examination in Professor Windberg, who is anything but starved. Mansfield, like von Arnim, was a serious musician and knew the cultural advantages men had in that field. The story opens with Herr Professor returning from playing Grieg's 'Ich Liebe Dich' ['I love you'] on his trombone out in the woods; he replenishes his saliva by eating cherries after 'those sustained blasts on "liebe"' (p. 214). His musical expression and his ego are both *fortissimo*, upending expectations for the pastoral. The professor is condescending to the narrator: if 'one wishes to satisfy the desires of nature one must be strong enough to ignore the facts of nature. . . . The conversation is not out of your depth?' (p. 214). The narrator shares a Wildean aside with the reader: 'I was grateful, without showing undue excitement' (p. 214). The narrator understands the dominant authority, and Fräulein Sonia is an example of how women are controlled: she is familiar with Heine, Ibsen and Japanese art, but both Windberg and her mother reinforce male superiority. When Fräulein Sonia observes 'swallows in flight' and says, 'they are like a little flock of Japanese thoughts', the Professor questions her: 'But why do you say "Japanese"? Could you not compare them with equal veracity to a little flock of German thoughts in flight?' (p. 216). Her mother offers an example of metaphor by her late husband: '"England is merely an island of beef flesh swimming in a warm gulf sea of gravy." Such a brilliant way of putting things' (p. 216). Such corrections send a clear message to Fräulein Sonia: do not express yourself.

Sydney Janet Kaplan observes that Mansfield's male biographers have had 'certain difficulties coming to terms with [her] feminism and with her youthful struggles for independence'.[22] Kaplan further contends, 'Mansfield's emancipation was to be through her efforts as an artist [. . .]. Her feminism, therefore, focused on the area of her greatest personal knowledge: sexuality and women's experience of it.'[23] Fräulein Sonia's confession that she is 'curiously sapphic' reveals another suppressed part of her self: she tells the narrator, 'I long to do wild, passionate things' (p. 219). Instead of expressing such desires, Fräulein Sonia accepts the tragic plot of an Ibsen drama with no 'possible light out of this darkness' (p. 220). In spite of latent insight into both her sexuality and her artistic needs, Fräulein Sonia is paralysed by thoughts that are far from modern. She retreats to Herr Professor and remains torn between her artistic ambition and filial obligation.

The narrator might at first appear as the foil to Fräulein Sonia's conventional thinking: she observes that marriage to the professor is better suited to the overbearing mother and later sees Fräulein Sonia's fainting episode in terms of performance, dramatic and 'quite beautiful' (p. 221). The narrator is 'cross' when she fetches the professor to help. Her evaluation is simple: 'Modern souls oughtn't to wear [stays]' (p. 221). Any brace, whether as a foundation for womanly appearance or as a support for marriage, is destructive for the modern soul. As in other Mansfield stories, the reader is given the opportunity for an epiphany that the character does not experience. The story's effectiveness rests in the empathy the reader feels with the woman on the verge of modernity; Sonia recognises that marriage is merely a 'solution' for the 'genius [who] cannot hope to mate' (p. 220).

'The Modern Soul' explores the struggle to define feminism. In 1926, when *In a German Pension* was republished, *The New York Times* recognised its importance in discussing 'the resentment of a certain type of woman against child-bearing'.[24] That 'certain type' of woman may be free of Victorian stays but she is, nevertheless, still conflicted. Fräulein Sonia is resigned to seek a man whom she views as a 'pillow' and who can help care for her mother, but the story does not conclude simply. The narrator adds the final words, 'I wondered'; yes, she might be referring to the Fräulein and the professor who are spending the day in the woods, but the observation simultaneously points inward (p. 221). Mansfield examines the complex position for women. The narrator's earlier cynicism does not mitigate her fright when Fräulein Sonia faints: in spite of another Wildean response, 'faint away; but please hurry over it', her return to the pension to get help escalates to running as she looks back at 'the dark form of the modern soul' (p. 220). That phrase includes a wide breadth: not only does it reference Fräulein Sonia, but it also questions the way women see themselves. The narrator does, after all, run for the help of a man.

In *Christine* (1917), von Arnim writes about the similar pressure of filial obligation and the practicality of marriage adding to women's struggle for artistic fulfilment. She writes an epistolary novel, which allows for an unmediated female voice. Indeed, early examples of the genre frequently place 'a female figure at the center of a male-authored text', and the form gained in popularity because it is essentially 'speaking in the private female voice [which reflects] cultural anxieties about the place of women in the literary marketplace and taboos against women writing, and more broadly about women's public voice'.[25] One might even read the form as a response to Mansfield's Fräulein Sonia, who reads writers' 'unedited letters [for] some touch, some sign of myself' (p. 219).

Christine was published under the pseudonym Alice Cholmondeley, and the press debated the identity of the author at the time of publication.[26] Von Arnim was writing *Christine* while in the United States and was likely to be conscious that the portrayal of the Germans as hard, 'brutal' and 'greedy' would help recruit American sympathy for the war.[27] The pseudonymous publication, however, should not imply that the novel is simply a work of anti-German propaganda.[28] Maddison explains that von Arnim's 'fierce repudiation of authorship, even amongst friends, is almost certainly because any connection with herself could have resulted in unhappy consequences for [her daughter] Trix', who remained in Germany.[29] Although it was widely reviewed and had strong sales at the time of publication, today it is largely unread and undervalued, dismissed as sentimental or even mawkish. The tone of Christine's letters, however, is not so different from that of von Arnim's when writing to Trix.[30] In those letters, von Arnim speaks in superlatives, accentuates adverbs with underlining, uses multiple modifiers to express her intimate tone, and addresses her daughter as 'My darling little Trixie'.[31]

Von Arnim writes in a similarly florid style in *Christine*. In her first letter, Christine writes,

> My blessed little mother, here I am safe, and before I unpack or do a thing I'm writing you a little line of love. I sent a telegram at the station, so that you'll know at once that nobody has eaten me on the way, as you seem rather to fear. It is wonderful to be here, quite on my own, as if I were a young man starting his career. (p. 1)

This reassurance goes further than confirming that all is well: after all, she has already sent a telegram. One of the tragic elements of the novel is that Christine, despite her talent and willingness for risk, can see her experience only 'as if' she 'were a [. . .] man'. Her vision for her material safety, she says, is as a 'son, and husband, [. . .] and I'm going to earn both our livings for us, and take care of you forever' (p. 2). By the end of the introduction, readers are already aware of the novel's ending; however, the novel's strength is not in picturing Germany on the brink of war, but, rather, its consideration of a different battlefield, the hostile mind-set towards a gifted female artist. Those attitudes cannot be blamed solely on a war between nations.

Von Arnim writes, 'The war killed Christine, just as surely as if she had been a soldier in the trenches,' but slyly adds, 'I will not write of her great gift, which was extraordinary' (p. vi). However, throughout the novel, readers are told of Christine's exceptional talent, one that mirrors both von Arnim's and Mansfield's musical skill. Von Arnim's musical references are not the simple melodies that she published in her *April Baby's Book of Tunes* (1900). Instead, the references to music reveal Christine's rare gift: in her youth, Christine played for both Joseph Joachim, a violinist who collaborated with Brahms, and Eugène Ysaÿe, whose compositions are still frequently performed (p. 13). Like Paganini's rival, Heinrich Ernst, whose *Pathétique Concerto* (opus 23) she plays, Christine is a prodigy. Her musical ability shows an important progression: her repertoire moves from the technically challenging to music that requires her to find her own voice. In one of her last letters from Berlin, Christine writes that she is practising Beethoven's *Violin Concerto*, a work that Itzhak Perlman considers 'the greatest concerto written for the violin [because] it's very transparent; you can't hide behind it'.[32] This reference might very well inform the reader's reaction to an important question: if Christine finds her voice in the Beethoven concerto, does it empower her to leave Berlin?

In spite of such extraordinary skill, Christine demeans her talent and falls victim to the hegemony of male authority; she refers to her talent as a 'lucky facility' (p. 2). Rather than elevate herself, Christine compliments her tutor's violin, on which she plays the *Kreutzer Sonata*: 'The Strad [...] seemed to be playing itself, singing to me, telling me strange and beautiful secrets' (p. 61). Even when playing her own violin, she credits the instrument rather than herself: 'And so is all this beauty of summer in the woods, and so is music, and my violin when it gets playing to me' (p. 128). She understates her talent because the culture demeans the woman artist: her teacher, Kloster, may concede Christine's 'unusual gift' but, after hearing her play Bach, he is none the less surprised by the 'well-washed, nice-looking, foolish, rich, nothing-at-all English Mees'. In Kloster's opinion, Christine may have talent but she must practise with a '*verteufelte Unermüdlichkeit*' [a devilish tirelessness], a phrase that suggests a woman must agree to a Faustian bargain to be an artist (p. 15). Kloster tells Christine that 'A woman should never be an artist. [...] It is sheer malice on the part of Providence to have taken you, a woman, as the vessel which is to carry this great gift about the world' (pp. 152–4). Kloster further explains that a woman is, as the culture demands, expected to be a wife:

'a woman artist who falls in love neglects everything and merely loves. [...] I urge you to marry quickly. Then the woman, so unfortunately singled out by Providence to be something she is not fitted for, having married and secured her husband, prey, victim, or whatever you prefer to call him [...] succeeds in steering clear of detaining and delaying objects like cradles, is cured and can go back with proper serenity to that which alone matters, Art and the work necessary to produce it. But she will have wasted time,' he said, shaking his head. 'She will most sadly have wasted time. [...] Marry quickly. Then there may be recovery.' (pp. 153–4)

Kloster regards Christine not as an artist but as a woman with the talent of a gifted male. She possesses a *Beethovenkopf*: '"you have the real Beethoven brow," Kloster continues, " – the very shape – and I must touch it [...]. You might be his child"' (p. 45). Kloster, sounding like Tolstoy in his 'Kreutzer Sonata' with its indictment of marriage, reveals a cautionary warning: Christine's acceptance of marriage is the real tragedy of the novel. Kloster ignores Christine's attempt to express her preference for the word 'husband' rather than his choice of 'prey [or] victim' (p. 154). He dismisses Christine as a woman with a 'precious, immortal gift, placed in such shaky small hands' (p. 155). Ultimately, the novel closes with Christine vulnerable and victimised. Music offers no safety; she is, in the end, travelling without her violin in its case.

Mansfield, in 'The Singing Lesson' (1920), pursued von Arnim's observations that a woman's knowledge of the arts does not ensure her self-knowledge. Mansfield's Miss Meadows, like von Arnim's Professor Kloster, dominates rather than nurtures the young artist's experience. Despondent after receiving a letter from her fiancé ending their engagement, Miss Meadows, in her position of authority over younger women, directs her students in singing the lyrics of Mendelssohn's 'Herbslied', chosen because the words echo her own despair: 'Fast! Ah, too Fast Fade the Ro-o-ses of Pleasure; / Soon Autumn yields unto Wi-i-nter Drear.'[33] Miss Meadows not only is absorbed by self-pity, but overrides her students' youthful optimism and 'gleeful excitement'; she commands impressionable female students to '"Repeat! Repeat!"' or to keep absolute '"Silence [...]!"'[34] Later, the class is interrupted when Miss Meadows receives a telegram from her fiancé asking forgiveness, and she, in turn, is scolded by the dour headmistress, who assumes the message is frivolous. Miss Meadows returns to the classroom to lead the same group of young women in a celebratory song of love. Only a naïve reader could see the conclusion as romantic; instead, Miss Meadows's reaction is reflected in the clinging leaves on the willow trees outside the classroom window, wriggling 'like fishes caught on a line'.[35] Here, as in *Christine*, tragedy lies in women who trust in convention. By this time in her writing life, Mansfield had found a distinctive style. She writes a story free from traditional form, and she scores a contrapuntal masterpiece, weaving Mendelssohn's lyric, Miss Meadows's thoughts,

Basil's letter and ambient sounds, exhibiting her confident writer's voice.

Even if von Arnim's popular writing did not develop into what Maddison calls Mansfield's 'oblique and allusive style that is thought to epitomize' modernism, contemporary readers should recognise that both writers were dealing with challenges for women in the arts and questioning 'the validity of marriage as the ultimate female destination'.[36] Neither offered simple solutions; Mansfield was angered when the publisher, Constable, marketed her as a voice for women. She particularly objected to the blurb on the dust jacket for *Bliss*:

> I think it so insulting & disgusting and undignified that – well – there you are! Its no good suffering all over again. But the bit about 'women will learn by heart and not repeat' – God! Why didn't they have a photograph of me looking through a garter![37]

While the political climate and the writer's relationship to her art are important in understanding both writers historically, contemporary readers may glean more from discussions of the cultural demands and the weight of marriage on the woman-artist. In a review in 1919, Mansfield dismissed characterisations that would outlive both her and her cousin, women who 'come to recognize the old, old charm of man's strength and woman's weakness'.[38]

Notes

1. May Sarton, 'My Sisters, O My Sisters', in Serena Sue Hilsinger and Lois Brynes, eds, *Selected Poems of May Sarton* (New York: Norton, 1978), pp. 192–3.
2. G. H. Scholefield, 'Katherine Mansfield', in Sir Harold Beauchamp, *Reminiscences and Recollections* (New Plymouth, NZ: Thomas Avery & Sons, 1937), p. 191.
3. Isobel Maddison, *Elizabeth von Arnim: Beyond the German Garden* (Farnham: Ashgate, 2013), p. 85.
4. Valerie Raoul, 'Women and Diaries: Gender and Genres', quoted in Deborah Martinson, *In the Presence of Audience* (Canton: Ohio University Press, 2003), p. 4.
5. Elizabeth von Arnim, *Elizabeth and Her German Garden* (London: Macmillan, 1899), p. 16. All further references to the novel are to this edition and are cited in parentheses.
6. Martinson, p. 14.
7. Antony Alpers, ed., *The Stories of Katherine Mansfield: Definitive Edition* (Auckland: Oxford University Press, 1984), pp. 547–8.
8. Isobel Maddison, 'Mansfield's "Writing Game" and World War One', in Gerri Kimber, Todd Martin, Delia da Sousa Correa, Isobel Maddison and Alice Kelly, eds, *Katherine Mansfield and World War One* (Edinburgh: Edinburgh University Press, 2014), p. 49.
9. The BBC appears to have responded to the consistent voice by compressing several stories from *In a German Pension* in their dramatisation of 'Germans at Meat'. Robin Chapman, *A Picture of Katherine Mansfield*, directed by Alan Cooke (UK: BBC2, 1973), DVD 2015.
10. CW2, p. 10.

11. Alice Cholmondeley, *Christine* (New York: Macmillan, 1917), p. 102. All further references to this novel are to this edition and are cited in parentheses.
12. W. Todd Martin, '"Unmasking" the First Person Narrator of *In a German Pension*', in Janet Wilson, Gerri Kimber and Delia da Sousa Correa, eds, *Katherine Mansfield and the (Post)colonial* (Edinburgh: Edinburgh University Press, 2013), p. 84.
13. Maddison, *Elizabeth von Arnim*, p. 57.
14. CW1, p. 198. All further references to stories in *In a German Pension* are to volume 1 of the Edinburgh Collected Works and are cited in parentheses.
15. The idea shocked even Mansfield, who wrote that von Arnim 'only wants a *male appearance*. Theres her essential falsity.' *Letters* 4, p. 105.
16. Andrew Marvell, 'The Garden', in Margaret Ferguson, Mary Jo Salter and Jon Stallworthy, eds, *The Norton Anthology of Poetry: Shorter Fourth Edition* (New York: Norton, 1997), pp. 275–6.
17. Hopkins, 'God's Grandeur', in *Norton Anthology*, p. 662.
18. Scholefield, p. 193.
19. Amanda Gilroy and W. M. Verhoeven, eds, *Epistolary Histories* (Charlottesville: University Press of Virginia, 2000), p. 2.
20. Jenny McDonnell, *Katherine Mansfield and the Modernist Marketplace* (Basingstoke: Palgrave Macmillan, 2010), p. 37.
21. McDonnell, pp. 37–8.
22. Sydney Janet Kaplan, *Katherine Mansfield and the Origins of Modernist Fiction* (Ithaca, NY: Cornell University Press, 1991), p. 125.
23. Kaplan, p. 129.
24. John Crawford, 'Katherine Mansfield Reconsidered: Her First Book Contains the Germs of Her Later Work', *New York Times Book Review*, 31 January 1926, p. 2.
25. Gilroy and Verhoeven, pp. 4–5.
26. Maddison, *Elizabeth von Arnim*, pp. 78–9.
27. Jennifer Walker, *Elizabeth of the German Garden: A Literary Journey* (Brighton: Book Guild, 2013), p. 202. Also see Maddison, *Elizabeth von Arnim*, p. 64.
28. While Mansfield distanced herself from her first collection of stories and did not allow it to be reprinted, Vincent O'Sullivan states that it was Mansfield's 'distaste for fashionable jingoism during the hostilities [that] led her to refuse the re-issue of *In a German Pension*. [She] did not want [her writing] turned to the ends of propaganda' ('Introduction', in *Letters* 2, p. xi).
29. Maddison, *Elizabeth von Arnim*, p. 81.
30. See Juliane Römhild's essay in this collection.
31. Elizabeth Russell, letter to Beatrix von Hirschberg, 1 September 1929, Huntington Library (Countess Russell Papers, ER1433).
32. 'Itzhak Perlman Talks About the Beethoven Violin Concerto', available at <https://www.lovenurturedmusic.org/itzhak-perlman-talks-about-the-beethoven-violin-concerto/> (last accessed 6 August 2018).
33. CW2, p. 236.
34. CW2, pp. 238; 235.
35. CW2, p. 237.
36. Maddison, *Elizabeth von Arnim*, pp. 100–1.
37. *Letters* 4, p. 137.
38. Katherine Mansfield, 'A Post-War and a Victorian Novel', in John Middleton Murry, ed., *Katherine Mansfield: Novels and Novelists* (New York: Knopf, 1930), p. 132.

'Not a Feminist, but...': Elizabeth von Arnim and Female Resistance

Alison Hennegan

Although Katherine Mansfield is today usually far better known to most readers than her older, Australian-born cousin, Elizabeth Beauchamp, the two women had some very important things in common, the most important perhaps being their dedication to writing. It is easy not to know or realise that during Mansfield's poignantly short life, von Arnim was by far the better known author. A second disastrous marriage would make her, briefly, Countess Russell, unhappy wife to Bertrand Russell's brother. Thinly disguised as the tyrannical husband, Edward Wemyss, he provided rich copy for her 1921 novel, *Vera*.

Von Arnim, like Mansfield, was accordingly a 'colonial' (though politically British), who became and remained a European. It was her first book, *Elizabeth and Her German Garden*, which quickly established her critical reputation and popularity with readers in 1898. Publishing thereafter as 'the author of *Elizabeth and Her German Garden*', she produced a steady stream of novels until her death in 1941. In them, she identified and addressed many of the same perplexities and struggles of women's lives that also preoccupied her younger cousin. Although Mansfield is invariably hailed as a modernist whereas von Arnim has often been disparagingly categorised as 'middle-brow', both those terms have, of recent years, been rightly subjected to increasing scrutiny.[1] Mansfield was often personally irritated by von Arnim, yet she recognised affinities of thought, attitude and values between the two of them, and she understood and acknowledged how important her cousin had been to her, as a woman and as a writer. I hope some of the reasons for that will become clear in what follows.

Most of my first copies of von Arnim's novels, bought for a few pence, were purchased from Cambridge bookshops and market stalls between 1970 and 1972, so I seem to have started reading von Arnim some forty-eight years ago, almost half a century away. That pre-dates, or is in the very earliest stages of, Second Wave feminism's 'rediscovery' of neglected women writers and reconsiderations of ways of reading them, and it is well before the emergence of the current concern with the middle-brow. Much of what I offer here comes, therefore, in the form of quite personal meditations and ponderings, prompted by my recent rereadings – undertaken for the talk on which this essay is based – of von Arnim.

My title, 'Not a Feminist but ...', points both backwards to the emergence of First Wave feminism, from the mid-nineteenth century onwards, and forwards to the decades after von Arnim's death and into our own times. It echoes a very familiar formulation often heard from women who, for whatever reason, do not wish to associate themselves formally with feminism, but who will then go on to voice their complete and often ardent support for clearly feminist demands and positions.

While I was rereading this time around, I was constantly aware of how much of von Arnim finds a parallel with Virginia Woolf, especially with *A Room of One's Own* (1928) and *Three Guineas* (1938). Questions Woolf raises there constantly present themselves in von Arnim's work, and her characters of both sexes grapple with them, with varying degrees of success. What, for example, are women for? What do they want? Who/what do they *think* they are? What or who tells them that? Are they *anything*, if marriage and motherhood are removed from the equation? And what really is 'a woman's work'? And I found myself turning time and again to those other basic and recurring preoccupations that Woolf identifies and that trouble von Arnim's characters and shape the broader feminist struggle from the mid-nineteenth century onwards, well into our own time.

A profound awareness of the economic infrastructures of men's and women's lives runs constantly through the novels. Sometimes, in the earlier works, those are discussed in ways that make comparisons between German and English economic, legal and matrimonial systems. These are usually to the disadvantage of the German ones, as in the opening pages of *Fräulein Schmidt*, where she argues that the different economic infrastructures of courtship and marriage in Germany and England have implications of greater or lesser freedom and choice of partner for young German women.[2]

Later works open out into more general discussion within a purely English context. Those economic infrastructures in von Arnim's work are constantly shaping, dictating and distorting many human relationships, but especially marital and parental/filial ones. Fräulein Schmidt's childhood, for example, would have been a lot happier if her widowed father had not gone for the 'cheaper' option of an unloving second wife and stepmother for Rose-Marie, rather than the more expensive option of a governess. How expensive the second wife has been: 'She has ruined us in such things as freedom, and sweetness and light' (p. 23).

Dependency corrupts many things. It is hard to reach *truthful* assessments of one's genuine love for those on whom one is dependent, whether for affection or for the more basic material necessities of life. It is hard to know, reliably, for example, if one is the provider, whether one is loved for oneself or for the things one provides – a roof, food, protection, status, a father for one's children, insurance against poverty or homelessness. But even a tiny amount of money might be enough to make possible a break for freedom: Jennifer, in *Father*, has only a meagre £100 a year, left to her by her mother, but she can make it sufficient for a Sussex cottage at 5 shillings a week rent, with her own garden produce. That she is exactly the right age matters here:

> Her decision had arrived in the nick of time, just when she was the exact right age – young enough to adore the fun of adventurously setting out like this, without an idea of where she was going to sleep that night, and old enough for no one to be able to say that living entirely alone wasn't proper.[3]

Up until this point, one of Jen's main tasks, apart from providing very skilled and free secretarial assistance to her writer father, has been to reflect her father to himself at twice his natural size (as Woolf, in *A Room of One's Own*, insists women have been doing for millennia), or as von Arnim puts it in *Fräulein Schmidt*, 'dreary men were endured by women in a way in which dreary women were *not* endured by men' (p. 58). Incidentally, and in an aside, it is even more interesting to discover the statement that Fräulein Schmidt knows that 'she's expected to sit in a draught if there is one' (p. 30) – said some twenty years before the publication of *A Room of One's Own*, in which Woolf makes the same statement of the Angel in the House.

But men also know something of those confusions about genuine affections and less elevated material concerns and anxieties, as we see in Devenish, the widowed clergyman in *Father*, living unhappily alone. He seems to find it genuinely difficult to work out what is simple relief at the delirious prospect of having his material needs met and what might be genuine gratitude to the woman who could provide that – Alice Ollier, James's sister, for example. And might gratitude come to constitute a form of love?

Whether or not 'souls' have space to expand and flourish is one of von Arnim's continuing concerns. There is nothing 'mere' about rooms, for example, and she often uses them symbolically to figure the emotional, psychological and moral lives of those within them. See, for example, in *The Pastor's Wife*, the farcical but also rather terrible conversation on the train to Lucerne between Ingeborg and the German pastor, Robert Dremmell, who will become her husband. The subject is the true function of windows. Clearly, the function of a window is to block – and to keep permanently blocked – the aperture it fills. To wish to open it is, in Robert's view, the height of mindless illogicality, and one to which the English – a profoundly unreasonable people – appear addicted. Yes, it is high comedy, but it also becomes deeply chilling as the symbolic meanings become ever clearer. (Even with a window closed, it seems, the emotional atmosphere may remain cold.) The discussion of the window opens out into a more general revelation of the man's rigidity and imperviousness, also indicated by the way he uses his clothes – scarf, coat buttoned to the neck – to form a carapace, resisting all incursions of unwelcome ideas or views.[4]

Later, Ingeborg is figured by her father, the enraged Bishop of Redchester, as an expensive path which he has had laid and maintained, and which now has the audacity to develop a gaping fissure in its smooth surface, threatening to trip or even swallow him. Woman here is seen as an aspect of a man-made landscape and, because made by him, also replaceable by him (p. 15). Furniture, too, may carry and impose meanings. We might consider the Bishop's wife's sofa, presented as a form of fortification that she refuses to allow him to scale: that is, she will not permit him to talk with her about anything serious concerning their marriage or parenthood. And anyway, her 'well trained' doctor has colluded by 'prescribing' silence as a necessary health measure (pp. 93–5).

Some of von Arnim's most interesting work is to be found in her explorations of types of tyranny, as practised by both men and women. She constantly expresses an intense loathing of it and explores the complex nature of its workings. Tyranny appears in almost every book, and often male: the Man of Wrath in *Elizabeth and Her German Garden*, the Baron in *The Caravaners*, the Bishop and Robert in *The Pastor's Wife*, Wemyss in *Vera*, Ernest in *Expiation*, Father in *Father*. Constantly, she employs the language of slavery and of mistreated animals, especially dogs, used throughout the books to figure the suppressed and downtrodden. And the price paid by the enslaved is to be reduced to half-persons, as Jen, in *Father*, realises:

> With father she had never, once, in her whole life, been natural. Probably no obedient creature, she thought, could be so, no creature whose time

was spent carrying out orders, and dodging round as the shadow and echo of another human being; no person, that is, who was in any way a slave. (p. 103)

Von Arnim's awareness of the degree of violence implicit in the male desire for mastery of women can be truly shocking, as when, in *The Pastor's Wife*, the Bishop of Redchester, Ingeborg's father, full of angry resentment against her, comforts himself to some extent by realising she can properly be returned to her former state (obedient and unquestioning submission), at which point, he tells himself, 'she would be put back in her grave' (p.98). This is a particularly shockingly naked revelation of male hatred for the resistant woman. Interestingly, although *The Pastor's Wife* is a book with both German and English settings, von Arnim does *not* set up a division between bad Germans and good Englishmen (as she does, for example, in the 1909 *The Caravaners* and elsewhere): here the 'class' of men, and their maltreatment of women, transcend narrow national divisions.[5] Similarly, the 1907 *Fräulein Schmidt and Mr Anstruther* has much to say about the destructive shortcomings of English practices and attitudes.

And *male* tyranny is not her only subject: she is also very aware of tyrannous women: for example, sister Alice in *Father*, and the constant humiliations she inflicts on her younger brother, James; or Ruth and Edith, manipulative and cruel wives in *Expiation*. She is very aware of the tyranny of a particular sort of cloying wifely love that suffocates, cutting the beloved off from others, whilst implicitly rebuking the husband for daring to complain. I am thinking here of Alec in *Expiation*, married to Ruth, who, at a time of family crisis precipitated by the discovery of Millie's adultery, has borne him away to an hotel and into suffocating isolation, convinced that by so doing she is safeguarding their marriage:

> Meekness, devotion, virtue, accompanying his every step – what could a man want more? He didn't want more, he wanted less, Alec said to himself after being shut up with these attributes for a fortnight.
> Shocked at this, he grew very quiet; and the quieter he grew the more she plied him with devotion, and he was more glutted than ever.[6]

When James Ollier in *Father* tells Jen that his sister, Alice, 'has devoted her whole life to me', he is astonished when she, 'with genuine and obvious sympathy, unexpectedly replies, "How awful!"' (p. 105).

Male reverence for women, so powerfully instilled in aspects of nineteenth-century social training of young men, can be corrosive when exacted rather than earned: that reverence which is demanded of all men for the child-bearing sex, even if individual women have borne no children and will not be going to – for example, Alice, as older sister, who constantly holds that over James, her younger brother. But James ponders how not all women, taken individually, quite fit the version of their being weak and fragile creatures: 'Taken singly they sometimes didn't perhaps seem quite like that. Taken singly, they sometimes seemed almost tough' (pp. 61–2). Things commonly deemed female virtues are sometimes vices, and von Arnim has a keen eye for them. James, for example, usually 'comes to heel' when sister Alice dictates, being, as he is, courteous and patient, but 'being, also, *weak*' (p. 64).

We see here a constant concern of von Arnim's – what is it that dictates whether certain sorts of behaviour, responses, judgments, reactions are to be admined or deprecated? And how is one to do the impossible arithmetic of deciding between one's own needs and other people's? James, we learn later, has such a terror of developing tyranny in himself that he has a horror of exercising authority over anyone, including his own parishioners. Is this virtue? Does it do him credit? Or is it a shirking of responsibility? And, interestingly, at a time when Jen is discovering the joy of freedom from what she calls 'concentrations' – obligations to family, especially her father – James has very different feelings, and, 'except from Alice, felt he didn't want to be as free as all that, and could picture mutual concentration, under the right conditions, as very happy indeed' (p. 106).

Von Arnim's work often reveals a keen awareness that the threat of male *physical* violence is never that far away when men seek authority over women. She notes in her description of the dynamic between Ingeborg and her husband that Ingeborg begins to realise the sheer power of men to terrorise women, and she has occasion to understand and feel the undertow of physical menace that accompanies it (pp. 88–92). We might also think of Ingeborg's father, when 'she had caused him to lose self-control' (and note here the familiar trope of the man who blames the woman who 'made' him have recourse to violence). We watch him envying the 'navvy', whose way with difficult women (that is, 'sorting them out' with his fists) is so much to be preferred to verbal chilliness, rebuke and sarcasm, the weapons of a 'civilised' man. And we see, too, his chafing under the constraints of 'gentlemanliness', which forbid the deeply desirable violence unfairly available to the working man. Von Arnim tells us wryly that the Bishop's supposed Christianity takes a back seat in his deliberations (pp. 92–5).

Women in von Arnim's work often experience a painful tension between the desperate desire for solitude and the equally fierce desire to be, in some sense, 'completed' by another. Escape is sometimes essential. Ingeborg, at the very beginning of *The Pastor's Wife*, finding herself free from her father when she is released into London where a very good dentist has relieved her pain and given her an unexpected ten days alone in the city, realises that she is free to roam; she sets off for a seven-day package holiday to Lucerne. Ironically, that is when she meets Robert, her future husband, thereby marking the beginning of a new and different form of subordination.

And here is Jen in *Father*, realising that 'There came a moment, she imagined, in the lives of most unmarried daughters, and perhaps in other people's too, when they must either bolt or go permanently under. Bolting would be what she would do' (p. 103). Jen realises, too, the necessity of always going back to the freedom, healing and self-development of solitude: 'How was one to think, if one was never alone? Or find the quiet necessary for realizing how deeply happy one was?' (p. 103).

The vital necessity of solitude is a recurring theme throughout the works. Having the freedom to discover it is so often denied, especially to women trained in endless service. However, von Arnim is keenly aware of the extent to which the hunger for love makes women vulnerable, both to the first person who appears to offer it, and to the capacity for delusion. Here is Millie, in *Expiation*:

> It came to this, Millie thought, that what one wanted beyond everything else in the world was love, and one would do anything to get it, and if it wasn't there, one invented it. The least little word, the smallest encouragement, set one off inventing love. (p. 142)

And it makes women especially, with their desperate desire for love, so vulnerable.

This takes us to the battle going on in this period and many others, to work out whether this desperate female desire for love is indeed a universal truth or a socially constructed, dismantle-able, temporary, historical 'truth'; and the struggle goes on throughout the nineteenth century and well beyond to decide whether or not any of this might be a deeply displeasing and regrettable truth, rooted in evolutionary necessities to do with links between sexual and maternal love. This is an idea that Millie herself approaches a few pages later, when she asks why women cannot just *shake* themselves after betrayal and start again:

> Yet it was what happened to women, to all that immense long category of fools who let themselves become absorbed in some particular person, betrayed by their maternal instincts, those instincts which dressed themselves up in so many tender and lovely names, while all the time they were ruthlessly intent on being nothing less to the object they had focused on than God Almighty – dispensers, that is, of happiness, insisters on dependence, absorbers of freedom. (pp. 224–5)

We might think here of a rather similar insight that comes to Ingeborg in *The Pastor's Wife*, when she realises that she is falling into her own type of tyranny, by her passionate desire that Robert should need her more than anyone – or anything – else.

On the subject of confusions or conflations of the sexual and the maternal, I find myself here making a rather unexpected sideways move to a very different work, Radclyffe Hall's banned 1928 novel of lesbian love, *The Well of Loneliness*, and the point in the narrative at which, after the first raptures of the fully consummated relationship between Stephen Gordon (female) and Mary Llewellyn are over, Stephen, the novelist, is wishing to get back to her writing, but for Mary it feels too soon. Were this a heterosexual relationship, Hall writes, children would have arrived at this point and Mary's passionate emotions would have made their 'natural', and necessary, transition from the sexual to the maternal. We might not like the model but it is a common one in the period, with clear links to the notion that, for women, maternal emotions are the truly passionate ones, and procreative sex is simply the necessary way, the price to be paid, to get to them.

Certainly, von Arnim's work abounds with examples of women who are not really very sure about sex – Ingeborg, for example, who hates 'clutchings' (p. 50), and who realises on the fourth morning of her honeymoon 'that probably she had no gift for honeymoons' (p. 130). Or Jen, in *Father*, enraged by the inexperienced James Ollier's first desperate kiss:

> If this was lovemaking then she didn't think much of it. But it wasn't lovemaking. It was gobbling – just gobbling, she said to herself, outraged, thumping her clenched fists on the mattress; as if one were a plate of food, with no say in the matter, and no wishes, and bound to be gulped down, whether one wanted to be or not. (p. 128)

This is an instance of something that reappears throughout von Arnim's work – many of her female characters have an intrinsic dislike of male desire nakedly expressed. And this is something her characters sometimes share with Mansfield's: think, for example, of Sabina in 'At Lehmann's'.

One of the things that von Arnim explores is whether intense love need be confined to only one sort – erotic, marital love, mainly – or whether it is better found elsewhere (as in old Mrs Botts's love for Millie, which will, at the book's end, offer her sanctuary, blameless affection, full acceptance and 'blessing', a word on which the book closes). Von Arnim is constantly inviting us to question the nature of the relations between sexual desire, sexual activity, love, marriage and motherhood.

Are any of them really essentially connected with each other in the manner we have been traditionally encouraged to assume? And those, of course, are the key questions that many nineteenth-century feminists had already identified and were addressing. Fräulein Schmidt finds herself wondering whether only men can afford the grand romantic notion. Women must always be more cautious because they will pay the higher price, an ancient theme for women writers, whether 'conservative' or 'radical'. Fräulein Schmidt also finds herself wondering how things *might* have been for Tristan and Isolde if Death had not, in some senses, solved everything (p. 39). Here we have the deconstruction of one of the greatest and most powerful love myths. (It is Wagner here but similar questions arise about the 'afterlife' of Romeo and Juliet: had they lived, how desperately wrong might it all have gone a few years down the line?)

Whether or not women do actually *want* sexual lives, and, if so, whether they want them with their *husbands*, are recurring questions in the work. Ingeborg wrestles throughout much of *The Pastor's Wife* to work out what love *is*, but she finds it far easier to define what it is *not*. And it is never clear what part sex plays or should play in this, other than that, once she summons the courage to insist to Robert that the multiple pregnancies (and multiple infant deaths) must now cease, he takes it as evidence that she never loved him. And it is a part of the misery, which von Arnim may hint at but does not or cannot spell out, that a less ignorant and fear-filled sexual world would at least make possible some forms of satisfying sexual exchange other than full intercourse, let alone contraception. Ingeborg, who rather ludicrously has become engaged 'by accident', wonders why no one is willing to talk to those not yet married – and who therefore most need to know – about the sexual and emotional 'mysteries' of marriage.

Sex might, of course, not really have anything much to do with love. We might think of Millie in *Expiation*, whose love-making with her middle-aged lover, Arthur, though present in the earliest stages of the affair, became

> a rather elaborate but sweet way of saying, How do you do, after which they composed themselves to tea and talk on calm things, *i.e.* excavations, which was what Arthur in his off times was chiefly interested in – the love making latterly become quite unidentifiable as such. (p. 35)

It is not entirely clear whether Millie regrets that development, although when Arthur later falls heavily for a woman more than young enough to be his daughter, he salves his conscience by reassuring himself that Millie, at forty-five, cannot possibly be really interested in any of that.

Which is just as well, because, in his judgment, she is not really any longer eligible for love-making.

'Ineligibility' for sexual love will be an enduring and intensifying concern in von Arnim's fiction: women, it is commonly held, age earlier than men, which renders them, apparently, of little interest to men. What is a woman to do when that part of her identity that resides in her physical beauty fades and her sense of her own desirability is severely undermined or even obliterated? And what happens when desire, most inconveniently, seems not to know that its day is over? That is clearly a theme of the greatest importance in *Love* (1925) and *Mr. Skeffington* (1940), even though they are two of the novels I am not focusing on here.

Freud famously asked 'What do women want?',[7] and von Arnim is very aware of the struggle for women to know *what* they actually think and want. How are women to understand themselves, value themselves, form themselves if marriage and maternity – which appear, in one version of the world, to be the only things that really matter – are never on offer, or are rejected, or are tried and found wanting to the point of impossibility? A long procession of these women weaves its way through von Arnim's novels: 'Elizabeth' (as in *Elizabeth and Her German Garden*), Vera, Millie (*Expiation*), Ingeborg (*The Pastor's Wife*). Or what of those with widowed fathers, incarcerated in the prison of spinster daughterhood (Jen, in *Father*)? All these women grapple with Freud's question of 'What do women want?'

Work might of course, constitute an answer, if only one could work out what 'a woman's work' ought to be: work and its importance for women – the destructive effects of the lack of it and of any adequate education, skills or training for middle-class women, which might enable them to be self-supporting. That goes straight to the heart of mid-nineteenth-century feminism's diagnosis, most notably articulated by Nightingale's plea, 'Give us work!', and her celebrated cry, 'better pain than paralysis!'(although, to that, we might also add Ingeborg's awareness that the function of bad provincial dentists was to keep you in pain because pain prevents thought and an understanding of the less physical wretchedness of one's state; certain sorts of pain *are* paralysis, or are at least paralysing).

But if women have difficulty in finding work for themselves, von Arnim's novels are also full of the potentially toxic effects – for women – when *men* are so married to their work that there is no real room for women (as with the Baron in *The Caravaners*, Jen's father, Ingeborg's husband, Herr Dremmel, and many of the brothers and brothers-in-law in *Expiation*). Women's difficulties in working out who they are and what they want are exacerbated by the unhelpful and confusing ways in which they are perceived by men and other women (all those comparisons of Ingeborg with small, furry animals, which Robert Dremmell goes in for, and which recall Torvald in Ibsen's *A Doll's House*). And the struggle for self-knowledge and self-awareness is constantly made more complicated by the very thin line between 'benign' complementarity and an eroding dependency, something especially strongly explored in *The Pastor's Wife* (Fräulein Schmidt, tussling with that very question, decides quite early on – and tries to stick to it – that clinging to one's dignity might be a way of avoiding clinging to a man [p. 37]).

Von Arnim also recognises very clearly what a struggle it is for women to know *what* they actually think and want, and recognises, too, the inward struggle to be as *honest* as possible about it all, which might include questioning the nature of 'unhappiness' (real, or fed by 'habits' of emotional response?). This is something with which so many of von Arnim's female protagonists struggle constantly, including Ingeborg, Jen, Millie and Vera. How do we even know if we feel what we think we feel? Fräulein Schmidt, for example, ponders the connections between *Weltschmerz* and three good meals a day. The poor and hungry do not, she says, suffer from 'Soul sickness'! Here she might be seen to be questioning and dismantling the model of her Goethean world view, set up in the first chapter and now much more sceptically viewed. Her scepticism might be aided by her choice of convalescent reading matter – the eighteen- and early nineteenth-century English and Irish women writers, Fanny Burney, Maria Edgeworth and Jane Austen: women writers far from indifferent to personal pain and suffering, but insistent throughout that women must see reason as a friend, not an enemy, and a quality to which they have as much right, and of which they stand in the same need, as any man. (This reminds me, fairly irresistibly, of John Middleton Murry's familiar consoling joke to von Arnim, rather cast down after some disobliging reviews, that the critics, faced with *Wuthering Heights*, written by Jane Austen, of course did not know what to do with it.)[8]

Possibly braced by those earlier women's keen sense of the necessity for rigorous self-scrutiny and emotional discipline, one of many undertakings that Fräulein Schmidt gives herself is *not* to write 'inappropriate' things, or to reveal 'unacceptable' thoughts and feelings, or to display aspects of herself that are 'better' suppressed: she rebukes herself with constant adjurations for more efficient self-censorship. That has been a consistent feature of her letters in the first fortnight of the correspondence that comprises this epistolary novel. But too much self-censorship can, of course, become its own problem, pushing further out of sight the distressing, the angering, the frustrating, the intractable. Ingeborg, like Fräulein Schmidt, turning to literature as a possible guide and trainer, embarks early in her marriage on a formidable course of reading, but the endless annual pregnancies, with their exhaustions and bereavements as the babies begin to die, saps her energy, both physical and mental, and the reading lapses. It had been one of the few ways available to her to escape her intellectually and emotionally stifling and barren life.

Given how much thought and effort women are often putting into marrying and being married, do *men* actually want to marry? This is a question also faced by the men in Mansfield's 'A Married Man's Story' and 'Marriage à la Mode'. In *The Pastor's Wife*, the Bishop reflects how much better it would have been if he had not married; many of von Arnim's men are as ambivalent as the women – though often for different reasons – about the desirability, the inevitability, the necessity of marriage. Robert Dremmell, having pursued it and Ingeborg initially, and having had a noisy strop about the end of their sexual relationship, does not really need marriage; he is happy to withdraw into his laboratory and pursue his endless measurings and weighings in pursuit of the creation of the perfect manure. But then, as he has crushingly explained to Ingeborg, husband and wife cannot be *friends* and if they are no longer to *be* husband and wife – because, without sex, how could that be? – they may continue to share a roof but any form of significant relationship is, in effect, now at an end.

Individual women's difficulties in finding their way through to answers to some of the questions I have mooted are often exacerbated in von Arnim's novels by women's rivalry for men and male attention. A mixture of economic terror, social pressure, versions of 'femininity' and 'real women' often drives mutual female hostility and suspicion – something von Arnim explores particularly fully in the 1901 novel, *The Benefactress*, and in *Expiation*, where the sisters-in-law are deeply resentful and angrily bewildered that Millie, who in so many ways does not conform to conventional ideas of attractiveness and desirability, nevertheless clearly has a sort of power over men that they know they lack. The fact that she never consciously uses it, and possibly does not even realise she has it, is no extenuation. Their other rivalries with each other, over houses, servants, clothes and status, are necessarily all filtered through their husbands' achievements or lack of them, since the women themselves have no autonomous existence, and their situation is all the more precarious because of it. One might say that their only autonomous possession is their virtue, narrowly understood as virginity before marriage and chastity within it. In *Fräulein Schmidt*, we see the married women's delight in others' general sins and the especial relish that they reserve for sins against love that 'breaks the law' (p. 30). Female relish of that sort is one of von Arnim's persistent themes, and it comes to an especially pustulant head in *Expiation*, allied with von Arnim's always keen awareness of the double standard.

And she runs up against that rather horrid female freemasonry of the matrons who intimate menacingly and frighteningly but will not tell the darker truths of birth and maternity (as the local Baroness eventually does). It is perhaps worth reminding ourselves at this point that the young Vera Brittain, a highly intelligent and well-read young woman, seeking from her mother accurate information about intercourse, was denied it. It can be very difficult for us to place ourselves, imaginatively, back in such a world. This – the struggle to acquire and impart sexual knowledge – is, in part, a two-fold problem: Ingeborg's and her inexperience, and von Arnim's (writing in 1914) and how much she can make explicit. In later works, we can see similar constraints at work – constraints both on the characters and on von Arnim. We might, for example, consider Netta and Jen in *Father*, where Jen refuses to respond to Netta, her young sister-in-law, who is clearly desperate to be listened to, sympathetically, as she discloses that her recent marriage to Jen's father was consummated by a rape and that it is continuing the way it began. (Von Arnim's cousin, Mansfield, was also keenly alive to the horror of marital rape, as the ending to 'Frau Brechenmacher Attends a Wedding' makes clear.) Jen's hopeless inadequacy in dealing with the younger woman's desperate distress is compounded by the fact that, as a virgin spinster daughter, she 'should not' really know what Netta is talking about. She both cannot and must not respond. There is clearly, then, a challenge for many of von Arnim's female characters in their efforts to think decorously but clearly about sex; and there is also a challenge for von Arnim in *writing* decorously, or at least in publishable form, over a period in which boundaries of 'the acceptable' were shifting dramatically.

Letter XI of *Fräulein Schmidt* is especially rich in its exposition of the double standard as it works in relation to youth and beauty, fidelity and the survival of love, and of the plight of the patient, forbearing wife who is there to be returned to, eventually, by the errant husband, who sinks back into the comfortable world of endless nurturing while she has been wearing herself away in enduring and ageing. This is a familiar world, of course, in which *male* sexual infidelities and transgressions are par for the course, but female ones are punished unforgivingly (the given of one of von Arnim's richest novels, *Expiation*).

In some senses, this is of course very familiar territory, and one we find nineteenth-century authors wrestling with as they try to adjudicate between the 'cold' virtues of self-abnegation, denial and the moral judgment of others *versus* the 'warm' and 'generous' fleshly sins: we might consider here Mrs Gaskell's *Ruth*, George Moore's *Esther Waters* and Dickens's Little E'mly – the whole familiar panoply of 'the fallen woman', the soiled 'dove'. And the corresponding debate about just how virtuous a suppressed or frozen female sexuality is is something that certainly seems to apply to many of the women we encounter in von Arnim's work, including the Bott wives in *Expiation*. Millie, with her own notions of good and bad, is often rather repelled by the Botts' version of goodness: 'What would happen if the bad began to pray for the good, Millie sometimes wondered but hadn't dared ask' (p. 41). She knows that she finds conventional notions of wifely virtue hopelessly inadequate: '"Will it be enough", she sometimes anxiously used to wonder, "when God, at the end, asks me what I have done with my life, to point to Ernest and say, I saw to it that his meals were good!"' (p. 37). But even those men who pay lip service to the conventional code of Virtuous Women and Fallen Ones, and the great gulf fixed between them, may have – and voice – their doubts. Here is Fred Bott, in *Expiation*, alarmed to find himself, when comparing his virtuous wife and the sinful Millie, wondering

> whether perhaps sinning made a woman soft and kind, educated her, helped her to wisdom and understanding – the sort of sinning, he meant, in which, in some form or other, must have been Millie's and Bertie's, there was love. But when he realized what he was thinking he was much shocked, and dismissed it sternly from his mind. Was he, in his anxiety, losing his sense of moral values? (p. 360)

We also see, in the brothers' responses to their womenfolk's hostility to Millie, a resentment of the marginalising of sibling bonds in deference to marital ones.

We are reminded that von Arnim also often explores the impossible weight imposed by the idealisation of romantic love and a particularly nineteenth-century notion of an all-sufficing marital love, even though there are clear signs that romantic love and that model of marriage cannot sustain the weight. We might see here too a reflection of the growing general discontent in the period with the tyranny of marriage as the only truly significant relationship (think, for example, of D. H. Lawrence's *Women in Love* and the men's warning to the women that if they cannot find a space in which to honour and leave room for male friendship, they risk losing everything).

Which brings us back to the question: Does sex matter? And if so, how and why, and in what contexts? The books include a constant questioning of the importance, or not, of sex, and its meanings for von Arnim's characters, as well as some enquiry into whether there is an unalterable difference between the sexes about it. Perhaps there are points at which von Arnim herself is defeated by the problems of what may or may not be told. In *The Pastor's Wife* there is maybe a slight problem, in that, although we are well informed about the toll the six pregnancies take and the horror of the first labour casting a long shadow of fear and dread over all the rest, von Arnim does not really indicate anything about the shared sexual life that creates them. We know that Ingram, the English Painter, enraptured by Ingeborg, feels sick when he thinks of those six births, and we also understand that what really makes him feel sick is imagining the acts that resulted in the conceptions, but we know little about Ingeborg's experience of them, other than a general dislike of 'clutchings'. It is, however, generally true, I think, to say that we look with some difficulty for a straightforward, uncomplicated picture of marital sexual happiness in von Arnim's work. Things *might* be going to work for Jen and James in *Father*, but von Arnim is not taking us there.

And yet the deep fear of enforced solitariness, of isolation, is intense for many female characters. Millie's relationship with her sister is far from close, and yet when they meet after a long estrangement, 'their minds were empty of everything except the blessed comfort of there being two of them. Two. In a desolate, frightening world, what magic in just that! "Oh, nobody should ever be only one" sobbed Millie' (p. 91). What *is* going to work, it seems, what is going to save Millie from the desolation of being 'only one', is Millie's future life with the materfamilias, old Mrs Bott, that wonderful creation of a character who has acted throughout *Expiation* as a sort of benign Greek chorus. Having sorted everything and everybody out and restored order, she dismisses all her embattled offspring and their spouses from the late-night family conclave (held in her bedroom) because she is tired now, and because she anyway wants to be alone with Millie, her daughter-in-law. *Expiation* ends with her words to Millie:

> 'Come here, my dear,' interrupted the old lady in a commanding quaver, 'and kiss me good morning. You haven't yet, you know, and we must keep up our manners, mustn't we, as we're going to live together. Besides, Milly my dear' – she held out both her unsteady hands – 'I want to bless you.' (p. 381)

Milly's hard-won expiation is at last complete, and redemption is granted by a woman approaching the end of her life, who has, throughout the novel, watched her offspring endlessly failing to understand what really matters: 'It seemed as if these poor children had no sense whatever of proportion. They wasted their short time in making much of what was little, and little of what was much. Well, they must settle their own affairs' (p. 355).

And so they must, as, too, must Fräulein Schmidt and Mr Anstruther, Ingeborg and Robert, Alice and Mr Devenish. And how very fortunate we are to be able to watch them do it, accompanied every step of the way by their creator's remarkable combination of gifts – tremendous skill in plotting, a wonderfully accomplished use of free and indirect style, an unsentimental compassion and impeccable comic timing, all in the service of great psychological acuity, and never greater than when anatomising the painful confusions of women struggling in the first half of the twentieth century to make sense of their rapidly changing world.

Notes

1. See Erica Brown, *Comedy and the Feminine Middlebrow Novel: Elizabeth von Arnim and Elizabeth Taylor* (London, Routledge, 2012).
2. Elizabeth von Arnim, *Fräulein Schmidt and Mr Anstruther* (London: Smith, Elder, 1907), pp. 4–5. All further references to this volume are placed parenthetically within the text.
3. Elizabeth von Arnim, *Father* (London: Macmillan 1931), p. 29. All further references to this volume are placed parenthetically within the text.
4. Elizabeth von Arnim, *The Pastor's Wife* (London: Virago 1987 [1914]), pp. 15–18. All further references to this volume are placed parenthetically within the text.
5. See Isobel Maddison, 'Complementary Cousins: Constructing the Maternal in the Writing of Katherine Mansfield and Elizabeth von Arnim', in Christoph Ehland and Cornelia Wächter, eds, *All Granite, Fog and Female Fiction: Gender and Middlebrow Fiction, 1890–1945* (Amsterdam: Brill/Rodopi, 2016), pp. 79–98.
6. Elizabeth von Arnim, *Expiation* (London: Macmillan, 1929), p. 313. All further references to this volume are placed parenthetically within the text.
7. Quoted in Ernest Jones, *Sigmund Freud: Life and Work*, vol. 2 (London: Hogarth Press, 1953, p. 421.
8. Quoted in Isobel Maddison, *Elizabeth von Arnim: Beyond the German Garden* (Farnham: Ashgate, 2013), p. 106.

Digging Out Characters: Elizabeth von Arnim in Virginia

Ann Herndon Marshall

Elizabeth von Arnim's letters to her daughter Liebet in 1917 reveal von Arnim's profound grief and struggle to justify a reconciliation with her second husband, the tyrannical Francis, Earl Russell. Working in a draughty cottage that cold Spring, the middle-aged von Arnim displayed a soldier's stoicism at Clover Fields, a farm in Keswick, Virginia, United States. The baleful news of the war, the conflicts in her marriage, and the experience of being a stranger at Clover Fields helped to shape the novel *Christine*, a romantic critique of German militarism. Von Arnim had come to regard the Germans, or 'germs', as 'a pestilential brood of vampires',[1] while her cousin Katherine Mansfield, in her diary that same Spring, mocked the British leadership for attitudes that trivialised the sacrifice of Britain's youth.[2]

Von Arnim was drawn back to Virginia in 1939 at the age of seventy-three; the small pleasures of independent life in Charlottesville tempered her grief and anger. She was exiled from a beloved home in France, and her return to Albemarle County, Virginia, evoked both the saddest and the happiest memories of her life. She discovered the perfect landlady, Charity Pitts, who ran a refined boarding establishment, Preston House, close to the University of Virginia. She also developed a fascination with the author Amélie Rives, whose novels share with von Arnim's own a focus on women and the great houses they occupy, a position that could either liberate or entrap them. For Rives, Castle Hill presides in her novels just as Nassenheide dominates von Arnim's novels, *Elizabeth and Her German Garden* (1898), *The Benefactress* (1901) and *The Pastor's Wife* (1914).

The nostalgia for lost places and people led von Arnim in 1940 to see a resemblance between a Virginia professor and her first husband, Henning von Arnim, the father of her children and patriarch of

Nassenheide, where von Arnim emerged as a writer before his untimely death in 1910. The journal von Arnim kept in Charlottesville upholds the values better known in her novels: her elevation of beauty and wit, and corresponding derision of dullness. Her resentment of those who outsize her – 'They are all so fat and hardy'[3] – conveys her sense of her own dwindling existence: 'What an absurd, contemptible life,' she writes after another evening spent drying her rain-soaked spaniel.[4]

Von Arnim's 1939–40 journal reflects a compassion expressed in the collection of three novels republished as *One Thing in Common* (1941), its 'Foreword' written in Charlottesville. There she insists that the best and worst of all her characters are aspects of her, with the exception of the monstrous Wemyss from *Vera*. They all have in common 'me': 'every person in my stories [. . .] old or young, male or female, objectionable or less objectionable has been dug out of some part of me'.[5] This essay will highlight evidence of the digging out of characters in von Arnim's private writing in Virginia, salient examples of the unity of her life and writing.

The Excavation of Christine *at Clover Fields*

Linking the novel *Christine* to von Arnim's biography highlights her habit of self-extraction: 'every person [is] dug out of some part of me'. Christine is as much a projection of von Arnim as her daughter Felicitas, whose death was one inspiration for the novel. Like Alice Cholmondeley, *Christine*'s fictional author, von Arnim insisted that her daughter Felicitas was killed by the war. Nicknamed 'Martin', she had been expelled from school for theft, and von Arnim subsequently placed her in a strict German school and forbade her the piano.[6] To get back at her mother, Martin claimed allegiance to her German homeland.[7] The report of her contracting pneumonia while playing the violin by an open window evoked guilt, which von Arnim reshaped into patriotic pathos.[8] Martin was a devoted musician, as was von Arnim, and Christine is likewise a particularly gifted one. She comes to Germany to study but falls victim to prejudice when Britain enters the war. Unlike the resentful Martin, Christine writes loving letters to her mother. Von Arnim drew on her own immediate experience to dramatise Christine's isolation.

Although Francis Russell had helped von Arnim through her grief over Martin, by the Autumn of 1916 his overbearing behaviour had precipitated her flight to America. From the time of the couple's wedding day, when he sulked over a change in von Arnim's will to benefit her children, he had attempted to assert a maddening control over her. At the same time, he allowed himself liberty to stray. Her daughter Liebet accompanied her mother from New York to California, but after devoting two months to her emotional restoration, she watched helplessly as her emotionally weakened mother reconciled with Russell. When Russell arrived unannounced in California in January, he quickly regained dominance. According to Liebet, 'Elizabeth [. . .] bowed to it all.'[9] Von Arnim justified her reversal as a new perspective on the fragility of life in wartime; however, she did not follow Russell home until May. His departure left her with the opportunity to finish *Christine* and reconnect with Liebet.[10]

By choosing Virginia, von Arnim sidestepped the invitation of American journalist Poultney Bigelow, an old friend, who encouraged her to join his family and work at Malden-on-Hudson, New York. Bigelow was also a friend of Kaiser Wilhelm II, and von Arnim planned to give the Germans no quarter as she completed her novel *Christine*. Bigelow may even have reminded her of the domineering Russell, as she soon came to dread entering 'Poultney's jaws'.[11] She avoided New York society and its prominent German sympathiser by heading to a rural retreat, where she hoped to find independence and further intimacy with Liebet, the 'Sun Child', whose leadership she acknowledged: 'I'm going to Virginia <u>of course</u> you're going to join up with me & resume your role of Cortez.'[12] Von Arnim slips in a reassurance: 'Dad's very sweet & will probably sail Saturday,'[13] as she satirises her escape to Virginia:

> I've bought a pair of yellow boots in which to deal with the mud [. . .]. There are the most <u>awful</u> thunderstorms [. . .] with different coloured lightning! Also there are a great many horses on each of which one is expected to ride.[14]

She longs for the outdoors; she knows she is forcing Spring 'so early in the year',[15] but her New York apartment is an 'awful *Kalte Pracht*' [cold splendour].[16] The impulse to escape New York recalls von Arnim's transport from a Berlin apartment to Nassenheide. In her debut novel, *Elizabeth and Her German Garden*, 'Elizabeth' maligns 'the horrors of a flat in town'.[17] The later character, Christine, revisits this preference for 'the sweet and blessed country' over the 'grim splendours' of residence in Berlin.[18]

Von Arnim's travel from New York to Virginia was more than a rural escape, however. The train trip south also allowed the author to gauge American enthusiasm for the war:

> I stayed a night in Washington on the way, to see some of the excitement about Congress & war or no war, & never was a place more calm & empty & unruffled – & then I read descriptions of it in the papers blazing with flags & enthusiasm![19]

Whether or not she met with anyone on the new Creel Committee, responsible for American war propaganda, her observation of a calm Washington added purpose to *Christine* as a rallying text to awaken the conscience of America. Isobel Maddison suggests von Arnim's awareness of Wellington House, Britain's propaganda bureau, which encouraged works with 'a clear, if covert, political agenda'.[20]

Katherine Mansfield's Indirect War Writing: *'I wish we could find a new country'*[21]

Von Arnim's disappointment at the lack of flag-waving in Washington stands in stark contrast to Mansfield's distaste for patriotic enthusiasm. Shortly after von Arnim comments on Washington in her letter of 3 April, Mansfield mocks chipper euphemisms of leaders:

> [Lloyd George in a speech on 12 April 1917] tells us that we have grasped our niblick and struck out for the open course [. . .]. Ah, God! But what <u>does</u> rather worry me [are t]hose crowds of patient Russians, waiting in the snow [. . .] what dreadful weapon will it present to their imagination?[22]

Mansfield resents war represented as proper British sport, an enigma to allies and anathema to her whose heart was broken by the war. She herself had lost her beloved brother and three dear friends.[23] Yet her grief did not take a direct expression like that of von Arnim, who, in *Christine*, fanned her readers' ire over German militarism.

Mansfield contrasts her indirection with John Middleton Murry's approach: 'the difference between you and me is [. . .] I couldn't tell anybody *bang out* about these deserts [of vast eternity]. They are my secret. But they must be there.'[24] At the same time, Mansfield was disgusted by the 'pro-Germanics' of two friends, Frank Harris and W. L. George.[25] Indeed, her fiction shows a subtle form of war resistance. Mansfield had emphasised the war's presence in her manuscript of *The Aloe*. Alex Moffett observes, 'A word here possesses a double meaning; a description there evokes an image from the front.'[26] The story includes young Kezia's belligerent response to the Samuel Josephs, escalating the conflict by tricking her adversaries into tasting burning arum lilies. Richard Cappuccio cites martial images and subtle absences in *The Aloe*, connecting fragments in the deserted family house to absences that Allyson Booth highlights as the civilian 'experience of disembodied death'.[27] However subtle *The Aloe* is, Mansfield may have considered the parable too overt when she reduced the Samuel Josephs episode in her subsequent revision of the work as 'Prelude'. There she omitted the suggestive images of a 'swarm' with boys jumping 'out at you', 'impossible to count them'; she also subdued the bellicose image of Mrs Samuel Joseph encouraging the children's 'airing their lungs', which amounts to a 'pitched battle'.[28]

Liebet, in the biography of her mother, observes the opposite trend in von Arnim, a shift toward demonising Germans after the death of Martin: *Christine* 'would, in fact, be Elizabeth's contribution to the war effort and make amends, perhaps, for having, since *The Caravaners*, treated Germans no less than English according to their individual merits'.[29] After Martin's death, her mother, who once resisted the popular genre of anti-invasion books, 'relinquished [her reservations] one by one'.[30] Few characters in war fiction are as bloodthirsty as Christine's landlady in Berlin, Frau Berg, who celebrates after the assassination in Sarajevo with an atavistic chant: '"War", she repeated; and began to tread heavily about the room saying, "War. War [. . .]. It must come. [... E]vil-doers must be emptied of all their blood."'[31] Like other Germans in the novel, she reveres the Prussian military.

There is no evidence that Mansfield disapproved of *Christine* but she was reluctant to have her first collection of stories, *In a German Pension* (1911), republished, for fear of its reduction to propaganda. Vincent O'Sullivan evaluates Mansfield's decision as a 'distaste for fashionable jingoism'; he highlights her disgust at 'the rampage of victory'.[32] For Mansfield, the enthusiasm of senile survivors sadly overshadows meagre commemorations:

> These preparations for Festivity are too odious. [...W]hen I think of all these toothless old jaws guzzling for the day – and then of all that beautiful youth feeding the fields of France [. . .] my mind fills with the wretched little picture I have of my brother's grave – What is the meaning of it all?[33]

It would be wrong to suggest that Mansfield resists all tropes of war or that von Arnim relies entirely on them. Erika Baldt emphasises that Mansfield dramatises the betrayal of youth in her story 'The Daughters of the Late Colonel' (1920): the daughters, still cowed by their dead father, mirror the victimisation of soldiers in combat and dispel the notion of sheltered non-combatants.[34] Von Arnim too is keen to show non-combatants swept up in suffering: German fury turns Christine into a scapegoat. At the same time, von Arnim relies on myth in portraying Frau Berg as a type of civilian harridan, whose vengefulness recalls a 'Jewish Prophetess'.[35] The old characters abuse the young: a draconian colonel commands Bernd to remove a comforting hand from Christine's arm. Poor Christine's openness sets her up for bruising, enforced by those of lower rank, even by the gentle forester's wife. In the hierarchy of German militarism, all must toady to those above them.

War at Clover Fields

In her March 1917 letters before leaving New York, von Arnim repeats 'Virginia' as though it were a protective charm. Virginia was linked, in the minds of Americans at least, to the romances of author Amélie Rives.[36] In addition, Clover Fields was advertised as a Summer home in *The New York Times*, so any of von Arnim's New York set could have known of it. A broadside from the 1910s advertised Clover Fields and included the novelist Rives's name, playing up proximity to the Rives mansion, Castle Hill.[37] Clover Fields was frequently a retreat for wives who needed a break from alcoholic or otherwise burdensome husbands; in cold weather, New Yorkers predominated, and in heat, Southerners.[38] Two weeks into her stay there, von Arnim writes to Liebet of 'a sort of pale spring beginning':

> it's very queer & ramshackle & rough, & I'm going to get used to it I trust, or may, for I so badly want to settle in for a stretch of work [. . .] it's very windy & draughty [. . .] But it's sweet country, or will be soon [. . .] when it's real spring and warm [. . .] you would be warm & happy on the porch.[39]

This same letter has a direct bearing on *Christine*. Christine's embarrassment at the home of the Graf and Gräfin Koseritz mirrors that of von Arnim at Clover Fields: 'We have meals en famille at a large table making conversation all the time. I never felt so shy in my life! I keep dropping things & blushing!! It's the funniest experience I've ever had.'[40] Christine, similarly, writes to her mother: 'Grafin Koseritz was terribly kind to me, and that made me shyer than ever [. . .]. I blushed and dropped things, and the more I blushed and dropped things the kinder she was.'[41] Thus, the hosts at Clover Fields merge in the writer's imagination with Christine's aristocratic hosts. In their emphasis on manners, families in Virginia share the intimidating traits of Prussian *Junkers*, a ruling-class graciousness impervious to awkward moments. The Randolphs, the hosts at Clover Fields, were, after all, descendants of Thomas Jefferson, their property a land grant from George II.[42]

Table conversation was not the sole challenge for the busy writer. She grew cross with the casual handling of mail:

> the letters here get sorted out by any guest who happens to be about, & hours after they'll say casually 'Oh, there was a letter for you – I forget what I did with it' & then we'll all hunt and sometimes find it.[43]

Such anxiety supported the portrayal of Christine's isolation, especially after her teacher and the Koseritzes turn on her. Like Christine's letters to her mother, von Arnim's to Liebet allow her to find comfort and fault. There is an emphasis on self-denial in both Christine's and von Arnim's letters. Liebet comments on her mother's shame at her earlier comfort:

> The spirit of dedication and patriotic fervor in which she labored during her first weeks in Santa Barbara was heightened by an acute feeling of shame at finding herself immune from the dangers and inconveniences that were the lot of Englishmen at that time.[44]

Von Arnim's guilt about comforts that her countrymen lacked is akin to the psychology of survivor's guilt: self-denial as a tribute to the privation of sufferers back home. Such feelings are implicit in New York when she shares with Russell a resistance to American excess: 'we dissuaded the Driggses from taking us to supper in some haunt of gilded splendor, & being spiritless English retired to our lair'.[45] Once in a draughty cottage at Clover Fields, she stresses her English quality of sticking to it:

> It's so difficult not to go away from here before the day I've fixed [...] but I remind myself that I'm a daughter of the race that never lets go once it has started & so I'm going to stick to the very last minute.[46]

Her determination to endure hardship parallels Christine's resolve to stay in a hostile Berlin. Christine's patriotism catches fire when she learns 'England isn't going to fold her arms and look on. Oh, how I loved England then!'[47] Abandoned in a sudden way by the Gräfin and let down by her violin teacher, Christine, a stalwart Englishwoman, perseveres in Berlin. The rejections might have spurred a less idealistic woman to escape in a timely fashion. However, because Christine believes in love's power, and she is in love with a rare sensitive Prussian officer, she misguidedly extends her stay. Her tragedy recalls the *Liebestod* [Lovedeath] of Wagner's *Tristan und Isolde*, with the added feature of British national pride.[48]

The letters of von Arnim at Clover Fields and those of Christine share a similar quasi-religious, Wagnerian elevation of love. Von Arnim reassures Liebet about her engagement. Recalling her past caution to 'think twice' before marriage, she stresses her accompanying testimony: 'I've also told you how there was nothing in the world like one's own lover or husband, that all the happinesses are as pale compared to that as sleep is pale & unreal compared to being awake.'[49] Christine paraphrases her mother with similar terms: 'How right you were about a lover being the best of all things in the world!'. Of course, Christine's confidence that love offers sacred space, 'like being inside a magic ring of safety', betrays her.[50] The illusion of a 'magic ring' foreshadows her entrapment as an innocent *Engländerin* in 1914 Germany.

Had von Arnim's Prussian husband lived past 1910, she might have remained in Germany, isolated like Christine. Unlike the fictional mother of Christine, who is English, von Arnim was a German national in Switzerland in 1914. After her narrow escape to England with two of her daughters, she married Russell. For all his tyranny, she continued to value him as English. Her ambivalence toward Russell, as well as her need of him, is revealed in the letters from Clover Fields after von Arnim received word of the death of 'Cousin William', Charles Erskine Stuart, once tutor to the 'crabs', as she called her children, and her unrequited admirer:

> I don't know, my little Lieb, if you can guess what this means to me – I don't expect you can – I have laughed often enough at him and his devotion and doglikeness, & now that it has gone for ever I feel <u>lost</u>. I wouldn't, of course, if I had Dad – it's such years that I had that immense affection there. It's so extraordinarily dreadful to me that never, never again shall I have it.[51]

While she values Russell, she acknowledges his difference from devoted Cousin William. The claim that Russell is transformed appears wishful:

> Well, [Cousin William is ...] dead & life's getting very much whittled away of all that one has had. What a year this has been from March 1916 to this March! Martin, Johnnie, William, & Francis – gone. But thank heavens Francis's still in the world – the first one of him has gone, but the second & revised version is still here.[52]

The deeply felt loss of Cousin William, not to mention the loss of a daughter and a nephew, necessitated her viewing Russell as a new man, forestalling further whittling away of her supports. With Russell 'still in the world', she returned to England for a reunion with her soon-to-be nemesis.

Charlottesville Journals, 1939–40:
'Lucid Ridicule of Dullness and Brutality'[53]

Although she had little choice about remaining in the United States during the Second World War, von Arnim's return to Albemarle County suggests a stoic attachment to the region. She confided in her journal, 'thought for the 100th time in a Nazi-ridden world that the departed are greatly blest'.[54] From Germany, daughter Trix wrote to calm her mother – 'it is no good worrying' – and echoed her mother's point about the luck of the departed: 'Aunt Maggy died the other day. What a wise thing for her to do!'[55] Von Arnim's journal also shows her ongoing anxiety for her English relations, especially her sister, niece and

Fig. 4 Elizabeth von Arnim and Billy at Bonnie Hall Plantation, home of Nelson Doubleday in Yemassee, South Carolina, USA, 1940. With kind permission of Ann Hardham.

great-nephew. In Charlottesville, while maintaining her independence, von Arnim was comforted by visits from Liebet. Von Arnim could drive her new Chevrolet to the mountains in the Summer's heat. Some Virginians became true friends; others were drawn to the celebrity of a woman whose novel, *Mr. Skeffington* (1940), was a Book-of-the-Month Club selection. She dreaded star-struck acquaintances, like the 'Scotch' woman who insisted music could tame Hitler.[56] When the Nazis took Paris in 1940, von Arnim mourned her dogs, left behind in France, and focused on the wellbeing of her spaniel, first called 'Tommy' but rechristened 'Billy', perhaps in memory of Cousin William. Billy's wellbeing governed many of her choices. She took mischievous pleasure in kidnapping a playmate, 'Toto': 'Result was lovely exercise for both dogs.'[57] The popularity of 'Skeff' brought financial ease, and Billy's antics offered distraction from dismal war news.[58]

Proximity to the University of Virginia's library offered reading from Rousseau to Mann. There was convenient shopping too: 'This is true to type – all women buy something to put on when disaster overtakes them, most sensible.'[59] When particularly depressed about the war, she bought six hats, 'all saucy beyond words'[60]; while her car was washed, von Arnim walked to her manicure.[61] On the recommendation of friends, she chose Mrs Charity Pitts's Preston House for her lodging, a 'delicious place', where she coped with celebrity: 'Lieb telephoned to the unknown people who have invited us to things.'[62] In the Summer of 1940, she moved to a cottage beside the house.[63] Walks with Billy extended beyond the churchyard and woods to the 'links' at the Farmington Country Club: 'very delightful, but I prefer infinitely Mrs. Pitts's'.[64] By 1940, she had acquired stationery engraved 'Old Preston House', a sign of her adjustment to her wartime refuge.

In her Charlottesville journal, von Arnim reveals her opinions and confirms lifelong attitudes like her disapproval of weight gain.[65] She sometimes chose milk and bread in her rooms over lengthy meals where a tiresome guest might waylay her, 'the arch bore woman of the place – exhausting'.[66] Miss Grearson was 'the lonely other little tenant here' and represents von Arnim's worst fears for lonely women: 'Pathetic these derelict women.'[67] After a busy life of writing, von Arnim may have seen retirement as potential 'dereliction' and Miss Grearson as a cautionary example. She distinguishes devotion to dogs from Miss Grearson's overflowing sentimentality:

> After dinner Lieb and I sat out a while and were joined by Miss Grearson whose loveliness is such that she told us once a fly came in and annoyed her at first, but finally she loved it, because it was a <u>living</u> thing. She ought to of course have a darling dog.[68]

For von Arnim, Miss Grearson's 'loveliness' is a vapidity that amounts to vanity. Mr Twist's mother, in von Arnim's novel *Christopher and Columbus* (1919), is similarly vexing: 'She made a good deal of work, because of being so anxious not to give trouble.'[69] Of Agnes Rothery Pratt, the travel writer, von Arnim comments, 'An attractive woman [...] but I fear the kind that bores me.'[70] A painfully slow eater and talker, 'Ag' and her husband exhibit the 'highly upsetting American habit, to drop in in the evening'.[71]

Von Arnim's peevishness arose out of her exile from family. Thrilled as she was when Liebet arrived, she suspected that her daughter failed to note her 'utter desolation of loneliness': she 'doesn't grasp me, being taken in by my apparent courage, and independence'. She attributes better intuition to her faraway niece: 'Drischie wouldn't be taken in. She would <u>know</u>.'[72] Von Arnim sometimes resisted her own moodiness: 'I got over that mood, due partly to the steaming hot weather I expect.'[73] Her landlady often came to her aid: 'Of the whole lot here I like Charity Pitts best'.[74] She earned epithets: 'the dear and gracious one' and 'the ever delightful'.[75] When von Arnim sought the cool of the mountains, she writes, 'Charity appeared in the doorway of my cabin, coming up without getting into a shred of [...] an awful thunderstorm [...]. This seemed incredible to me.'[76] The enchantment eventually extended to Miss Carolyn Martin, the boarder who occupied the other half of von Arnim's cottage. Married women, on the other hand, were handicapped by husbands, a situation common in von Arnim's novels. Much like Mr Wilkins and Mr Arbuthnot in *The Enchanted April* (1922), Charlottesville's Mr Barr and Mr Pratt are 'immensely inferior to their wives'.[77]

The 'dreadful war news' once again provoked the author of *Christine* to indignation at American recalcitrance.[78] She was appalled by discussions she attended at the university's Institute of Public Affairs: 'A low level of intelligence. And the reactions of the audience proof too of this. What a job, governing this enormous, still uneducated country. To bed dejected.'[79] Charlottesville's newspaper paraphrases an equivocal speaker who must have maddened von Arnim: 'Germans [...] were not super-men nor was Germany invincible,' but it would be difficult to 'lay down the law' to them.[80] Von Arnim returned satisfied from the final programme, featuring Rabbi Morris Lazaron of Baltimore on the 'spiritual malady' in America: 'We have failed to be indignant at evil and wrong.'[81] The author of *Mr. Skeffington*, which includes a sub-plot of Nazi barbarism, applauds the Rabbi's plea for American involvement: 'Very good speaker indeed.'[82]

Von Arnim's anger at the repeated American reluctance to enter the war was coupled with, and perhaps found a surrogate in, her horror at their mistreatment of animals: 'How awful these cruel hard people are, all for want of imagination.'[83] Rives, the Virginia writer whom she came to revere in 1940, also supported the cause of animal welfare. Von Arnim had not visited Rives in 1917 but she probably knew of her for some time, because of her successful novels and the celebrity surrounding her first marriage to Archie Chanler, the eccentric Astor heir, who was forced into an asylum, only to escape and eventually move near his ex-wife and her second husband in Virginia.[84] Von Arnim probably knew this back story from her time in New York and at Clover Fields, as well as from her close friendship with actress Beatrice Ashley Chanler, the ex-wife of Archie Chanler's brother.

Rives was considered a scandalous writer at the turn of the century, after *The Quick or the Dead: A Study* (1898) portrayed a widow's struggle with her erotic feelings for her late husband's cousin. That novel, published with a striking portrait on the cover, became a best-seller. Although the sensation of her divorce from Archie Chanler and his subsequent antics exceeded the publicity surrounding Russell's litigiousness, von Arnim's separation from Russell also involved a dose of scandal.

By the time von Arnim visited Amélie, Princess Troubetskoy, in 1940, neither lady was 'ousted' from 'the slough of gentility', to borrow von Arnim's terms from another context.[85] In her journal, von Arnim describes the visits as a welcome enchantment and respite from American dullness:

> Amélie R. was in bed, and still wonderfully attractive and charming. Her lovely room, so beautifully proportioned reminded me somehow of Nassenheide. We drank iced tea by her bedside. She was charming to Billy – charming altogether [. . .]. A dream visit [. . .]. A fascinating afternoon, and the magnolias all flowering![86]

Von Arnim took Liebet to meet Rives: 'enchanting. Lieb loved it. So did Billy, who gets much petting there.'[87] She contrasts the scene when she drives Beatrice Chanler, to see her

> gross friend ... [in] a shockingly ruined house [. . .]. Afterwards, and with what thankfulness, drove to the magic Castle Hill and had tea with the utterly enchanting Amélie Rives [. . .]. As usual [I] was spell bound by Amélie and her perfect background. Had tea by blazing fire, strolled in garden, was bewitched.[88]

Three more visits in the Autumn of 1940 spur her to read Rives's novels, starting with *The Quick or the Dead*, which she finds 'pure Family Herald'.[89] She admires *Firedamp* (1930), however, a novel set at a grand English house. Rives had lived briefly in England, where she was introduced by Oscar Wilde to her second husband, the artist Pierre, Prince Troubetskoy. Like *Mr. Skeffington,* the novel *Firedamp* focuses on family and marriage conflicts; indeed, the family patriarch is almost as monstrous as Wemyss from *Vera*. Rives's character Emily resembles Rives herself, who became a quasi-recluse: 'She had been a beauty in her day. At fifty-seven there remained to her only a faded distinction and a classic profile rather blurred. Her given reason for living at Elmside was her love for country life and quiet.'[90] Von Arnim takes heart from Rives's longevity as a writer: '[I] found it very wonderful seeing she was [when *writing Firedamp*] well on in the sixties. Late to bed, because of it.'[91] The 'rose' of Castle Hill continues to captivate:

> The adorable Amélie was lying resting in bed, looking like a delicate rose – there were some roses exactly like her by the bed. She gave me tea, spoilt Billy, and was exquisite beyond words. So extremely intelligent as well. Parted reluctantly [. . .]. The whole thing is strangely lovely and I came away as exalted and purified by the beauty of spirit and setting as if I had been to the Eucharist early on Easter Sunday.[92]

Von Arnim made a final visit the day before she left Charlottesville. Her description suggests how the Rives mystique was intertwined with house and garden:

> Amélie in bed, lovely and delightful, but I think Liebet's presence made the darling thing shy. Anyhow she seemed to take refuge in blandishing with Billy, whom she spoils and who behaves there like the lord and master [...]. Went alone in the beautiful garden a few moments.[93]

Her courtship of Rives inspired a letter in which she tried 'feebly to convey to her her own charm'.[94]

Von Arnim venerates less, but still grows fond of, the retired professor, Richard Heath Dabney. Her attachment to 'Old Dabney' reveals her ongoing affection for her first husband Henning; she plays chess with the 'ex-professor of history here, very delightful'.[95] In a biography of Dabney, his son mentions 'Lady Russell' as an example of the platonic love affairs of his father:

> Lady Russell dined often at Edgewood, flirted with him, and insisted he reminded her of her first husband, whom she termed 'The Man of Wrath' [...]. Dabney was much disappointed when Lady Russell's sudden death prevented a chess game which had been scheduled between them.[96]

Dabney, who had a Prussian moustache, exhibited old-fashioned gallantry, 'courteous adherence to the principle of *noblesse oblige* and a sense of honor that was paramount'.[97] He appeared in von Arnim's life when she was haunted by memories of her late husband, memories that still arose on anniversaries. The first, a scene when Henning tried to force his way into her writing room, she recorded in her dictionary, her way of remembering the difficult day: 'When he died eleven years later I cut this vengeful inscription out. Funny it all is.'[98] The second was a commentary on trauma and memory:

> I was at Kissingen with H, who began this day his last week on earth [...]. Came home hungry, and were given a dickereise[99] mould, not cooked enough. What funny things stick in one's memory, and all that went before and afterwards vanished as though they had never been.[100]

The third is a recollection of Henning's arrest: 'Martin seven weeks old [...]. Dusty marigolds in the garden' and von Arnim's 'dark grey–green coat and skirt with striped shirt'. Here she refers to the Germans as 'Jolly people'.[101] The salient event may add to the antipathy expressed in *Christine*, as well as the scene of the arrest of Anna's lover in *The Benefactress* (1901).

In her friendship with Professor Dabney, she reconciled with Henning, now seeing once threatening memories as 'funny', calling to mind the evolution of her character, Fanny Skeffington. Six years her senior, 'Old Dabney' 'has to be shouted at' because of his deafness. After once again winning at chess with Dabney, she writes: 'I beat him, which dejects him.'[102] Von Arnim describes a poignant moment as he leaves her cottage: 'while he was here it started <u>snowing</u>! So telephoned to his home to come and fetch him and a charming tall son came and wrapped him up in his (the son's) overcoat and was terribly sweet to the old father.'[103] Dabney and son suggest the kernel of a novel never written.

If we recall the claim that all her characters were 'dug out of some part of [her]',[104] we can appreciate von Arnim's archaeology; a similar creative process is recognised as a feature of Mansfield's New Zealand stories. It is not just copying from life, as the naïve writer Minora practises in *Elizabeth and Her German Garden*. Digging out implies a risky self-scrutiny. We should include in von Arnim's 'me' the vivid characters of her Virginia journal, from the divine Amélie to the failing Dabney. At Clover Fields in 1917, she had experienced the isolation portrayed in *Christine*. While the novel lacks the subtle parable of Mansfield's war fiction, it speaks with the poignancy of exile. In 1917, von Arnim pursued a surrogate devotion: the loss of a dear admirer was a blow that pushed her to cleave to Francis Russell. Her experience of life's dwindling led her back to Virginia during a second difficult period. There, in her last year, she had no delusions about husbands. Henning was the husband whose memory she venerated in bittersweet recollections. At the end of her life, like Mansfield, von Arnim accepted frailty while showing a capacity for new love that does honour to her final year.

Notes
1. Elizabeth von Arnim, Letter to Liebet, Countess Russell Papers, Huntington Library, 17 March 1917. Hereafter, all letters to Liebet are cited as Letters with date only.
2. See CW4, pp. 224–5.
3. Elizabeth von Arnim, Journals, 1939–40, Countess Russell Papers, Huntington Library, 20 June 1940. Hereafter, von Arnim's journal entries are cited as Journal followed by date.
4. Journal, 17 July 1940.
5. Elizabeth von Arnim, *One Thing in Common: Three Famous Novels in One Volume* (New York: Doubleday, Doran, 1941), p. v.
6. Isobel Maddison, *Elizabeth von Arnim: Beyond the German Garden* (Farnham: Ashgate, 2013), p. 80.
7. Karen Usborne, *'Elizabeth': The Author of Elizabeth and Her German Garden* (London: Bodley Head, 1986), pp. 182–3.
8. Jennifer Walker, *Elizabeth of the German Garden: A Literary Journey* (Brighton: Book Guild, 2013), p. 203.
9. Leslie De Charms, *Elizabeth of the German Garden: A Biography* (New York: Doubleday, 1958), p. 190.

10. Letter, 27 March 1917.
11. Letter, 27 March 1917.
12. Letter, 22 March 1917.
13. Letter, 14 March 1917.
14. Letter, 27 March 1917.
15. Letter, 22 March 1917.
16. Letter, 16 March 1917.
17. Elizabeth von Arnim, *Elizabeth and Her German Garden* (London: MacMillan, 1899), p. 2.
18. Alice Cholmondeley [Elizabeth von Arnim], *Christine* (New York: Grosset & Dunlap, 1917), p. 85; p. 102.
19. Letter, 3 April 1917.
20. Maddison, p. 62.
21. *Letters* 2, p. 279.
22. CW4, p. 224.
23. As well as Leslie, she lost Rupert Brooke, Henri Gaudier-Brzeska and Frank Goodyear.
24. *Letters* 3, pp. 97–8.
25. On 'pro-Germanics', see Ann Marshall, 'Turning the Tables: Katherine Mansfield and W. L. George', in Todd Martin, ed., *Katherine Mansfield and the Bloomsbury Group* (London: Bloomsbury, 2017), p. 131.
26. Alex Moffett, 'Katherine Mansfield's Home Front: Submerging the Martial Metaphors of "The Aloe"', in Gerri Kimber, Todd Martin, Delia da Sousa Correa, Isobel Maddison and Alice Kelly, eds, *Katherine Mansfield and World War One* (Edinburgh: University of Edinburgh Press, 2014), p. 80.
27. Richard Cappuccio, 'War Thoughts and Home: Katherine Mansfield's Model of a Hardened Heart in a Broken World', in Kimber et al., pp. 84–97 (p. 85).
28. Vincent O'Sullivan, ed., *The Aloe with Prelude by Katherine Mansfield* (Manchester: Carcanet New Press, 1983), p. 27.
29. De Charms, p. 188.
30. De Charms, p. 188.
31. Cholmondeley, *Christine*, p. 75.
32. Vincent O'Sullivan, Introduction, *Letters* 2, p. xi.
33. *Letters* 2, p. 339.
34. Erika Baldt, 'Mythology and/of the Great War in Katherine Mansfield's "The Daughters of the Late Colonel"', in Kimber et al., pp. 98–112 (pp. 102–6).
35. Cholmondeley, *Christine*, p. 75.
36. Beginning with *The Quick or the Dead: A Study* (1898), Rives wrote a series of novels celebrating Virginia's natural beauty and the love of her heroines for their ancestral homes.
37. 'Clover Fields: Summer Home', Broadside 1922, Special Collections, University of Virginia. See also <https://www.hippostcard.com/listing/virginia-keswick-clover-fields-albertype/2005156> (last accessed 23 October 2018).
38. Margaret Anderson (descendant of the Randolph family at Clover Fields), Interview, April 2017.
39. Letter, 3 April 1917.
40. Letter, 3 April 1917.
41. Cholmondeley, *Christine*, p. 69. Von Arnim's publisher does not retain umlauts over *Gräfin*.

42. Edward C. Mead, *Historic Houses of the South-West Mountains of Virginia* (Bridgewater, VA: C. J. Carrier, 1962), p. 130.
43. Letter, 18 April 1917.
44. De Charms, p. 189.
45. Letter, 14 March 1917.
46. Letter, 18 April 1917.
47. Cholmondeley, *Christine*, p. 238.
48. Walker, p. 279; p. 362.
49. Letter, 21 April 1917 b.
50. Cholmondeley, *Christine*, p. 149.
51. Letter, 21 April 1917 a.
52. Letter, 21 April 1917 a.
53. Frank Swinnerton on von Arnim's work, quoted in Walker, p. 207.
54. Journal, 5 June 1940.
55. Card attached to Journal, 11 June 1940.
56. Journal, 21 June 1940. The visitor talked 'the vaguest hot air about some movement for reforming Hitler by waves of thought – music'.
57. Journal, 20 August 1940.
58. Journal, 14 June 1940. She meets 'a great admirer of Skeff, who at once invited me to a wedding tomorrow'.
59. Journal, 15 June 1940.
60. Journal, 17 September 1940.
61. Journal, 10 June 1940.
62. Journal, 19 October 1939.
63. Journal, 4 June 1940. Von Arnim had a top-floor bedroom 'facing southeast, a little hell'. For photographs of 611 Preston Place, see 'Landmark Survey' in *The Daily Progress*, 14 August 1977, available at <http://weblink.charlottesville.org/public/0/doc/652147/Electronic.aspx> (last accessed 23 October 2018).
64. Journal, 5 June 1940.
65. Journal, 21 October 1939.
66. Journal, 22 October 1939.
67. Journal, 4 July 1940.
68. Journal, 25 June 1940.
69. Elizabeth von Arnim, *Christopher and Columbus* (New York: Doubleday, 1919), p. 89.
70. Journal, 28 July 1940.
71. Journal, 13 July 1940.
72. Journal, 17 June 1940.
73. Journal, 17 June 1940.
74. Journal, 23 June 1940.
75. Journal, 15 October 1940.
76. Journal, 31 July 1940.
77. Journal, 11 August 1940.
78. Journal, 16 June 1940.
79. Journal, 17 June 1940.
80. *Daily Progress*, 18 June 1940, p. 1.
81. *Daily Progress*, 24 June 1940, p. 1.
82. Journal, 22 June 1940. Her ire suggests she might have gone further in her novel, had she not been known as mother to Trix, who was already under scrutiny in Nazi Germany.

83. Journal, 24 June 1940.
84. Donna M. Lucey, *Archie and Amelie* (New York: Harmony Books, 2006), p. 211 ff.; p. 266 ff.
85. Walker, p. 311.
86. Journal, 27 October 1940.
87. Journal, 21 August 1940.
88. Journal, 27 September 1940.
89. Journal, 1 October 1940.
90. Amelie Rives, *Firedamp* (New York: Frederick A. Stokes, 1930), p. 115.
91. Journal, 25 September 1940.
92. Journal, 12 October 1940.
93. Journal, 27 October 1940.
94. Journal, 16 October 1940. In Charlottesville, 1938–41, novelist Louis Auchincloss noticed the poverty at Castle Hill. He admires Rives's 'beauty, wit, charm, and inspiration': 'Her eyes were large and blue-gray; they were probingly curious and seemed to hide reserves of laughter.' *A Writer's Capital* (Minneapolis: University of Minnesota Press, 1974), p. 135.
95. Journal, 3 October 1940.
96. Virginius Dabney, *Richard Heath Dabney: A Memoir*, in *The Magazine of Albemarle County History* (Charlottesville: MACH, 1975–6, reprinted 1978), vols 33–4, pp. 53–140 (p. 120).
97. Dabney, p. 53.
98. Journal, 10 August 1940.
99. This may be a misspelling of '*dickerreis*' or 'thick rice', perhaps rice pudding fortified with egg. If undercooked, it would be runny.
100. Journal, 15 August 1940.
101. Journal, 23 September 1940.
102. Journal, 3 October 1940.
103. Journal, 19 October 1940.
104. Von Arnim, *One Thing in Common*, p. v.

'[P]assionate, magnificent prose': Tracing the Brontës in the Friendship and Writings of Elizabeth von Arnim and Katherine Mansfield

Charlotte Fiehn

Did Elizabeth von Arnim and Katherine Mansfield's engagement with, and awareness of, each other influence their work? In Mansfield's case, the answer is a resounding yes. Her first collection of stories, *In a German Pension* (1911), suggests von Arnim's influence in its title and in the subject choice of several stories.[1] In von Arnim's case, the answer is rather less obvious. Mansfield famously denied influencing her cousin – 'Never could Elizabeth be influenced by me.'[2] Yet, von Arnim's novel *Vera*, published in 1921 and written at the height of her friendship with Mansfield, offers an interesting comparison to Mansfield's short stories 'The Little Governess' and, even more particularly, 'Bliss', first published in 1918. In this essay I establish fresh resonances between the work of Mansfield and von Arnim through their engagement with the writings of the Brontë sisters, particularly Charlotte Brontë's *Jane Eyre* (1847).

Both von Arnim and Mansfield knew and greatly admired the work of the Brontë sisters. Von Arnim describes Emily Brontë's *Wuthering Heights* as one of her preferred books in *The Solitary Summer* (1899). She refers to the novel and Emily Brontë's poetry in *Vera*, and in her 'incomplete lecture' on the Brontës, written in the 1930s following a visit to Haworth, describes both *Jane Eyre* and *Wuthering Heights* as family masterpieces.[3] The Brontës also commanded a similar presence in Mansfield's life and writing. In a 1908 letter, Mansfield alludes to her ready acquaintance with 'all the Brontës',[4] and records show that she borrowed copies of the Brontës' works from the General Assembly Library in Wellington.[5] Mansfield's biographer, Jeffrey Meyers, identifies the Brontës as being among those authors Mansfield looked to, 'not only to learn how to write, but to learn how to live'.[6]

Both von Arnim and Mansfield seem to have responded to what one nineteenth-century critic, Wemyss Reid, describes as 'the Brontë cult'.[7] Although their reputation suffered a decline after Charlotte's death in 1857, the Brontës were nevertheless prominent figures in the nineteenth-century cultural imagination. As Patsy Stoneman notes, *Jane Eyre* was adapted into a stage play as early as January 1848.[8] There was also Charlotte Birch-Pfeiffer's *Die Waise von Lowood* or 'The Orphan of Lowood', performed throughout Europe and America, and James Willing's somewhat alternative play of 1879, wherein John Reed seduces Blanche Ingram as a mechanism for Willing to explore Rochester's attempted bigamy in more detail. Stoneman also speaks to the 'revolutionary impact of *Jane Eyre*' for women writers specifically, describing how other nineteenth-century writers such as Dinah Craik, Julia Kavanaugh, Rhoda Broughton and Mary Elizabeth Braddon, representing a kind of first wave of respondents, appeared to use Jane as a model heroine.[9]

At the end of the nineteenth century, the influence of Reid's *Charlotte Brontë: A Monograph* (1877) and Swinburne's *A Note on Charlotte Brontë* (1877, reprinted 1894) was sufficient to propel engagement with the Brontës' works into the new century. A contemporary of von Arnim and Mansfield, May Sinclair recognised the Brontës as a primary influence on her own work and wrote about them frequently, most notably in *The Three Brontës* (1912) and *The Three Sisters* (1914). The publication of Charlotte's letters to her Belgian teacher in 1913 fuelled interest in the sisters' lives and their creative practices, with renewed speculation that, at least in Charlotte's case, the writings were heavily autobiographical. Lucile Dooley's 'Psychoanalysis of Charlotte Brontë, as a Typical Woman of Genius', published in 1920 in the *American Journal of Psychology*, reflects new critical engagement with the Brontës in von Arnim's and Mansfield's lifetimes, whether or not either of them encountered this particular study.

The patterns and scope of the Brontës' influence on von Arnim and Mansfield have received relatively little attention. Patsy Stoneman calls *Vera* 'the first link in a chain of *Jane Eyre* derivatives',[10] and Erica Brown discusses it as a reversal of *Jane Eyre*'s 'romantic paradigm', situating it as part of a 'wave of interest in the Brontës among inter-war women writers'.[11] None of these studies considers the influence of the Brontës as a thread common to both Mansfield and von Arnim's work. By examining strong intertextual relationships between Charlotte Brontë's *Jane Eyre*, Mansfield's short stories 'The Little Governess' and 'Bliss', and von Arnim's novel *Vera*, produced at the high point of the cousins' friendship, I suggest that there are important insights to be gained, looking at precisely how von Arnim and Mansfield engaged with the Brontës and some of the ways in which, if not exactly shared, their engagement was at least parallel and the basis for striking, sometimes surprising, connections between their writings.

Published in 1915 in *Signature* and later reprinted in the collection *Bliss and Other Stories* (1920), 'The Little Governess' offers several intriguing parallels to Charlotte Brontë's *Jane Eyre*, perhaps with an additional nod towards Anne Brontë's *Agnes Grey* (1847), which features the attempted seduction of the eponymous character (also a governess) by an older male. The most obvious allusion is in the title and the repeated use of 'little' to describe the otherwise unnamed governess. Jane Eyre refers to herself as 'little' when acknowledging her sense of powerlessness. Other details about the governess's travel parallel Jane's experience of travelling from Lowood to Thornfield. The subtle hostility of Mansfield's governess towards her fellow travellers – perhaps it even rises to the level of xenophobia – gestures towards Brontë's *Villette* (1853). As the porter 'pounced on her dress-basket', the governess's reaction, 'What a horrible man!',[12] echoes Lucy Snowe's initial description of M. Paul as 'a harsh apparition' and 'irritable'.[13]

The anger of Mansfield's governess – its own particular violence – is also akin to Jane's: 'her anger, far stronger than she, ran before her and snatched the bag out of the wretch's hand', manifesting an almost out-of-body experience, gesturing at an othering of her emotions – or through her emotions – in relation to her sense of self (p. 140). The extreme and childlike petulance of Mansfield's character echoes Jane's behaviour at Gateshead. Although both her aunt and her cousins provoke Jane's reaction, she responds violently. Likewise, in the Red Room episode, she exerts a kind of energy that echoes Mansfield's governess observing the various servant characters, the porters and later the waiter, whom she instinctively mistrusts.

Another parallel to *Jane Eyre*, and a distinct example of othering for Mansfield – one that 'Bliss' notably offers as well – is a mirror episode: Mansfield's governess catches 'sight of herself in the mirror, quite white, with big round eyes' (p. 141). This – the event, if not the character's 'white' appearance and 'big round eyes' – recalls the episode in Chapter 20 in *Jane Eyre* when Jane recalls seeing 'a woman, tall and large, with thick black and dark hair hanging low down her back'.[14] She describes how the woman, later revealed to be Bertha Mason, took the

> veil from its place and she held it up, gazed at it long, and then she threw it over her own head, and turned to the mirror. At that moment, I saw the reflection of the visage and features quite distinctly in the dark oblong glass. (pp. 327–8)

Bertha's features reflected in the mirror are, to Jane, '[f]earful and ghastly', showing 'a discoloured face [. . .] a savage face' (p. 327). The parallels are even more striking within Mansfield's broader narrative structure because of the disparity between how the governess sees herself and how others perceive her.

Mansfield renders the governess's uncertainty about whether she should accept the old man's offer to show her the town as a betrayal of her naïvety:

> It was not until long after she had said 'Yes' – because the moment she had said it and he had thanked her he began telling her about his travels in Turkey and attar of roses – that she wondered whether she had done wrong. (p. 146)

Even as the governess is caught up in the details of the old man's adventures – no doubt as he intends – the reader can consider the possibility that the old man is manipulative, perhaps even predatory. The reaction of the waiter as he leads the governess into the 'dark bedroom' further compounds the suspicion brought on by the old man's initial invitation (p. 147). Although readers tend to ignore the hints about Rochester's shady past, Brontë notably employs a similar technique, emphasising Jane's own convictions about the source of the suspicious laughter and Rochester's own somewhat erratic behaviour, even as the reader registers other possibilities.

A final parallel between *Jane Eyre* and 'The Little Governess' is, of course, the painful anagnorisis. In a single episode, Jane learns of Bertha Mason's existence and Rochester's intention to lead her into a bigamous marriage, one that could very well expose her to the same kind of judgment as Mansfield's governess. And, while Jane has the opportunity to escape and Rochester to be appropriately chastised, the narrative allows space for a potentially happy resolution. Mansfield, however, takes full advantage of form and cuts her governess short. An exposed 'little girl [. . .] crying without a handkerchief', running through 'a world full of old men with twitchy knees' (p. 150), the little governess experiences the kind of scrutiny that Jane only barely avoids. The waiter and the manager allow the appearance of impropriety to go unchallenged, and Mansfield ends with the governess 'shuddering so violently that she had to hold her handkerchief up to her mouth', even as the waiter she previously abused enjoys a sense of triumph, 'mincing over the little governess's words', now devoid of power (p. 150).

Despite the various potential allusions to *Jane Eyre*, 'The Little Governess' (along with Mansfield's later story, 'Bliss') has rarely been considered in relation to Brontë's work. The value of such attention has various dimensions, not least the potential to render the story all the more clearly as a commentary on gender politics and the dangers faced by young and inexperienced women. The allusion to *Jane Eyre* heightens both the complexity of the dynamic between the governess and the old man, and the scope of the implications for the governess when she finds herself abandoned by her would-be employer. More significant to Mansfield's relation to von Arnim, though, is the evidence that Brontë had a fairly consistent influence on Mansfield's writing, with aspects of *Jane Eyre* also echoing in 'Bliss'.

The most immediate parallel between 'Bliss' and *Jane Eyre* concerns names: Mansfield's Bertha Young shares her first name with Rochester's wife. Her last name, 'Young', is an example of aptronym; it is a telling name, like the name of Charlotte Brontë's protagonist, Jane Eyre, who, integral to plot, is both a 'plain Jane' and an heiress. The parallels do not end there. One of the first things Mansfield reveals about Bertha Young is that her age renders certain behaviours inappropriate:

> Although Bertha Young was thirty she still had moments like this when she wanted to run instead of walk [. . .]. What can you do if you are thirty and, turning the corner of your own street, you are overcome, suddenly by a feeling of bliss – absolute bliss! (p. 69)

Mansfield clearly plays with the word 'young' here and uses it to striking effect, but Bertha's behaviour is also labelled as 'drunk and disorderly' by whoever judges her – perhaps the 'idiotic civilization' (p. 69). For reasons never made explicit, Bertha implies that she is expected to keep her 'body [. . .] shut up in a case like a rare, rare fiddle' (p. 69). Mansfield immediately creates the expectation of containment, creating resonance between Bertha Young and Bertha Mason, 'the madwoman in the attic'.

Mansfield's treatment of Bertha Young's laugh – presented as a mechanism for expressing 'bliss' – develops the association with Bertha Mason's madness even further. Described by Jane, Bertha Mason's is a 'curious laugh – distinct, formal, mirthless' (p. 126). A few lines later, Jane describes it as 'tragic' (p. 127), and then again she calls it 'demoniac [. . .] – low, suppressed, and deep-uttered' (p. 173). While Mansfield does not offer such an abundance of adjectives to describe her protagonist's laugh, she associates Bertha with a kind of laughter that implies hysteria and thus connotes a kind of madness: Mansfield's Bertha wants to 'stand still and laugh at – nothing – at nothing simply' (p. 69), and later she 'began to laugh' but censures herself from becoming 'hysterical' (p. 70).

Mansfield also employs a motif common to *Jane Eyre*, using a mirror reflection to convey Bertha Young's alienation and isolation. Mansfield reconfigures this scene in 'Bliss' when Bertha Young 'hardly dared to look into the cold mirror – but she did look, and it gave her back a woman, radiant, with smiling, trembling lips, with big, dark eyes and an air of listening' (p. 70). The scenes are framed differently, largely dictated by form. Jane's is the privileged perspective in Brontë's rendering, rather than Bertha's; Jane's narrative is heavily filtered because she relates her observations to Rochester with temporal and spatial distance. Jane also admits that she may have been in a dream state when she saw the vision. Yet, both Brontë and Mansfield render the scene as an encounter with the uncanny, apt for both Freudian and retrospective Lacanian readings.

In *Jane Eyre*, Brontë develops and gradually unveils a dynamic between Jane and Bertha Mason, drawing attention to key similarities and differences in their character and behaviour. Jane, for example, is physically unremarkable and attractive to Rochester because of the contrast to Bertha Mason, who was remarkably beautiful. When Rochester confesses his history to Jane, he describes Bertha as 'the boast of Spanish Town for her beauty [...] a fine woman, in the style of Blanche Ingram: tall, dark, and majestic' (p. 352). Jane mentions her 'want of beauty' and, of course, declares herself 'poor, obscure, plain, and little' before Rochester proposes to her (pp. 117, 293). Her emphasis on reason, demonstrated in the Lowood and Moorland episodes of the novel, and her 'seriousness', mentioned by Rochester, distinguish her from the psychologically unstable Bertha, but Jane is not always stable.

At times, Brontë reveals Jane's connection with Bertha Mason as being rather too close for comfort. The Gateshead servants describe Jane as being 'like a mad cat' (p. 15). One of the servants perceives her as 'a sort of infantine Guy Fawkes' (p. 31), making an awkward association with incendiarism, seemingly anticipating Bertha Mason's final arson. Mrs Reed insists that Jane is 'passionate', labelling this a fault of character, with Jane admitting that she gives 'furious feelings uncontrolled play' (p. 45).

In spite of her madness, Bertha Mason also recognises Jane as her rival, setting fire to her room 'like as if she knew somehow how matters had gone on, and had a spite at her' (p. 493). Brontë's use of indirect diction here and the double qualification ('like as if', 'somehow') are mimetic of Bertha Mason's powerlessness, suggesting an inability or unwillingness to articulate her concerns clearly or decisively. The association between Jane and Bertha Mason also offers a way of reading 'Bliss' and of recognising Bertha Young's hyperawareness of her behaviour, recalling the representation of madness in *Jane Eyre*: how, in effect, a hypercritical social and cultural context could mislabel women's extremes of emotion as madness when, as in Jane's case, such extremes expressed frustration in response to socially constructed female repression.

Von Arnim addresses the same hypercriticism of women's behaviour in *Vera*, representing a domineering husband who seeks to prevent his wife from demonstrating 'morbid' tendencies – the etymology of the term suggesting the association with disease. This and the various other resonances of *Jane Eyre* in *Vera* raise interesting questions about the cross-currents at work in von Arnim's and Mansfield's writings. Like Jane Eyre, *Vera*'s Lucy becomes an orphan, lacking an effective guardian. She is notably young and what von Arnim reveals of her physical appearance suggests she is relatively plain – another plain Jane. Wemyss also mentions being married to Vera, his first wife, for fifteen years (p. 17), which is the length of Rochester's marriage to Bertha Mason when he undertakes his bigamous marriage to Jane: 'a date fifteen years back' (p. 335). Rochester and Wemyss both have a propensity for locking their bookcases.[15] Vera falls from a window and is discovered 'smashed' on the flagged terrace (p. 15); Bertha Mason has a similar end, 'smashed on the pavement' (p. 493).

Vera and Bertha are both associated with the upper stories of the homes they share with their husbands: Bertha Mason is 'safely lodged in that third-story room, of whose secret inner cabinet she has now for ten years made a wild beast's den – a goblin's cell' (p. 356), from which she renders the whole of the top floor of Thornfield entirely 'strange' and, from Jane's perspective, 'the aspect of a home of the past – a shrine of memory' (p. 125). In contrast, Vera has her sitting-room in 'the top room of the house [...] because of the view' (p. 15), suggesting she has the same fondness for landscapes as Jane, who ventures to the third floor herself for the view and to enjoy a haven: her 'sole relief was to walk along the corridor of the third story, backwards and forwards, safe in the silence and solitude of the spot' (p. 129).

When Lucy ventures into Vera's rooms, she realises how they provided a retreat:

> Vera had managed, and her spirit wasn't beaten out. For years and years, panted Lucy – her very thoughts came in gasps – Vera lived up here winter after winter, years, years, years, and would have been here now if she hadn't – oh, if only Vera weren't dead! If only, only Vera weren't dead! But her mind lived on – her mind was in that room, in every littlest thing in it——. (p. 190)

Here von Arnim seems to borrow Brontë's association of the top floor of the house with the mind and memory, a thematic undercurrent similar to Mansfield's in 'Bliss', establishing connections between the behaviour of women and madness. In *Vera*, for example, Lucy is not mad, but Wemyss's attitude involves labelling her as such. Similarly, Mansfield suggests that others label Bertha Young's behaviour as inappropriate. In *Jane Eyre*, Brontë leaves little scope for Bertha Mason's sanity since her behaviour is the result of mistreatment. Nevertheless, the parallel between Bertha and Jane implies that women's passionate responses are frequently in danger of being labelled madness.

One of the most striking reverberations between von Arnim and the Brontës' works is the characterisation of Wemyss as self-absorbed, mercurial, controlling and vindictive, recalling both Rochester and Heathcliff. As Isobel Maddison notes, a review in the *New York Times Book Review* described *Vera* as the 'story of a modern Bluebeard', suggesting that the 'portrait of the hero makes him more brute than man'.[16] Wemyss is 'like a child in his misery' when he first appears and, a few lines later, he is 'all puckered, like an unhappy baby' (pp. 6, 7). He becomes increasingly petulant after his marriage, reacting vindictively when Lucy fails to conform to his ideal of wifely duty. Von Arnim's representation of this dynamic suggests Wemyss's objectification of Lucy and his complete failure to recognise her as an individual. Instead, he reduces her to a type, constantly comparing her to his first wife to imply that Lucy should simply function as Vera's substitute.

This, of course, is the psychological model developed in the narrative of the Bluebeard fairy tale – a tale to which Charlotte Brontë refers to by name in all but one of her novels and which is a significant influence on the structure of *Jane Eyre*. In *Vera*, Wemyss also locks Lucy out of the house during a storm, echoing the episode in *Wuthering Heights* in which Cathy's ghost begs to be let in. Emily Brontë's novel is also the book that both Vera and Lucy read, with Lucy showing a particular awareness that it is a violent romance (p. 210). Wemyss, on the other hand, 'hadn't read it, but he fancied he had heard of it as a morbid story' (p. 210). Von Arnim uses this detail, I think, to suggest that Wemyss is excluded from understanding how either of his wives bears witness to his abuse. He thus refuses to engage with these narratives of women writers – the Brontës – who present testimonies about the actions of men who torment and instigate the death of women.

The comparison with Rochester is even more profound if we look at specific episodes in *Jane Eyre*. For instance, when Jane describes the month prior to the wedding, she makes out that Rochester's behaviour is rather childlike: 'He fretted, pished, and pshawed' (p. 315), she says at one point, and describes him as fuming and fidgeting. Eventually, she 'worked him up to considerable irritation' such that he 'retired, in dudgeon, quite to another end of the room' (p. 315). There is also a trend in *Vera*, 'Bliss' and *Jane Eyre* to associate courtship with trees. In Chapter 23, for example, Jane finds Rochester waiting for her in a 'shrubbery' (p. 287), and then he proposes to her beneath a 'great horse-chestnut' that is struck by lightning (p. 296). In 'Bliss', there is a pear tree that Bertha sees as 'a symbol of her own life' and which she associates with Pearl Fulton (p. 72). In *Vera*, von Arnim repeatedly refers to a 'mulberry' tree, which has particular associations with Shakespeare's *A Midsummer Night's Dream* (pp. 10, 18, 21, 27, 29, 39, 44), it being 'midsummer' when Rochester proposes to Jane (p. 286).

Vera also echoes the pivotal scene of *Jane Eyre* by establishing a temporal context aligned with trickery and deception. Rochester waits for Jane in the garden at Thornfield Hall, bullies her into believing that he will send her away and then, when she is worked into an emotional frenzy, proposes marriage, vehemently denying, of course, that he does not already have a wife. Charlotte Brontë's treatment of this episode, so often seen as romantic, is something Mansfield and von Arnim acknowledge as really rather unsettling in their fictional appropriations. Whereas both Bertha Young and Lucy Entwhistle believe their significant others are acting out of love, Mansfield and von Arnim expose these perspectives as, at best, misguided. As Brontë does in *Jane Eyre*, both Mansfield and von Arnim reveal the repression of the female protagonist even as they appear to have the means for self-expression, of bearing witness to their experiences.

Far from being the only connection between 'Bliss' and *Vera*, von Arnim and Mansfield's concurrent echoing of the Brontës may help explain Mansfield's problematic response to Dorothy Brett in 1922, when she insisted that her cousin's novel, *Vera*, was in no way influenced by her own writing. When she said they were 'worms of the same family',[17] Mansfield was denying her influence on von Arnim and, at least initially, doing so confidently: 'Only one thing, my hand on my heart, I would swear to. Never *could* Elizabeth be influenced by me. If you knew how she would scorn the notion, how impossible it would be for her.'[18] In the very next sentence, however, Mansfield makes a tremendous concession: 'There is a kind of turn in our sentences which is alike.'[19] As Maddison argues, Mansfield's assessment here is 'disingenuous'[20]: Mansfield and von Arnim read and commented on each other's work with considerable regularity and had done so for some time. Because they were cousins as well as fellow writers, they had been conscious of each other for most of their writing careers.

Beyond *In a German Pension* (1911), Mansfield acknowledged von Arnim's influence in various other texts.[21] Jane Nardin demonstrates how Mansfield borrowed from *Vera* in the opening paragraph of 'The

Garden Party' and how Mansfield draws on Lucy's viewing of her father's body in *Vera* for a similar scene in the same story when Laura Sheridan views the body of Mr Scott.[22] The textual similarities are remarkable:

> lying so **remote** from her, so wrapped, it seemed, in a deep, absorbed attentiveness ... [W]hen dusk came ... she would be alone ... and upstairs that strange, **wonderful**, absorbed thing that used to be her father, and whatever happened to her ... he would still lie there, **content, content**. (p. 2)

> There lay a young man, fast asleep. ... Oh, so **remote**, so peaceful. ... He was given up to his dream. ... He was wonderful, beautiful. ... Happy ... happy. ... All is well, said that sleeping face. This is just as it should be. I am **content**. (p. 209, all Nardin's emphases)

As Nardin argues, the textual similarities suggest a close literary and stylistic connection between Mansfield and von Arnim while von Arnim was working on *Vera* and Mansfield on 'The Garden Party'. Such a connection is also evident between 'Bliss' and *Vera*, particularly where the female protagonists struggle to interpret their lives as happy. Bertha Young self-edits, forcing herself to represent her life as entirely 'happy' by consciously ignoring or reframing most of its details:

> **Really – really** – she had everything. She was young. Harry and she were as much in love as ever, and they got on together splendidly and were **really good pals**. She had an adorable baby. They didn't have to worry about money. They had this **absolutely satisfactory** house and garden. And friends – modern, thrilling friends, writers and painters and poets or people keen on social questions – just the kind of friends they wanted [...].
> '**I'm absurd. Absurd!**' She sat up; but she felt quite dizzy, quite drunk. It must have been the spring. (p. 73, all my emphases)

Similar strategies are used in *Vera* just before Lucy realises she is locked out in the rain:

> Everard – **why, of course** – Everard had only spoken like that out of fear – fear and love. The window – **of course** he would be terrified lest she too, trying to shut that fatal window, that great heavy fatal window, should slip [...]. **Oh, of course, of course** – how could she have misunderstood – in moments of danger, of dreadful anxiety for one's heart's beloved, one did speak sharply, one did rap out commands. It was because he loved her so much [...]. **Oh, how lunatic of her** to have misunderstood! (p. 186, all my emphases)

Here both Mansfield and von Arnim use free indirect speech as their characters try to convince themselves of a particular interpretation of reality. Bertha rattles off her reasons for being happy in short, deliberate clauses. The broken first line, disrupted by repetition, encloses the more abrupt outburst in direct speech, 'I'm absurd. Absurd!' The placement of the qualifiers, 'really' and 'absolutely satisfactory', enclose and flatten the potentially positive statements about her relationship with her husband and her child.

Lucy likewise uses grasping expressions, loaded and broken with repetition, as she accounts for her husband's behaviour. Like Bertha's 'really', the exclamation 'of course' disrupts Lucy's argument and forces her thoughts towards a positive explanation by closing down alternatives, '[he] had only spoken like that out of fear' and 'he would be terrified'. The exclamation, 'Oh, how lunatic of her', like Bertha's 'I'm absurd. Absurd!', accentuates a connection between self-doubt and madness that is integral to the representation of both women in relation to their husbands. As with the episode from 'The Garden Party' paralleling *Vera*, the textual linkage hints at a profound connection between the two writers, even beyond their familial relationship and parallel interest in the Brontës.

Both Maddison and Juliane Römhild discuss the relationship between von Arnim and Mansfield in terms of shared interests affected by their familial connection.[23] Describing von Arnim and Mansfield as 'complementary cousins',[24] Maddison reflects on the various elements common to their writings:

> both share a preoccupation with the organisation of space, portraying fictional episodes that represent periods of actual, or psychological, confinement. Both construct motherhood as alienation [. . .] – particularly in von Arnim's *The Pastor's Wife* (1914), and Mansfield's 'A Birthday' and 'At Lehmann's'. Both writers also consistently address Anglo-German tensions in the early twentieth century.[25]

Even if these connections may have been prompted, in part, 'by the historical context and the residency of both authors in Germany in the 1890s and early 1900s', and by the many other experiences von Arnim and Mansfield shared,[26] their familial relationship was important to both of them and had implications for their work. From June 1921 to January 1922, and June to July 1922, von Arnim and Mansfield lived '1/2 an hours scramble away'[27] from each other and spent a good deal of time in each other's company, allowing them even more opportunities to engage with each other as fellow writers.

Just as Mansfield felt acutely conscious of her cousin's example – both personal and literary – there is tantalising evidence that von Arnim felt equally challenged by her young cousin, especially when they spent time together. As Römhild notes, von Arnim confessed to John Middleton Murry how much Mansfield intimidated her: 'I always came away feeling as if my skin were off, and miserable with the conviction I must have bored and repelled her. Yet I adored her.'[28]

Although Mansfield categorically denies influencing her cousin, von Arnim's construction of *Vera* qua the Brontës – as a response to *Jane Eyre* and *Wuthering Heights* – echoes some aspects of Mansfield's 'The Little Governess' and 'Bliss'. In particular, the connections between *Jane Eyre*, 'Bliss' and *Vera* suggest the importance of the Brontës to both Mansfield and von Arnim, and to how they may have related to each other as fellow writers. The Brontës provided three remarkably compelling examples of professional female writers whose works exposed the constraints upon women in the early Victorian period. In the connections between their own writing, the Brontës also provide a model for female writers within a family. When Mansfield suggested that she and her cousin were 'worms of the same family', she might very well have meant 'bookworms', acknowledging that they not only read the same types of literature, but experienced a mutual creative influence because of how they read it.[29]

Notes

1. Isobel Maddison, *Elizabeth von Arnim: Beyond the German Garden* (Farnham: Ashgate, 2013), p. 93.
2. *Letters* 4, p. 346.
3. Maddison, pp. 107–8.
4. *Letters* 4, p. 51.
5. Jeffrey Meyers, *Katherine Mansfield: A Darker View* (London: First Cooper Square Press, 2002), p. 25.
6. Meyers, p. 25.
7. Wemyss Reid, *Memoirs of Sir Thomas Wemyss Reid, 1842–1855*, ed. Stuart J. Reid (London: Cassell, 1905), p. 235.
8. Patsy Stoneman, 'Adaptations, Prequels, Sequels, Translations', in Marianne Thormählen, ed., *The Brontës in Context* (Cambridge: Cambridge University Press, 2012), pp. 207–14 (p. 207).
9. Stoneman, p. 207.
10. Patsy Stoneman, *Brontë Transformations* (London: Harvester Wheatsheaf), p. 94.
11. Erica Brown, *Comedy and the Feminine Middlebrow Novel: Elizabeth von Arnim and Elizabeth Taylor* (New York: Routledge, 2013), p. 90.
12. Katherine Mansfield, 'The Little Governess', in *The Collected Stories of Katherine Mansfield* (London: Wordsworth, 2006), p. 140. All further references to Mansfield's stories are to this edition and are cited parenthetically in the text.
13. Charlotte Brontë, *Villette*, ed. Margaret Smith (Oxford: Oxford University Press, 2008), p. 129.
14. Charlotte Brontë, *Jane Eyre* (London: Penguin, 2011), p. 327. All references are to this edition and will be cited parenthetically.
15. Brontë, *Jane Eyre*, p. 122; Elizabeth von Arnim, *Vera* (London: Virago Press, 1941), p. 2. All further references are to this edition and will be cited parenthetically.

16. Anonymous, 'Latest Works of Fiction', Review of *Vera*, by von Arnim, *New York Times Book Review*, 27 November 1921, pp. 24 and 28. Quoted in Maddison, p. 35.
17. *Letters* 4, p. 346.
18. *Letters* 4, p. 346.
19. *Letters* 4, p. 346.
20. Maddison, p. 108.
21. Maddison, p. 93.
22. Jane Nardin, 'Katherine Mansfield and Elizabeth von Arnim's *Vera*', *Notes and Queries*, 62, (2015), pp. 450–1.
23. See Maddison and also Juliane Römhild, '"Worms of the Same Family"': Katherine Mansfield and Elizabeth von Arnim', in Sarah Ailwood and Melinda Harvey, eds, *Katherine Mansfield and Literary Influence* (Edinburgh: Edinburgh University Press, 2015), pp. 93–104.
24. Maddison, p. 87.
25. Maddison, p. 87.
26. Maddison, p. 87.
27. *Letters* 4, p. 252.
28. *Letters* 5, p. 297.
29. *Letters* 4, p. 346.

CREATIVE WRITING

SHORT STORY

Vessel

Sarah Laing

Laura had been worried all day about crashing the car – the last time she'd driven Monica, she'd overtaken a cyclist on a blind rise and Monica had flinched, anticipating the crunch of a head-on collision that would ricochet the oncoming car against the Frida Kahlo mural on the concrete retaining wall. The mural was primitive, done by a midnight gang with no council mandate. Ian Curtis's death date was up there too, and either someone continued to touch up the paint, or it had everlasting properties. Why were people in Wellington so fixated on Ian Curtis's death? Other people had suicided subsequently. Kurt Cobain, Robin Williams, Antony Bourdain. There were no retaining walls near where she lived and the hill crumbled, cascaded, little slumps of ochre rock strewing the road. There was also a sign, warning drivers about low-flying kereru, but the last time she'd biked up the hill, she saw a wood pigeon on the road, its wings iridescent green and blue, scarlet blood starbursting its head. It was the first time she'd seen one with its eyes shut.

She was that cyclist, and she felt bad to have been so reckless. She also felt that crunch, every time she pulled out. *Crunch*, and the side of her car cratered, her children crushed. *Crunch*, and her neck whiplashed back, her vertebrae displaced, herself in a foam brace for months to come, having to buy orthopaedic pillows for her bed, a burgeoning opioid addiction, turning to heroin when the doctor stopped the scripts. *Crunch*, as she failed to give the ochre rock a wide enough berth and flew off her bicycle at 40 kilometres an hour, the road ripping off her skin like cellophane from a package.

It wasn't as if she crashed the car often – she hadn't done so for at least four years. It was her husband who dinged the car last, grinding it against the concrete pillars in the supermarket carpark. The panel beaters weren't surprised – they got a lot of local business because of those pillars – but she'd been annoyed, another day pockmarked by cleaning up messes she hadn't even made. She hated being the good wife. She was exhausted by motherhood. She told her husband this morning that she didn't want to be married any more, even though she knew it was professional suicide, knew that she wouldn't be able to support herself on the sales of her speckled, pale bowls. He said he'd been having similar thoughts.

Laura was picking Monica up for their Women in Ceramics group, where they all brought their latest bowls and glaze innovations and artist statements and poems to make them feel more Zen. Laura hardly ever felt Zen. She mostly felt agitated. Her *kupu o te rā* popped up in her inbox: *He tou tīwawaka!* Bottom like a fantail. Always flitting erratically to catch her prey. The only time she felt in the least bit quieted was when the rim of the bowl had risen up into a pleasing circle and the spiral of clay hypnotised her. But if it veered off – if it collapsed – then she was full of rage, unable to accept the impermanence and the imperfection and her own failure to coax this goddamned lump of dirt into a receptacle of happiness, or tea, or chrysanthemums, like the ones Katherine Mansfield floated in a bowl when John Middleton Murry came to visit her for the first time.

Monica was Zen. Monica had been making ceramics for over thirty years, and she said it took twenty years to even begin to get good at it. Monica had been to Japan and had studied under a master, and she could speak Japanese. When it came time for her to host the ceramics circle, she made exquisite layered jellies flavoured with matcha powder, pillowy rice flour buns with red bean paste inside them – she'd learnt how to make all these herself; she didn't go down to the store to buy them. The last time she'd hosted, she'd placed white cotton gloves on her work table and pointed at a papery-thin bowl.

'I made this with my Sensei, Daisuke, in his forest studio. It was one of those days where the humidity was at least 90 per cent – the water was dripping off the trees, and I felt like I was going to faint. We got the clay on to the wheel, and just as Daisuke pressed his thumbs into the centre, there was this great green presence rushing in through the windows. It was sucked into the spiral, and Daisuke said it was a spirit. When I got back to my apartment there was a message on my phone – my cousin ringing me to say that my mother had died of a massive stroke that morning. I don't believe in God, but … well, the spirit world revealed itself to me.'

The back of her neck tingled in spite of her scepticism. Laura pulled the cotton gloves on – of course, too short, leaving her own fingers webbed, and accepted the bowl as it was passed from hand to hand.

'Oh, yes, I feel it,' said Saskia, always the most eager to please of them all, but also the oddest, and the most likely to be attuned to the spirit level. 'I think I can hear the harmonics – the vibrations – it's as if there's a pulse in there. It's like – you know – when you're pregnant and you feel the quickening. Hardly noticeable at all but once you've sensed it, it's unmistakeable.'

She was reluctant to hand it on, and her eyes closed, her mouth opened a little. Laura was sickened by the glistening strand of spittle that attached her top teeth to her lower lip and seemed to quiver. She wanted to slip a knife in there to sever it. Saskia's eyes snapped open and she passed the bowl on to Laura, who admired how fine the ceramic was, how light it felt, but did not sense any vibrations beyond the tremor of her own anxiety. She felt a surge of envy for Monica – why had the spirit revealed itself to her, not Laura? She'd had trouble feeling her babies too, because the placenta attached itself to the front of her uterus. She couldn't tell if it was the baby kicking off, diving into the amniotic deep, or if it was an air bubble in her intestines, negotiating its way past a stool. She obsessively counted the kicks to make sure there were enough each hour, unsettled by the women at her prenatal yoga classes who said their babies were beating them up from the inside, like ninjas or future footballers.

Laura had been doing ceramics for four years, about the same time as she began to think she should leave her husband, a year before her youngest son was born. 'You still have sex,' her friend had incredulously said when she'd told her she was pregnant. Laura had laughed and said *hardly ever* and wondered if nobody had sex after ten years of marriage, or if some people were still hot for each other into old age. There were so many bowls. She thought of sex as she pressed her fingers into the wet clay, and it parted for her, making a sucking sound. She had to give most of them away, even though she had an Instagram following and an Etsy shop and every few weeks got a request to package her baked cunts up, to send them somewhere in America, Tasmania, Timaru. Sometimes they arrived in pieces despite the cardboard bracing and copious tissue paper she stuffed the box with. She felt fury at the couriers of the world, hurling things into their cargo holds and vans like they were all made of rubber and steel.

She'd found her first ceramics posse at the beleaguered local night school – no longer fully funded – and would drop the children off at her mother's place so she could spend three hours with other wannabe artists. There was a cluster of post-menopausal women, and a young woman with too many tattoos and facial piercings, always wearing her beanie inside, never talking to anyone. There was a single man, of Czech extraction, who didn't make bowls but instead made monsters – strange nightmarish distortions with hungry maws and reaching arms. He'd fashion hearts torn from bodies and fire them separately. It was good to have something of her own, something that felt real and not like the business analyst job she'd had before, which was lucrative but also made her feel conflicted, feeding the capitalist machine that was eating the planet alive. Besides, her husband earned enough – they had met on the job, and he'd been her junior, but now he had moved into management while she treaded water, drowning a little in freelance contracts. She wanted ceramics to be her vocation but she worried that she was seen as a housewife with a hobby. The Czech man, Dušek, complained about New Zealanders, how they only wanted to talk about sports and renovations and politics, how they were not interested in art or poetry at all, and Laura had wanted to say LOOK AT ME, what the hell do you think that I am doing? Instead she sympathetically agreed. He probably put her into the renovations camp, making bowls to decorate her house.

It was on the way home from ceramics class that the last crash happened – at least the last one she'd caused. She'd picked the children up from her mother's, only two of them at the time, and her mother had provided a list of all the things that she had done, ostensibly to help, but surreptitiously to criticise. Laura was not allowed to take offence at the implicit criticism because her mother would be hurt that her ministrations were not appreciated. 'Eamon's hair was a rat's nest – I got rid of the dreadlocks. He really needs it cut – I don't know why you let him keep it so long. And we wandered down to the Warehouse to buy Charlie some new shorts because his ones had too many holes; it was a little embarrassing for me.' Laura would bite her tongue and say thank you, thank you, how wonderful, because she *had* wanted to comb Eamon's hair and she *had* wanted to make sure Charlie was in some decent shorts but she'd been in such a hurry and in danger of missing the first part of the class, where they drank coffee and Dušek complained, and the older women talked about their friends dying of cancer, that she'd thrown the boys into the car in a state. Now they were ratty and tired, overstimulated by her mother's educational games and nutritionally balanced snacks. It was late – going on five, the traffic already gnarled and infuriating, and the boys were fighting over something in the back. What were they even fighting over? A car that their grandmother had given them. She'd bought them each a matchbox hot rod from the Warehouse as a treat for walking there but now the older one wanted to see the younger one's car, but the younger one wasn't handing it over as he knew he wouldn't get it back. 'GIVE IT TO ME!' he screamed. 'JUST GIVE IT TO ME. I WILL GIVE IT BACK.' The traffic was starting and stopping as one lane merged into another lane, a tributary into the three lanes that traversed the east to west road. The older one had now grabbed the younger one's hair and was pulling it and the younger one was screaming. Start stop. Start. Stop. Start –

'Stop it! Stop fighting, or I will –'

CRUNCH

It didn't feel like much. It didn't feel like much apart from the strap cutting into her shoulder and the fact that the bonnet of her car was steaming and the traffic was definitely stopped.

The car was quiet. The boys were quiet. The steam was coming up, or was it smoke? Perhaps it was smoke and the car would soon blow, billowing yellow flames, shrapnel flying. 'Quick, boys, out of the car!' She unbuckled herself and jumped out in between two lanes. She unbuckled Charlie, cursing the stupid seat that had been designed with carelessness, the designers knowing that women were the main operators of these buckles, and their time wasn't money. She pulled him out, his hoodie catching behind the straps, the thought of dislocating his shoulder zig-zagging her mind. Eamon tried to climb over him as she yanked.

'WAIT,' she yelled.

The boys were now on the footpath and they were both crying. 'Our car!' they cried. 'Its eye has fallen out!' And it was true – the left light had popped out as the front bonnet had crumpled and dangled on a cable.

The woman whose car she'd run into also hopped out, running her hand across her bumper. She had golden skin and wore her hair in a curly bob. There was no obvious damage – hers was an SUV with a number plate that spelled AROMAT. Laura wondered if she owned a fragrant laundromat, or an archery vending machine.

'Are you ok, boys?' she asked. 'I have some Rescue Remedy in the car – I could give it to them.'

Aromatherapy perhaps.

'Um, maybe?'

The woman disappeared and then reappeared with a little tincture bottle. 'Open your mouths, boys. Lift up your tongues.' She gave Laura a look, like she was a bad mother, like she did this on purpose, and she could call the authorities. The boys, still crying, did as she said and Laura had a fleeting worry that there wasn't any Rescue Remedy inside the bottle, but instead there was cyanide. But the boys still stood there, shoulders heaving in unison, perhaps slightly quieted, and Laura was peeved that the woman hadn't offered her Rescue Remedy too.

A police truck pulled up, and two women in blue dungarees hopped out with a stack of orange road cones between them. One of them, looking at the shards of plastic on the road, got a brush and shovel out of the back and swept it up. The other one questioned Laura, writing her responses in a flip notebook with a creaky ballpoint. She was Scottish and had dark blonde hair and heavy-framed glasses, and Laura remembered her from the time when her buggy was stolen off the front steps and she'd spotted it for sale on Trade Me. The policewoman hadn't been able to do anything then, and Laura had had to buy a new one. She hoped she wouldn't be prosecuted for this – it was the boys' fault anyway. If only they wouldn't fight.

They were sniffling now, as the policewoman told her that the tow truck would be coming to take her car away, because she was definitely not driving it anywhere with a busted radiator. The car had stopped steaming, but it looked disconsolate, and she remembered how pugs were meant to sneeze their eyeballs out sometimes, and how they were so inbred they had trouble breathing. The policewoman was very attractive, and Laura wondered if she was attracted to her. She didn't know who she was attracted to. Not to her husband any more. She was unsure if she'd ever wanted him, or had mistaken his desire for her own. Sometimes she thought she fancied Dušek, wondering if he'd plunge his arm into her chest and rip out her heart. The policewoman's skin was very pale and she was slender in her dungarees, with a proper waist and an air of competency and compassion. Laura would not be prosecuted – people made mistakes like this all the time. She imagined going to live with the policewoman, who would grow extraordinary cabbages and chase away the rabbits while Laura placed bowls and cups into their garden kiln and drank coffee on the sun-baked patio, plaited ropes of garlic hanging out to dry on the rafters. There were no children in this fantasy. She imagined unlacing the police officer's heavy boots, easing them off to reveal her creamy, delicate feet. She ran her tongue along her instep, up her calf, her inner thigh –

'You will have to call a taxi home, I'm sorry. This is the tow company's business card – you can call them once you've contacted your insurance company.'

'We can walk – we're not that far.'

'But it's raining.'

'Come on, boys,' she said, taking their hands.

The drizzle was persistent. Her house wasn't so near after all – it was a twenty-minute walk, which was perfect exercise for her, but an eternity for a three- and a five-year-old who had already walked to the Warehouse with their grandmother. What were they going to have for dinner?

'Keep walking and I'll buy you an ice block at the dairy.'

She was a bad mother. She used food bribes way too often. The kids would associate all physical activity with treats and grow fat and diabetic as a result. She bought them each a lemonade ice block at the bottom of the hill but then realised there was another fifteen minutes' walk and she should've held out until the next dairy. Suddenly she remembered her bowls – they were good ones this time, her favourites so far, a green glaze gradating into a violet grey – and how the tow truck would tip the car up so they smashed against each other, even though she'd wrapped them in tissue and newspaper, placed them in a packaged soup box. She wondered what her husband would say about the crash. Probably nothing. He would be so nice about it all. If he'd crashed the car she would've sighed and rolled her eyes, used it as evidence that he was useless and careless, but she knew that he would be understanding, and that enraged her. He was so calm, so stagnant, and she felt duped by his early confession that he was writing a film, and he wouldn't work a desk job forever. She'd read the script – it was about unconventional relationships, Katherine Mansfield's and John Middleton Murry's in particular. She was entranced by the story, and how this ordinary-seeming young man could harbour another secret world inside his head. She'd told him to be bold, to quit his job, but he hadn't secured funding after the second round, and she got sick of him spending weekends at film incubators rather than with her. He set the script aside once they had children, and she was pleased. She could be the primary caregiver, the artist. She wanted him to yell at her for rear-ending that SUV, to call her a stupid bitch, and then she could yell at him, throwing the china that they'd bought from Briscoes on the tiled floor – *smash, smash, smash* – and she could kick him out, bringing home irregular cups and bowls each week from class to stack in the cupboard.

The boys had finished their ice blocks and they were crying again, asking her to give them a piggy back. Their hands were all sticky and their cheeks were red from the chill of the rain. They were walking so slowly, as if through a muddy estuary where the mangroves stretched out their roots, trying to ensnare their ankles and turn the boys into mangroves too.

'Just a little bit further, boys. If you make it to the next dairy I'll buy you a lollypop each.'

'Can I have a coke?'

'No, you may not have a coke. Not at all. It's bad for your teeth.'

'Toby gets cokes all the time.'

'Well, Toby's mother is irresponsible. Come on boys, walk a little faster. Pretend you're on the moon and there's no gravity and you can leap metres at a time.'

'But there is gravity. It's pulling me down. It's like we're on Neptune.' Eamon collapsed on the footpath, his knees and ankles folding beneath him.

'Get up!' Laura resisted the urge to kick him. Charlie kneeled down beside him, forever in his brother's thrall. She let them sit there on the footpath, the rain soaking their pants.

'Will the car get its eye pushed back into its socket, Mummy? Will it be able to see again?'

'Yes, darling, of course.'

'I miss our car, Mummy.'

'Get up, keep walking. It's only another five minutes to the next dairy.'

'I'm sorry that happened to you,' her husband said, sweaty and damp from his bike ride home. He tried to give her a hug. She sent him out again immediately to buy the fish and chips and opened the bottle of wine. She wondered if they'd get on better if he lived elsewhere and they wrote letters to each other. Then she wouldn't be confronted by the physical reality of him – his flushed, freckled skin, his pungent sweat. Everyone told her what a nice bloke her husband was. Everybody said that Katherine Mansfield should've left Murry because he was so squeamish, and shied away from her because of her illness. But in those letters were moments of exquisitely rendered love. They had pet names for each other. They read the same books. Her husband only read management books now, and he talked about sports and politics at parties, while Laura discussed renovations and children with the women in the kitchen. He didn't shy away from her – that was the night she got pregnant. Sex was infrequent enough post children that she could easily pinpoint the day. The boys ate half their chips and some of their fish, and then she let them watch a DVD while she finished the food off, along with the bottle of wine. She'd felt mellow and acquiescent by the end of the evening, an air of hilarity gripping her as she urged her husband to describe his workmates' foibles, as she made fun of the aromatherapy woman, who was so reasonable and so judgmental. He must've come a little before putting on a condom, and she couldn't bring herself to have an abortion in case the baby was a girl.

Laura pulled down Monica's gracious street in Wadestown – not a suburb that suited her, she was more of an Aro Valley or Mount Victoria type – but she'd inherited her mother's cottage. Laura lived further out in the northern suburbs now because she needed a big house to fit her three boys, who broke things all the time. One of them was on crutches, having turned his ankle at soccer, and the other had fractured his scaphoid bone falling off his bike last year and had to have his hand in plaster for six weeks. Everything was cracking and breaking and so was Laura, no longer a reliable vessel to contain them in. They were spilling out and running down the drains, which themselves were fissured from the last big earthquake. They were seeping into the soil, beyond her control.

Already waiting on the street, Monica's coat was a multi-layered, unstructured affair with unfinished edges on angles. Her long dyed black hair was cut in a blunt fringe and she had a crow look to her in the dark. A giant Japanese crow. Behind her, she could see the silhouette of her garden in the night light – sculptural plants and ceramics resting on poles like totems. If she were a child, she'd be terrified. She wondered if the neighbourhood children thought of Monica as a witch, if their parents thought she was a disgrace. Pulling into the drive, Monica jumped aside, as if anticipating that Laura might run her over.

'I'm so grateful you're driving. I hate driving at night.' Monica didn't have anything in her hands today apart from a packet of wasabi peas. Laura wondered if she'd memorised her poetry. Laura had remembered hers at the last minute and had scrolled through Instagram, settling on a faux-philosophical stanza by a twenty-one-year-old with four million followers.

'You're welcome. I come past your place anyway. Makes me feel less guilty about driving when I probably could bike.'

'I wouldn't feel safe. Not that I bike – not since I lived in Japan. I always biked there, but I think drivers are a little more respectful.'

'You're right – drivers here are full of rage. We're all so mild-mannered on the outside that cars are an expression of our psyche. Seething and roiling underneath. I just read an opinion piece that said bikes should be banned in Wellington, and 54 per cent of people agreed.'

'I'm a nervous driver myself, especially behind bicycles. And I've such a day.'

'Oh no,' said Laura. She wasn't going to tell her about ending her marriage. She wasn't sure if it was real or not.

'You know my bowl? The spirit bowl, the one I showed the group?'

'Of course.'

'My cat Mitzi jumped up on the shelf and somehow got behind it and knocked it over. I thought I'd blue-tacked it down, but maybe the blue-tack had dried out.'

'Is it ok? Sometimes they bounce.'

'No, I was in the kitchen when I heard the crack. It's in four pieces now.'

And when she said that word, Laura felt it too. The crack. For a moment she wondered if the bowl spirit had found her, and had collided with her body at force. Then she realised there was a real crack, or more a CRUNCH, because she had reversed into the black SUV parked on the other side of the road.

'Oh shit.'

'It's my fault – that car doesn't normally park there. I would've told you to watch out, had I seen it.'

'I didn't see it either. It was so dark and the car is dark too.'

She got out of the car, and went to inspect the damage. There was a small dent on the side of the glossy black SUV. Why did everybody have such huge cars these days?

'Don't worry, I've done this too. Not to this car though. I know whose car it is. It's my neighbour's – they've just had renovations, double-glazed everything. They totally rebuilt their house.'

Laura climbed the steps to their double-glazed front door and knocked, admiring the original art, the immaculate sofas. Everything gleamed.

The woman leaned against the door frame as she listened to Laura, her arms folded.

'It's my husband's car,' she said. She was wan in contrast to the scarlet and saffron oil paint palette-knifed on to the canvas behind her. 'He just bought it. He's in New York – he can sort it out when he gets home. I can't be bothered.'

Laura wrote down her name, her phone number, her insurance details. The woman gave her hers.

'I am so sorry,' Laura said again. 'I am so sorry,' she said to Monica as they walked down the stairs.

'He's a futures trader,' said Monica.

'What even is that?' Laura had a brief vision of people trading Jetson-style apartments, hover trains, small pockets of usable mountain land after the ice caps melted and the continents turned into burning deserts.

'You know – stocks, bonds. Anticipating booms and busts. Filthy rich.'

'I know – I meant more rhetorically. How is that even a job.' Laura felt a sudden hatred for him and his stupid car, which was so unnecessarily big and black, like a vortex.

'He normally parks it in the garage.'

The aromatherapist's car had been a black SUV too. Laughter – or was it hysteria? – bubbled up inside her. She'd manifested this. She'd been so worried about crashing the car that the first thing she'd done was crash it. Had she done it on purpose? She wondered what her husband would say when she got home and told him. Her bumper was split and there was a dent in the metal. Would he be so understanding now she was going to leave him? Was he inherently understanding or provisionally so? She thought of her three boys and the life they'd made. They'd be asleep by the time she returned. That's when she loved them the best. They'd be curled up around their blankets, their hair messy over their flushed faces, their books splayed by their pillows, the spines cracking a little. She wondered how she would tell them, and how they would take the news that their mother and father were no longer whole, that they would soon be week-about kids, with two sets of clothes and two different bedrooms, demanding computers and bikes in each home. Would they be irreparably damaged? She wondered if, as much as she longed for solitude, she'd miss them, and missing them would be more than she could bear.

'Of course, I will try kintsugi on my bowl. I can't just throw it out.'

'Kintsugi?'

'You know, the Japanese art of mending broken china with gold.'

'I think I've read about it. How do you get the gold to make the china stick together?'

'It's not gold – it's gold-dusted epoxy. At least the kind that I learnt. It makes the piece more beautiful. Instead of trying to hide the cracks, the imperfections, you fill them with gold. It adds a vitality to the bowl.'

'Perhaps I could do that with my bumper bar. Forget about the panel beater and the insurance claim.'

'Well, your car is Japanese.'

'Exactly. But I don't think kintsugi will make it more beautiful.'

'I wonder where my spirit is now. I'm hoping that it's hovering and it will re-enter the bowl when I've made it whole again. I don't want Mum on the loose, haunting me because I haven't done the vacuuming.'

Did she really think it was her mother? 'Perhaps it's like worms – chop it in half and you make two worms. You'll have four spirits now. They might fight.'

'That's not true, you know. Worms die when you chop them in half. You chop them in half to make more chicken snacks. The chickens like it when their dinner wriggles.'

Monica had chickens, of course. Laura thought of Baba Yaga's house on chicken legs, the fence of skulls on sticks like Monica's ceramic totems.

Cresting the hill down to Thorndon, Laura saw the city glued together with sodium lamps. *Kintsugi.* That part of Wellington hadn't even existed before the 1855 earthquake and the shaking had lifted the land from below the sea. The beach that Katherine Mansfield ran down the zigzag path to, it was a freshly made one, a crust of rock butted up by sparring plates. Jetties had been put out of service. Weatherboards had to be hammered back on to building skeletons. A shipping basin became a cricket ground.

They perched so tentatively on this land; they didn't even know if it wanted them in the long term. It might rise up and shake them off its back, a great wet dog, a waking taniwha, the god Rūamoko turning in his mother Earth's stomach, kicking like a ninja. Nothing was permanent. Everything was provisional. Laura and Monica glided down into the basin, the once-was-underwater world.

POETRY

If Katherine Mansfield Were My Best Friend

Nina Powles

'It was only when she came out of the tunnel into the moonlight or by the sea or into a thunderstorm that she really felt herself.'
    Katherine Mansfield, 'The Daughters of the Late Colonel' (1921)

1.
She would teach me how to apply winged eyeliner
in a moving vehicle.

She would write long, passionate texts to her high-school crush,
then screw up her eyes and ask me to press 'send'
quickly before she changed her mind.

She would let me borrow her vintage coats,
her bright silk scarves, her oversized sunglasses
and her Frida Kahlo socks.

When I'm in the middle of a break-up
she would come over when I can't get to sleep
and we would sit on the floor eating Russian fudge
watching documentaries about serial killers.

2.
once we'd saved up enough money
we would go see the cherry blossoms like she always wanted to
and drink chrysanthemum tea beneath the moon
and we would climb mountains that look
just like the mountains in Chinese paintings
and we would sit on the cliff edge
eating mangoes out of our hands
dangling our feet into the clouds

3.

then we would move cities / then countries / at the beginning we would write / then we wouldn't anymore / but sometimes I'd get an email from an unknown address / (subject line: MAGNOLIA FLOWERS) / and then we'd collide / by a river in Shanghai / or on a crosswalk in New York / and we would spend one sunburst afternoon / running through art galleries / watching dogs at the dog park / taking pictures of each other's / shadows

the years would pile up / and she'd get harder to find / but I would always remember that one New Year's Eve / when we were young / when she decided not to turn up to her own party / sneaking out instead to light sparklers / and swim naked in the cold sea / white-gold fireworks / exploding like lightning / in the sky over the harbour / lights blooming in her eyes

CRITICAL MISCELLANY

Of Bliss and Blushing: Cities and Affect in Katherine Mansfield and Jean Rhys

Andrew Thacker

At the Bookshop

Writing to Dorothy Brett in March 1922, Katherine Mansfield extolled the pleasures of France as a 'remarkable country' in which the people are 'always alive, never indifferent as the English are', and praised Paris for the way in which its newspapers were written and for the fact that 'Bookshops swarm in Paris.'[1] I want to start with an imaginary scene set in one of those swarming bookshops, some time in October of 1922, the time of Mansfield's last visit to Paris, where she stayed at the Select Hôtel, next to the Sorbonne. Let us imagine that, one morning, Mansfield strolls into a nearby bookshop, browses a little, picks up a copy of Gertrude Stein's *Three Lives*, and then observes a well-dressed young woman flicking through the same author's *Tender Buttons*. The two women exchange glances and then, tentatively, strike up a conversation on the merits and limitations of Stein's prose style. Mansfield then notices that the woman's English is heavily accented and she asks whether she is English or not.[2] 'That's an interesting question,' replies the other woman, 'no, I'm "hardly" English as I'm "a savage from the cannibal islands" of the Caribbean.' 'Oh,' says Mansfield ruefully, 'so you're a "little savage" from the colonies too.'[3] 'Yes,' replies the other woman, 'my name is Jean, and where are you from exactly?'

This imaginary meeting between two colonial 'savages' – Katherine Mansfield, born in New Zealand, and Jean Rhys, born in Dominica – may have occurred in Shakespeare and Company, the bookshop opened in 1919 by the American Sylvia Beach and since 1921 located in rue de l'Odéon, only a couple of minutes' walk from Mansfield's hotel.[4] Shakespeare and Company was a quintessential site in the geography of European modernism, a cultural institution that disseminated the great works of modernist literary experimentation and also served as a place for writers and artists to gather and meet.[5] Shakespeare and Company, of course, published the first edition of *Ulysses,* but it is another feature of its role within the institutions of modernism that I am interested in here. This bookshop not only sold books but also famously ran a lending library, and it is from the records of this library that I take the rather fanciful scene that Rhys and Mansfield met on a day in October 1922.

The borrowers' cards for Shakespeare and Company (held in the Beach archive at Princeton University and now the subject of a digital humanities project there)[6] offer us a tantalising glimpse into the reading habits of many key modernists and intellectuals in Paris in the 1920s and 1930s, from familiar habitués such as James Joyce and Ernest Hemingway, to young French intellectuals such as Jacques Lacan and Simone de Beauvoir. Katherine Mansfield's card (Fig. 5) offers but the briefest peep into what she was reading in the last months of her life, revealing an intense interest in recent American writing. In addition to *Three Lives* (1909) by Stein, there are four books by Sherwood Anderson: his acclaimed debut volume of short stories, *Winesburg, Ohio* (1919); his follow-up collection of stories, *The Triumph of the Egg* (1921); and the novels, *Windy McPherson's Son* (1916) and *Poor White* (1920). Then there is *The Brimming Cup* (1919), an early feminist novel by the American social activist and educational reformer Dorothy Canfield Fisher; and Carl Van Vechten's *Peter Whiffle: His Life and Works* (1922), a parody of bohemian New York figures such as the hostess Mabel Dodge. This reading not only opens up an intriguing image of what Mansfield was reading in Paris, but also points to possible influences that might have shaped her work, had she not died in 1923.

There are also cards (compiled in a rather rough and ready bibliographic format) for the books held in the library, including a card for the volumes by Mansfield that a 'bunnie' (Beach's term for her library members, from the French for subscriber, *abonné*) could borrow from the library: here (Fig. 6) we find a good selection of Mansfield's works, including two copies of *The Garden Party and Other Stories* (1922) and two copies of *Bliss and Other Stories* (1920), along with the posthumously published *Journal* (1927) and *Letters* (1928). A borrower from the library in the early 1930s would thus have been able to read all of Mansfield's major works, including other posthumous publications such as John Middleton Murry's edition of her collection of book reviews, *Novels and Novelists* (1930), and the first biography, *The Life of Katherine Mansfield* (1933) by Ruth Elvish Mantz and Murry, for which another card exists in the archive.

There are small references to Beach in Mansfield's letters, which indicate that she felt a certain ambivalence towards the proprietor.

Cities and Affect in Mansfield and Rhys

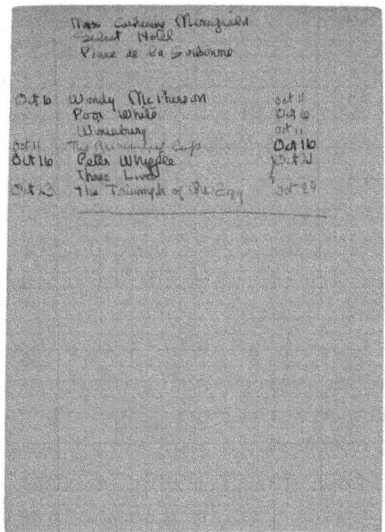

Fig. 5 The borrower's card of Katherine Mansfield from the library of Sylvia Beach's bookshop, Shakespeare and Company. Image reproduced courtesy of the Firestone Library, Princeton University.

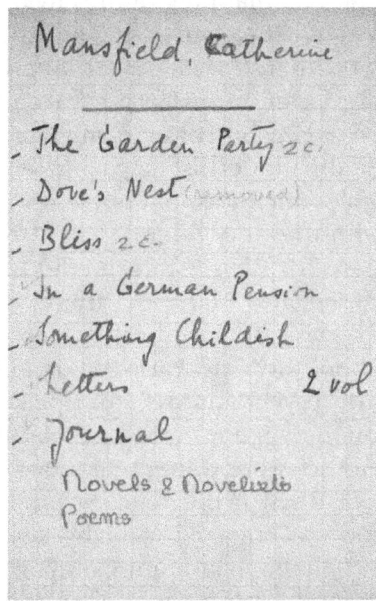

Fig. 6 Index card from the library of Shakespeare and Company showing volumes by Mansfield for borrowing. Image reproduced courtesy of the Firestone Library, Princeton University.

In June 1922, in another letter to Brett, Mansfield asks, 'What are you reading out of Sylvia Beach's library? I am glad you have changed your opinion of her. Im sure she is kind and very decent. She knows Paris inside and out like a sleeve, I think.'[7] This positive appraisal of Beach is tempered in a later letter to Ida Baker, after Mansfield has left Paris in October: the letter ends cryptically, 'I shall not write again just now. I do not want to hear about Miss Beach.'[8] Regardless of her personal feelings about Beach, Mansfield's use of the lending library reveals a fascinating engagement with this most significant of cultural institutions for Anglophone modernists in Paris.

While Mansfield's time in Paris is fairly well documented, Jean Rhys's stay in the only city she 'really loved' and which forms the setting for several of her novels and short stories is much more obscure and difficult to date precisely.[9] Rhys has sometimes, even in Shari Benstock's pioneering *Women of the Left Bank*, seemed to drop off the map of expatriate female writers in Paris, and her connections to the many modernist networks existing in the city have always appeared tenuous.[10] This relative absence from the cultural geography of expatriate Anglophone modernism in Paris has always represented something of a puzzle for scholars of Rhys, particularly given her early connections with Ford Madox Ford and the precise mapping of the city from the stories of her first book, *The Left Bank* (1927), onwards. Indeed, in the second story in this collection, 'A Spiritualist', a character describes visiting a woman who lived in place de l'Odéon, just up the road from Shakespeare and Company.[11] Ford was a borrower from Beach's library, and the bookshop also stocked the modernist magazine he edited while in Paris, *The Transatlantic Review*, which was, of course, the place in which Rhys was first published, with the story 'Vienne', in 1924. There exists, however, no borrower's card for Rhys.[12] But she did use the bookshop and thus might have bumped into Mansfield there, as a reference in her unpublished Black Exercise Book indicates. Here Rhys refers to 'One day in Sylvia Beach's bookshop' in 'Paris rue de l'Odeon I think it is or was I wanted a book on psychoanalysis', and picked one up (probably Freud, who is mentioned by name) and read about women who 'imagined/fantasised' when they were young that they were seduced by older men.[13] This glimpse of Rhys in the bookshop points to the fact that, like Mansfield, she too was engaged with the key modernist networks that circulated around Shakespeare and Company, demonstrating the centrality for both writers of their experience of Paris and its cultural institutions, which is the topic explored in this article.

Critics have compared Rhys and Mansfield before, beginning as long ago as 1927 when, in a review of Rhys's first volume of short stories, *The Left Bank*, the *New York Times* reviewer commented that her tendency to 'reject the descriptive' along with 'structural plot' and the 'fullness of characterization' makes her resemble Mansfield 'more than she does any one else'.[14] More recently, Angela Smith has argued that, as 'colonial subjects' in Paris and London, Rhys and Mansfield often depict characters who use some form of masquerade to conceal a secret side of themselves.[15] Sydney Janet Kaplan long ago noted how Mansfield's position as an 'outsider in the city strengthened her powers of observation', a statement that also can be readily applied to Rhys's own representations of Paris in novels such as *Quartet* (1928) and *Good Morning, Midnight* (1939).[16] Further, Patrick Williams suggested that colonial writers such as Mansfield and Rhys raise the important question of whether their 'Voyage In' to the imperial metropolis is a case of them 'bringing modernism with them, or are they coming to the imperial centre precisely to become involved in it?'[17]

This essay brings Mansfield and Rhys together to explore how they experienced Paris by means of two sets of ideas. The first, echoing the arguments of Kaplan, Smith and Williams, is the notion of the outsider: that is, those modernist writers and artists who were, in multiple ways, 'outsiders' to European urban centres such as London, Paris, Vienna and Berlin. The perception of the linguistic outsider to a city has long been identified by critics as an important stimulus to modernists' creation, whose innovations were stimulated by living as 'exiles and émigrés'.[18] One aspect of the experience of the outsider was emphasised by Raymond Williams, many years ago: '[i]t is a very striking feature of many Modernist and avant-garde movements', he writes, not only that were they located within metropolitan locations, 'but that so many of their members were immigrants into these centres, where in some new ways all were strangers'.[19] This interaction between the stranger and the city in the early twentieth century, suggests Williams, focused upon the available mediums of expression:

> Liberated or breaking from their national or provincial cultures, placed in quite new relations to those other native languages or native visual traditions, encountering meanwhile a novel and dynamic common environment from which many of the older forms were obviously distant, the artists and writers and thinkers of this phase found the only community available to them: a community of the medium; of their own practices.[20]

Although the perception of language as a medium was more noticeable for those for whom English, say, was a second language, even to native speakers, argues Williams, 'the new relationships of the metropolis, and the inescapable new uses in newspapers and advertising attuned to it, forced certain productive kinds of strangeness and distance'.[21] Thus, for both Rhys and Mansfield, colonial outsiders in London and Paris, the 'strangeness and distance' they experienced in these cities directly shaped the production of their fictions.

Another way to think about 'strangeness and distance' in the city is through the language of affect. The cultural geographer Nigel Thrift summarises how cities can be understood in terms of a spatial politics of affect:

> Cities may be seen as roiling maelstroms of affect. Particular affects such as anger, fear, happiness and joy are continually on the boil, rising here, subsiding there, and these affects continually manifest themselves in events which can take place either at a grand scale or simply as a part of continuing everyday life.[22]

Thus, the second set of ideas the essay draws upon is a loosely articulated theory of affect and mood examining how particular cities are experienced by outsiders such as Mansfield and Rhys. Exploring the 'geographical emotions' of these writers entails a broad understanding of affect, encompassing features such as spatial phobias, sensory responses to urban locations, and how cities interact with one's moods.[23] In Mansfield and Rhys, particular spaces in London and Paris produce affective responses and changes in mood, registered in discourses of bodily reactions (such as smiling with joy or blushing) and sensory perceptions (such as smells or sounds). These can be positive moods of bliss and delight at the urban sensorium, or they can result in phobic responses to what are felt as strange and alienating spaces in the city. Heidegger's notion of '*Stimmung*', referring to a particular conception of mood, 'comes neither from "outside" nor from "inside", but arises out of Being-in-the-World'.[24] Moods thus do not solely belong to an individual as an internal state, but are instead part of a person's relationship or attunement (*Stimmungen*) to an external environment. As Jonathan Flatley puts it, moods can thus be regarded as a kind of 'affective atmosphere'; they are 'not in us; we are in them; they go through us'.[25] I thus adapt this notion of a reciprocal relationship between the mood of the individual and that of the spatial environment to explore how Mansfield and Rhys seek to capture the poignant moods provoked and sustained by locations within Paris and London: being in a city is always being in a mood nurtured by the spaces of that city, experiencing geographical emotions in a process of becoming attuned or orientated to one's environment.

Bliss and Other Affects

Many of Mansfield's stories are suffused with affects, perhaps none more so than 'Bliss'. Composed in February 1918 and set in London, 'Bliss' is the story of Bertha Young's misreading of a putative same-sex relationship with Pearl Fulton (who, we learn at the end of the story, has been having an affair with Bertha's husband, Harry). The story opens with Bertha being overcome with the affect of bliss while strolling through city streets:

> Although Bertha Young was thirty she still had moments like this when she wanted to run instead of walk, to take dancing steps on and off the pavement, to bowl a hoop, to throw something up in the air and catch it again, or to stand still and laugh at – nothing – at nothing, simply.[26]

Bliss is here characterised as an all-consuming sense of physiological pleasure, echoing one set of theorists who stress that affect is a form of vitality and 'intensity' that it is hard to translate accurately into a conventional language of emotion.[27] Bertha thus struggles to articulate what is happening to her:

> What can you do if you are thirty and, turning the corner of your own street, you are overcome, suddenly, by a feeling of bliss – absolute bliss! – as though you'd suddenly swallowed a bright piece of that late afternoon sun and it burned in your bosom, sending out a little shower of sparks into every particle, into every finger and toe? . . . (p. 142)

Affect here emerges from the external environment and is symbolically ingested by Bertha, provoking her overwhelming response and demonstrating how her bliss is a result of becoming attuned to the mood of the city. Bertha now protests against the social norms that prevent the outward expression of this bodily affect: 'Oh, is there no way you can express it without being "drunk and disorderly"? How idiotic civilization is! Why be given a body if you have to keep it shut up in a case like a rare, rare fiddle?' (p. 142). Kaplan interprets the story as one where a female character takes pleasure in the 'rapid movement of life in the London streets', a pleasure that is connected to a 'sexual restlessness' of urban experience that is also a 'symptom of rebellion against confinement within stereotypically female spaces'.[28] Significantly, Bertha's initial bliss is stimulated by being outside in an urban environment, imagining dancing on the pavement, rather than indoors, where she becomes transformed into a wife and mother, a body shut up in a case like a fiddle. As Bertha enters the interior space of her domestic home, she attempts to preserve the affect of bliss, enjoying physical contact with her baby and feeling the 'shower of little sparks' inside as almost 'unbearable' (p. 142). Looking in the mirror, she sees a woman 'radiant' and now the overpowering affect is registered in the stumbling disruptions to the free indirect prose Mansfield employs in most of the story: 'a woman, radiant, with smiling, trembling lips, with big dark eyes and an air of listening, waiting for something . . . divine to happen . . . that she knew must happen . . . infallibly' (p. 142).

A similar moment of linguistic disruption occurs when Bertha touches Pearl's arm to direct her into the dining room: 'What was there in the touch of that cool arm that could fan – fan – start blazing – blazing – the fire of bliss Bertha did not know what to do with?' (p. 147). Kaplan's reading of such moments is that here Mansfield is encoding 'sexuality in language, especially in the *rhythms* of language', and she points to the 'undercurrent of sexually charged intimacy' between Bertha and Pearl here.[29] This is persuasive, but I think there is something more happening in such moments, whereby sexual desire is articulated by what Brian Massumi terms the 'asignifying philosophy of affect'.[30] Thus the near breakdown in the language used by Mansfield here is, we might say, an example of the 'productive' effects of 'strangeness and distance' in the city. It also indicates a related point made by several affect theorists: that the intensity of an affect like bliss can overwhelm attempted representation in conventional discourse. Affect, in this sense, writes Lawrence Grossberg, comes to denote 'everything that is non-representational or non-semantic', particularly as experienced by the body during interpersonal contact.[31] Eve Kosofsky Sedgwick broadens the kinds of possible relations affect can possess: 'Affects can be, and are attached to things, people, ideas, sensations, relations, activities, ambitions, institutions, and any number of other things, including other affects.'[32] I want to follow this wider sense of affective relationships and focus upon moments when intense affects flow from cities to subjects, between subjects and spaces, and between bodies and urban environments, as with Bertha's initial desire to dance in the streets.

Though 'Bliss' is set in London, it is another city – Paris – that, I want to suggest, produces the most affective moments in Mansfield's life and works. Take, for example, one of her earliest descriptions of the city, from a letter to Garnet Trowell in 1908, where Mansfield's enthusiasm for the city coalesces with her love for Trowell:

> The picturesque aspect of it all – the people – and at night from the top of a tram – the lighted interiors of the houses – you know the effect – people gathered round a lamp lighted table – a little homely café. [. . .] I picture us with perhaps two small rooms high in the Quartier Latin – setting out

at night – arm in arm – and seeing it all and because we were together – a thousand times more.³³

Even if we remember that this is a private letter, composed by a twenty-year-old away from home and whose generic character encourages the note-like quality of the preponderance of dashes here, we can still see the resemblance to those incidents in 'Bliss' where affective intensity overwhelms conventional prose expression.

Later letters from Mansfield also illustrate the powerful geographical emotions provoked by Paris, as when she and John Middleton Murry briefly relocated to the city in 1913 and she wrote to her sister:

> The weather is icy, but Paris looks beautiful. Everything is white & every morning the sun shines & shines all day until it finally disappears in a pink sky. [. . .] I am going to enjoy life in Paris I know. It is so human there is something noble in the city – Then the river is so much more a part of it than the Thames. It is a real city, old and fine and life plays in it for everybody to see.³⁴

This is more formal in tone and mood, but her enthusiasm for the city remains, particularly in contrast to London, where Mansfield's colonial heritage and status as an outsider were more visible. A similar set of feelings can be found in Rhys's comments upon the two cities. In later life, Rhys described her first visit to Paris as a trip to 'a known world – a déjà-vu world' and noted that she had 'been very faithful and never really loved any other city'.³⁵ Paris produced a powerfully affective response from Rhys, one that contrasts with her largely negative feelings for London, to which she was sent from Dominica as a colonial migrant by her family in 1907. In *Voyage in the Dark* (1934), the fictional account of that voyage, London is a city that is perpetually cold and grey, with 'the streets like smooth shut-in ravines and the dark houses frowning down' and to which the initial response of Anna Morgan, the novel's heroine, is 'oh I'm not going to like this place I'm not going to like this place'.³⁶ The enduring strength of Rhys's attachment to the French capital is demonstrated in a later comment: 'When I say I write for love I mean that there are two places for me. Paris (or what it was to me) and Dominica.'³⁷

In Spring 1915, living alone in a flat near the Seine, Mansfield wrote a series of letters that recall similar geographical emotions to those evinced by Rhys. Mansfield draws upon her experiences of *flânerie* through the Luxembourg Gardens or along the river, of sitting in cafés, or simply what she observes from her window:

> The weather is so warm Im sitting with the windows wide open [. . .]. All the trees are popping and the air smells of mignonette. Big open barges

> full of stones are being towed by black & red beetles up the river – the steering men lean idly – legs crossed – you know their way – and the water froths against the bows.[38]

The view from a Paris apartment, of course, was to become central to the narrative of 'Feuille d'Album', composed a few years later (discussed below). Another wonderful letter to Murry captures an intense experience after lunching in a restaurant:

> As I came out it began to snow. A wind like a carving knife cut through the streets – and everybody began to run – so did I into a café and there I sat and drank a cup of hot black coffee. Then for the first time I felt in Paris. [. . .] And then you know the strange silence that falls upon your heart. [. . .] I felt that and knew that I should write here. I wish that you would write a poem about that silence sometime, my bogey. It is so *peculiar* – even one's whole physical being seems arrested. It is a kind of dying before the new breath is blown into you. [. . .] So after this intense emotion I dashed out of the café bought some oranges and a packet of rusks and went back to the hotel.[39]

The 'peculiar' and 'intense emotion' Mansfield tries to capture here is an indication of how the mood of the city infuses the writer, and her 'whole physical being seems arrested' by the affect of the city. She now feels herself finally to be 'in Paris', and the use of terms such as 'strange' and 'peculiar' points not only to her presence in the city as a *stranger*, but also to Williams's notion of modernism's productive quality of 'strangeness and distance'. The desire for a poem about 'the strange silence that falls upon your heart' might also be viewed as another attempt to capture the asignifying logic of affect.

The geographical emotions that Mansfield experienced in Paris clearly acted as a significant prompt to her creativity, as only a few days later she declared to Murry that she had fallen 'into the open arms of my first novel', then called 'The Aloe', which was to result in the breakthrough style of the story, 'Prelude'. It is fascinating to see how this story, characterised by Kaplan as a 'spatially ordered narrative',[40] was described by Mansfield, in a well-known letter to Murry, as originating in her Parisian location:

> Its queer stuff. Its the spring makes me write like this. Yesterday I had a fair wallow in it and then I shut up shop & went for a long walk along the quai – very far. It was dusk when I started – but dark when I got home. The lights came out as I walked – & the boats danced by. Leaning over the bridge I suddenly discovered that one of those big boats was exactly what I want my novel to be – Not big, almost 'grotesque' in shape I mean perhaps *heavy* – – with people rather dark and seen strangely as they move

in the sharp light and shadow and I want bright shivering lights in it and the sound of water.[41]

The 'queerness' of the modernist style Mansfield imagines here is thus a fascinating response to the geographical emotions she experienced in Paris; as she became attuned to its environment, the mood of the city, one might say, is translated into her vision for a story that could capture the weightiness of boats along with a sensorium of light and sound. Though 'Prelude' is set in New Zealand, this letter indicates how the narrative qualities of this story bear the influence of the mood of 'strangeness and distance' experienced by the author's outsider perspective in Paris.

At the Quai

It was another couple of years before Mansfield returned to address Paris directly in two more important stories: 'Feuille d'Album' (1917) and 'Je ne parle pas français' (1918). 'Feuille d'Album' offers a portrait of an English painter, Ian French, who is living uneasily in an artistic Paris of cafés and studios. French's lack of attunement to the city is noted by the anonymous female voices that narrativise his presence: he is 'impossible', 'too shy', has 'nothing to say for himself' and is such a 'weight' (p. 93). Three early paragraphs end with the narrator stating 'Hopeless', a reflection on French's inability to engage more fully with life. One woman tries to make him fall in love by attempting to visit him at his studio and forcing the boy to 'smell the enchanting perfume of her hair' (p. 94). Another takes him to Paris cafés and cabarets for a 'rousing', visiting 'thrilling' places 'where someone had always been shot the night before' (p. 94). But French does not respond to the delights of the demi-monde, and his manner remains as if he had 'walked home from church' (p. 94). His inability to attune to bohemian Paris is symbolised by his overly tidy studio, 'as neat as a pin', in which 'Everything was arranged to form a pattern', by his 'complicated list of expenses', and by a bedside note that commands 'GET UP AT ONCE' (p. 95). Indeed, we might say that Mansfield's choice of his surname ironically points to his inability to immerse himself in the mood of Parisian life: French is thus most unlike the French bohemians of Paris.

Janet Wilson has argued persuasively that 'Feuille d'Album' and the character of French represent Mansfield 'writing back' to T. S. Eliot's 'The Love Song of J. Alfred Prufrock', particularly in the 'representation of masculinity, gendered relations, and the psychological hesitation in thought, speech, and action' in Eliot's poem.[42] French's hesitations echo

Prufrock's in a number of ways, one of which appears in the disrupted textuality of the story itself: several paragraphs end inconclusively, with dashes or exasperated expressions ('Hopeless!'), but most noticeable is the repeated use of ellipses marked by dots. These are employed some twenty-five times in the story, an average of once every hundred words, and echoes those moments when ellipses appear in Eliot's poem, such as, 'I grow old . . . I grow old . . .'[43] French's incapacity to attune to the mood of Parisian cultural life produces a brief narrative album that, we might say, is missing some of its key leaves.

This textual registration of affect is paralleled by a puzzling manifestation in the character of French himself: his blushing. Blushing has occasioned much debate amongst theorists of affect, with one of the founders of affect theory, Silvan Tomkins, linking it to his influential discussion of shame. The metaphorical 'loss of face' in a person experiencing shame, writes Tomkins, produces an acute self-consciousness of the physical face itself as a form of communication:

> Blushing of the face in shame is a consequence of, as well as a further cause, for heightened self- and face-consciousness. [. . .] The face is the most common locus of blushing because the face is the chief organ of general communication of speech and affect alike.[44]

In literary history, shame and blushing have also been much associated, at least as far back as Shakespeare's *Hamlet*, whose attitude towards his mother's actions after his father's death famously produces the line: 'O shame, where is thy blush?' (III, iv). However, psychologist W. Ray Crozier's analysis of blushing in literature indicates that 'the blush has no single meaning', and in addition to shame, it can refer to modesty, or be inherently sexual in nature.[45]

In 'Feuille d'Album', French's blushing appears not to be triggered by shame. Possibly it is a manifestation of his embarrassment at not fitting into Parisian cultural life, but it definitely seems to have a coquettish quality to it. He is said to be able to 'blush his way out' of an awkward situation and is able to manipulate the affect at will to men and women, recalling Wilson's suggestion that French engages in a masquerade or performance: 'How could one resist him?', notes the narrator, recalling sitting in a café with French: 'one's heart was wrung at sight. And, as if that was not enough, there was his trick of blushing. . . . Whenever the waiter came near him he turned crimson' (p. 173).[46] At the story's conclusion, when French obsessively follows through the streets a woman who lives in the opposite flat, their encounter commences with yet another blush affect: 'Blushing more crimson than ever, but looking at her severely [. . .] almost angrily' (p. 179). Is this the blush of erotic appeal or of embarrassment? Its affective meaning is as inconclusive and mysterious as the final incident when French hands the woman an egg, which he claims bizarrely she has dropped.

However, I think that the affect of shame, if not its blush, still lurks in the story as a textual response to various spaces in the city. The narrative point of view of the story shifts, after the free indirect discourse of the female voices commenting upon French, to a passage mainly in third person that offers an extensive description of its Parisian location, which, as Wilson notes, employs something like a cinematic panning shot from the rooftop studio:[47]

> Perched up in the air the studio had a wonderful view. The two big windows faced the water; he could see the boats and the barges swinging up and down, and the fringe of an island planted with trees, like a round bouquet. The side window looked across to another house, shabbier still and smaller, and down below there was a flower market. You could see the tops of huge umbrellas, with frills of bright flowers escaping from them, booths covered with striped awning where they sold plants in boxes and clumps of wet gleaming palms in terra-cotta jars. (p. 175)

The view is recognisable as being one from the flat where Mansfield stayed during the Spring of 1915, the period of the letters to Murry quoted earlier, and one that renders an intense set of geographical emotions. The flat was at 13 quai aux Fleurs, on the Île de la Cité, and was owned by Francis Carco, a poet and chronicler of French bohemia, with whom Mansfield had conducted a brief affair earlier in the year and which formed the backdrop to her story, 'An Indiscreet Journey', also composed while living in the flat in May 1915.

Can the blush of shame, therefore, be discerned in 'Feuille d'Album', albeit in a disguised fashion, but one experienced by Mansfield herself? In depicting Carco's flat in this story, whose spaces must have been suffused with the intense memories of her recent affair with him, did Mansfield feel something like the affect of shame, triggered, as Tomkins argues, by the 'incomplete reduction of internal joy'?[48] The description of the view from Carco's flat is full of an affective vocabulary that renders a complex mood derived from the urban setting: the building is 'mournful', but can look 'romantic' yet also 'forlorn'; it 'smells so unromantic', and the imagery of the concierge trapped in a 'glass cage', 'wrapped in a filthy shawl' with a 'swollen old dog' for company, only adds to this melancholy mood (p. 94). However, the description of the barges and boats 'swinging' along the river and the 'bright flowers' and 'gleaming palms' of the flower market on the quai present a slightly more appealing scene. The mood registered in the text is thus one that vacillates between the 'romantic' and the 'unromantic', a conflicted perception in keeping with Mansfield's own feelings and illustrating Tomkins's notion that shame is the affect of 'transgression' and is 'felt as an inner torment'.[49] Though there is no overt blush of shame here, the affect nevertheless seems to seep into the very textual spaces of the story.

Almost three years later, just after composing 'Bliss', Mansfield returned to her experience with Carco in Paris. He became the model for the writer Raoul Duquette in 'Je ne parle pas français', who, in manner and attitude, is almost the reverse of Ian French: Duquette, as was Carco, is an habitué of Parisian bohemia, a self-confident Lothario at ease in its environment and attuned to its moods. The blush of shame, we surmise, would never appear on Duquette's face. The opening of 'Je ne parle pas' is located within a 'dirty and sad' café (p. 112), but one in which Duquette experiences a moment of revelation about life. The story he recalls while sitting in the café, told in the first person by Duquette, concerns his meeting with an English couple, loosely modelled upon Murry and Mansfield. Mansfield's story is a complex exploration of her own relationship with both Carco and Murry, but it is also what she described as a 'cry against corruption'[50] and a protest against the kind of predatory male sexuality represented by Carco, as she recorded in a notebook at about the same time as she wrote the story: 'Lord! How I do hate the French. With them it is always rutting time. See them come dancing and sniffing round a woman's skirt.'[51] The shameless behaviour of Carco and Duquette is now the target of Mansfield's narrative.

Rhys's fiction, too, often reveals the difficulties faced by solitary women in cities, particularly when they encounter predatory male figures of the Raoul Duquette or Francis Carco variety. One example is her 1930 novel, *After Leaving Mr Mackenzie*, in which Julia Martin meets and is discarded by a series of men in London and Paris. The final section of her novel is, like 'Feuille d'Album', set on the Île de la Cité, and sees the heroine take a room in a hotel there. As in Mansfield's story, the view from the window is significant for revealing Julia Martin's mood, alone in the city after a disastrous trip to London:

> Her hotel looked out on a square in the Île de la Cité, where the trees were formally shaped [. . .]. The houses opposite had long rows of windows, and it seemed to Julia that at each window a woman sat staring mournfully, like a prisoner, straight into her bedroom.[52]

The sense of imprisonment is a common motif in much of Rhys's Paris fiction, and Julia's geographical emotions only improve when she leaves the hotel: 'out of doors she felt calmer and happier', partly because the room itself was 'so narrow' but also because 'it was so horrible not to be able to open the window without having several pairs of eyes glued upon you'.[53] Walking along another quai on the Île produces a feeling of hope and possibility: 'Anything might happen. Happiness. A course of face massage.'[54] Her mood thus partially revived, Julia now shops for a new dress and hat, has lunch in a café, and visits another café nearby in the place St Michel.

In much of Rhys's fiction, this sort of desperate *flânerie* by her characters is a strategy to ward off unhappiness and escape a certain claustrophobia associated with the many dingy hotel rooms that produce a melancholy mood of despair in her heroines. *Quartet* (1928) offers one such example of the female outsider in Paris, and in the heroine, Marya Zelli, Rhys fictionalises her own affair with the writer Ford Madox Ford.[55] In a preface to Rhys's first publication, *The Left Bank,* Ford had criticised the book of stories for its supposed lack of topographic detail, and *Quartet* appears to rebut that charge in the precision of its geographical references.[56] Almost every café, restaurant and hotel can be located on a map of Paris, and just as Marya's life is said to sway 'between two extremes, avoiding the soul-destroying middle',[57] so the novel oscillates between two key Parisian geographies that provoke strong geographical emotions in Marya: Montmartre, on the Right Bank, and Montparnasse, on the Left Bank. In Montparnasse, Marya lives a shame-filled existence, symbolised by her meetings with Heidler (the fictional Ford) in a shabby hotel room that exudes an 'atmosphere of departed and ephemeral loves … like stale scent'.[58] For Rhys in *Quartet*, then, Paris presents a much more negative set of geographical emotions overall than those found in Mansfield's 'Feuille d'Album'.

Conclusion: In the Café

Rhys's relationship with Ford not only produced the material for *Quartet*, but also provided another curious link with Mansfield. Ford asked Rhys to provide a translation of one of Carco's novels, *Perversité* [*Perversity*]. Publishers of this novel have often made the most of the material, which concerns a Parisian prostitute, Irma, and her brother, Emile, and which ends with Emile killing his sister, as seen in the many sensationalist covers used for the book over the years. However, when the English translation first appeared, it was Ford's name on the cover, not that of Rhys.[59] Though the error was that of the publisher, Pascal Covici, rather than Ford himself, Rhys always believed that it was Ford's doing, after he had finished the affair with her.[60] Some of her anger at this perceived slight (and the rejection by Ford overall) clearly fuelled the mood and affect that we discern in *Quartet*.

I have tried to offer a sketch of some of the complex ways in which these two colonial outsiders experienced Paris and of how their texts are replete with geographical emotions capturing the mood of the spaces in which they moved and their various attempts to attune themselves to these moods. Let us leave Mansfield and Rhys, as we commenced, with that imaginary encounter in October 1922 in Beach's bookshop. Perhaps we might envisage that, after becoming acquainted in the bookshop, they decided to repair to some little café nearby for an early aperitif. Maybe they compared notes on the geographical emotions of the cities they had visited, or discussed their feelings towards men such as Carco and Ford, feelings that sometimes made them blush and sometimes felt like bliss. Or perhaps they pondered, finally, what it meant to write as outsiders in Paris.

Notes

1. *Letters* 5, p. 95. This article is based upon a keynote address given at the Katherine Mansfield Postgraduate Symposium, March 2018, at Queens' College, Cambridge. I am grateful to Gerri Kimber and Joe Williams for inviting me to talk at the conference.
2. From an early age, Rhys's accent was regularly commented upon by British people; see Carole Angier, *Jean Rhys: Life and Work* (Harmondsworth: Penguin, 1992), p. 46.
3. The narrator of 'Luft Bad' describes herself as 'hardly' English; see Katherine Mansfield, *In a German Pension* (Harmondsworth: Penguin, 1964), p. 64. Rhys described how, as a child, she was 'suspected [...] of being a Savage from the Cannibal Islands'; see Jean Rhys, *Letters 1931–1966*, ed. Francis Wyndham and Diana Melly (London: Penguin, 1985), p. 201. Mansfield had been called a 'little savage from New Zealand' by the principal of Queen's College in London during her time there; see *The Katherine Mansfield Notebooks*, vol. 2, ed. Margaret Scott (Canterbury, NZ: Lincoln University Press, 1997), p. 31. For a discussion of such images see Anna Snaith, *Modernist Voyages: Colonial Women Writers in London, 1890–1945* (Cambridge: Cambridge University Press, 2014).
4. Mansfield stayed at the Select from 2 to 16 October 1922. She had previously stayed in the same hotel in the Spring of 1918 but this was before Beach's bookshop appeared.
5. See Sylvia Beach, *Shakespeare and Company* (Lincoln, NB: University of Nebraska Press, 1991); Noel Riley Fitch, *Sylvia Beach and the Lost Generation: A History of Literary Paris in the Twenties and Thirties* (New York: Norton, 1983); and *The Letters of Sylvia Beach*, ed. Keri Walsh (New York: Columbia University Press, 2010).
6. See <https://mep.princeton.edu> (last accessed 24 October 2018).
7. *Letters* 5, p. 199.
8. *Letters* 5, p. 312. The editors speculate that Ida had passed on some story about Beach.
9. Rhys, cited in Angier, p. 107; see pp. 122–5 for the difficulties of precisely locating Rhys's whereabouts in Paris in the early 1920s.

10. Though Benstock discusses Rhys's works, she does not place her upon the map of writers in Paris included in the preface to the book; see Shari Benstock, *Women of the Left Bank: Paris, 1900–1940* (London: Virago, 1987), Preface, n.p.
11. Jean Rhys, *The Collected Short Stories* (New York: Norton, 1987), p. 7.
12. There is, though, a record of a subscriber in 1924 named Mlle Lenglet, the name of Rhys's then husband, Jean Lenglet, from whom she became estranged some time in the early 1920s (see Angier, p. 128). Rhys certainly used Jean Lenglet's name throughout the 1920s (envelopes addressed to her using the name 'Madame Lenglet' up to 1929 can be found in the archives of the British Library). Given the uneven nature of the record-keeping for Beach's lending library, it is entirely plausible that a clerk in the shop recorded Rhys as a 'Mademoiselle' rather than a 'Madame'.
13. Black Exercise Book, Jean Rhys Archive, Special Collections, McFarlin Library, Tulsa.
14. *New York Times Review*, 11 December 1927, pp. 28–30.
15. Angela Smith, '"There is always the other side, always": Katherine Mansfield's and Jean Rhys's Travellers in Europe', in Janka Kascakova and Gerri Kimber, eds, *Katherine Mansfield and Continental Europe: Connections and Influences* (Basingstoke: Palgrave Macmillan, 2015), pp. 142–53 (p. 143).
16. Sydney Janet Kaplan, *Katherine Mansfield and the Origins of Modernist Fiction* (Ithaca, NY: Cornell University Press, 1991), pp. 69–70.
17. Patrick Williams, 'Theorising Modernism and Empire', in Howard J. Booth and Nigel Rigby, eds, *Modernism and Empire* (Manchester: Manchester University Press, 2000), pp. 13–38 (p. 25).
18. The phrase derives from an early account of this phenomenon in Terry Eagleton's book, *Exiles and Émigrés: Studies in Modern Literature* (London: Chatto and Windus, 1970).
19. Raymond Williams, *The Politics of Modernism: Against the New Conformists*, ed. Tony Pinkney (London: Verso, 1989), p. 77.
20. Williams, p. 45.
21. Williams, p. 46.
22. Nigel Thrift, 'Intensities of Feeling: Towards a Spatial Politics of Affect', *Geografiska Annaler: Series B Human Geography*, 86:1 (March 2004), pp. 57–78 (p. 57).
23. Here I am adapting and extending the phrase 'geographical emotions', found in Bryher, *The Heart to Artemis: A Writer's Memoirs* (London: Collins, 1962), p. 26. Heidegger's discussion of *Stimmung* (meaning being attuned to one's surroundings) occurs in his *Being and Time*, trans. John Macquarrie and Edward Robinson (Oxford: Blackwell, 1962), pp. 172–9; 388–96.
24. Heidegger, p. 176.
25. Jonathan Flatley, *Affective Mapping: Melancholia and the Politics of Modernism* (Cambridge, MA: Harvard University Press, 2008), pp. 19; 22.
26. CW2, pp. 141–2. All further references to Mansfield's stories are to this volume and are placed parenthetically in the text.
27. For the Deleuzian notion of affect as 'intensity' see Brian Massumi, 'The Autonomy of Affect', *Cultural Critique*, 31 (Autumn 1995), pp. 83–109. Some critics distinguish sharply between 'affect' and 'emotion', but I tend to follow those who see them as points on a scale, such as Sianne Ngai in *Ugly Feelings* (Cambridge, MA: Harvard University Press, 2005).
28. Kaplan, pp. 69–70.
29. Kaplan, p. 148.

30. Massumi, p. 88.
31. Lawrence Grossberg, 'Affect's Future: Rediscovering the Virtual in the Actual', in Melissa Gregg and Gregory J. Seigworth, eds, *The Affect Theory Reader* (Durham, NC: Duke University Press, 2010), pp. 309–38 (p. 316).
32. Eve Kosofsky Sedgwick, *Touching Feeling: Affect, Pedagogy, Performativity* (Durham, NC: Duke University Press, 2003), p. 19.
33. *Letters* 1, pp. 77–8.
34. *Letters* 1, p. 133.
35. Rhys, *Letters*, p. 284; Angier, p. 108.
36. Jean Rhys, *Voyage in the Dark* (Harmondsworth: Penguin, 1969), p. 16.
37. Rhys, *Letters*, p. 171.
38. *Letters* 1, p. 165. See also her letter to Murry, c. 13 May, p. 186.
39. *Letters* 1, pp. 157–8.
40. Kaplan, p. 103.
41. *Letters* 1, p. 168.
42. Janet Wilson, '"Feuille d'Album": Katherine Mansfield's Prufrockian Encounter with T. S. Eliot', in Todd Martin, ed., *Katherine Mansfield and the Bloomsbury Group* (London: Bloomsbury, 2017), pp. 73–89 (pp. 76–7). Another intertext here might be that of James Joyce's story, 'Araby', which concerns a boy gazing at a woman and desiring, but failing, to enter into a relationship with her. See Joyce, *Dubliners* (Oxford: Oxford University Press, 2000), pp. 19–24.
43. T. S. Eliot, *Collected Poems 1909–1962* (London: Faber, 1963), p. 17.
44. Silvan Tomkins, *Shame and Its Sisters: A Silvan Tomkins Reader*, ed. Eve Kosofsky Sedgwick and Adam Frank (Durham, NC: Duke University Press, 1995), pp. 136–7.
45. W. Ray Crozier, 'The Blush: Literary and Psychological Perspectives', *Journal for the Theory of Social Behaviour*, 46:4 (2016), pp. 502–16 (p. 503).
46. Wilson, p. 80.
47. Wilson, p. 79.
48. Tomkins quoted in Elspeth Probyn, *Blush: Faces of Shame* (Minneapolis: University of Minnesota Press, 2005), p. xii.
49. Tomkins, *Shame and Its Sisters*, p. 133.
50. *Letters* 2, p. 51.
51. CW4, p. 238.
52. Jean Rhys, *After Leaving Mr Mackenzie* (Harmondsworth: Penguin, 1971), p. 129.
53. Rhys, *After Leaving*, p. 130.
54. Rhys, *After Leaving*, p. 131.
55. For accounts of the background to the novel see Angier, and Max Saunders, *Ford Madox Ford: A Dual Life*, vol. 2 (Oxford: Oxford University Press, 2012), pp. 281–99.
56. On the limitations of Ford's criticism see David Armstrong, 'Reclaiming the Left Bank: Jean Rhys's "Topography" in *The Left Bank* and *Quartet*', in Mary Wilson and Kerry L. Johnson, eds, *Rhys Matters: New Critical Perspectives* (New York: Palgrave Macmillan, 2013), pp. 169–85.
57. Jean Rhys, *Quartet* (Harmondsworth: Penguin, 1973), p. 20.
58. Rhys, *Quartet*, p. 87.
59. Francis Carco, *Perversity*, trans. Ford Madox Ford (Chicago: Pascal Covici, 1928).
60. See Angier, p. 164. Letters in the British Library indicate that when Ford sent the typescript to the publisher, he indicated that the translation was by 'Miss Jean Rhys'; see British Library, Jean Rhys archive, RP6206, box 150c.

Beatrice Hastings in Paris

Chris Mourant

In the major exhibition of Amedeo Modigliani's work staged at Tate Modern in 2017–18 there hung two portraits of his lover, Beatrice Hastings (Fig. 7), accompanied by a short caption that, for most visitors, will have raised more questions than it provided answers. The fiery affair that Modigliani and Hastings conducted from 1914 to 1916 in Paris coincided with – and was perhaps the primary catalyst for – one of the most important and productive periods in the artist's brief career. During these years, Hastings was a significant creator in her own right, producing often highly experimental prose and regularly contributing articles to the influential British periodical, *The New Age*, but in both her life and her work she cultivated multiple personae, regularly adopting a variety of masks to parody fellow artists or pillory the political establishment. For this reason, her œuvre remains obscure and she continues to be a shadowy presence, frequently marginalised or misrepresented in accounts of the period.

The name 'Beatrice Hastings' was itself a mask. Born Emily Alice Haigh in 1879, she was raised in Port Elizabeth, South Africa, the daughter of a successful wool merchant, before being sent to an English boarding school near Hastings, which probably accounts for her choice of name later on. Like her friend and rival Katherine Mansfield, Hastings was taught as a child to see England as 'home' but instead found herself isolated and alone when sent to boarding school, becoming a sullen, precocious teenager who was mistrustful of authority. As a young woman, Hastings set out to defy the bourgeois conventions of her parents, courting scandal with two brief marriages, including one to the pugilist Lachlan Thomson. A photograph taken in 1898 shows her sporting a low-cut dress and staring boldly into the camera, an image to which she appended the inscription: 'In full revolt'.[1] While few details

Fig. 7 Amedeo Modigliani, *Beatrice Hastings*, 1915, oil paint on paper, 40 x 28.5 cm. Private Collection. © Bernard Bonnefon/akg-images.

from this period in Hastings's life are known for certain, her fictionalised autobiography, *Pages from an Unpublished Novel*, suggests that she may have travelled to New York with a theatre troupe, become pregnant with a child who died in infancy, and possibly attempted suicide by jumping into the Hudson. When she moved to London and began to write frequently for *The New Age*, however, her life story becomes easier to trace.

Hastings met A. R. Orage, the editor of *The New Age*, at a talk on Madame Blavatsky given at the Theosophical Society in London in 1907. From this moment, she became a regular contributor, eventually becoming Orage's partner and shadow co-editor. In one of the most temperate assessments of her position on the periodical, her fellow contributor Philip Mairet observed: 'She was the one woman who held her place for years amongst the regular writers of the paper and she did it by sheer force of character and volume of production.'[2] In total, Hastings contributed nearly 400 articles to *The New Age*, regularly sparking controversy with intentionally provocative pieces written under a dizzying array of pseudonyms. These included: 'Pagan', 'Annette Doorly', 'Beatrice Tina', 'Robert á Field', 'A Reluctant Suffragette', 'Hastings Lloyd', 'Mrs Beatrice T. Hastings' ('B. H.'), 'D. Triformis', 'Alice Morning' ('A. M.'), 'Mrs Malaprop', 'T. K. L.', 'E. Agnes R. Haigh', 'Edward Stafford', 'Sydney Robert West', 'H. M.', 'G. Whiz', 'J. Wilson', 'T. W.', 'A. M. A.' and 'Cynicus'. There are undoubtedly other *noms de plume* that remain untraceable and numerous items that were published anonymously. Indeed, Hastings later observed that her writing had relied on 'Disguise! [. . .] Many rôles, and all doubled.'[3] As a result, the prominent position that she occupied on the London literary scene of the early twentieth century has often gone unnoticed.

In literary and art history scholarship, Hastings rarely appears other than as an occasional footnote to the life stories of her more famous contemporaries. In a move that disregards her literary output, for instance, she has frequently been characterised merely as the 'fiery mistress' to various male protagonists of modernism.[4] Jeffrey Meyers, for example, dismisses Hastings as a 'rabid feminist', responsible only for fulfilling the sexual appetites of Orage, Wyndham Lewis and Modigliani, and possibly for arranging an illegal abortion for Mansfield.[5] Similarly, in their introduction to the first volume of Mansfield's collected letters, Vincent O'Sullivan and Margaret Scott credit Hastings with instructing the younger writer only in 'swank and bitchiness'.[6] And Antony Alpers, Mansfield's most authoritative biographer, reflects the critical consensus when he states that the 'raging' Hastings was 'fanatically jealous' of Mansfield.[7] There have been some significant recent attempts at revision, however. In 2004, Stephen Gray published a monumental, meticulously researched biography of Hastings that is indispensable for the dedicated reader of her works, but sadly this is now out of print and available only through specialist booksellers.[8] Likewise, in articles and book chapters, Ann Ardis has argued for Hastings's centrality on *The New Age*, Lucy Delap has shown her importance to the feminist avant-garde, Robert Scholes has examined the contributions Hastings made to *The New Age* from 1914 while living in Paris, and Carey Snyder has considered the predilection for satire and parody shared by both Mansfield and Hastings.[9] A selection of Hastings's writings was included in the ground-breaking anthology edited by Bonnie Kime Scott, *Gender in Modernism* (2007), and a book published in 2016 for 'The Unsung Masters Series' of the Pleiades Press reproduced selections of her writings across multiple genres alongside six critical essays examining her output.[10] All of this points to increasing interest in Hastings's work.

Hastings's writing is marked by acerbic wit, uncompromising position-taking and stylistic fastidiousness. In her first years as a professional writer, she used her different personae to provoke fierce debate in *The New Age* about feminist politics. In *Woman's Worst Enemy: Woman*, for example, a pamphlet of her essays published in 1909, she suggested that women did not universally seek motherhood, arguing that it was the conventional gender roles of marriage and maternity that inhibited the imaginative, creative development of independent women. She also argued forcefully and consistently against the middle-class, autocratic leadership of the suffragists, anticipating the individualist feminism of Dora Marsden's radical journal, *The Freewoman*, by several years, and became a vocal opponent of capital punishment, writing with compassion on humanitarian issues. Hastings was also a central figure in London's pre-war avant-garde, frequently clashing with Ezra Pound. 'The state of things in Art which Mr Pound deplores', she wrote, 'is somewhat due to just such florid, pedantic, obscurantist critics as himself.'[11] Her parodies and critiques of Futurism, Vorticism and John Middleton Murry's magazine *Rhythm* established her importance as a 'critical friend' of the avant-garde. In addition to publishing her poems and short fiction, *The New Age* also serialised three of her books: *Whited Sepulchres* (1909), a novella about the horrors of forced marriage and motherhood; *The Maids' Comedy* (1910–11), a retelling of *Don Quixote* from the female perspective; and *Pages from an Unpublished Novel* (1912).

In May 1914, Hastings left London for Paris. Writing as 'Alice Morning', she sent a regular column titled 'Impressions de Paris' to *The New Age*, chronicling her experiences in Montparnasse as she familiarised herself with its artistic scene and café culture. Hastings developed a unique style of journalistic reportage and collage in this series, cutting abruptly from the chaos of a street scene, for example, to fragments of overheard conversation. One scene described by Hastings neatly encapsulates her own approach: 'nothing maudlin, no sleepy couples; all quick and fireworky, impressionist'.[12] At some point in mid-1914, she was introduced to Modigliani, either by Nina Hamnett, Ossip Zadkine or Max Jacob, each of whom claimed to have been responsible for arranging the meeting. 'Impressions de Paris' is invaluable as a window on to the world in which these writers and artists circulated. Hastings is remarkably reticent about her own life, however, and Modigliani is mentioned by name only three times throughout the series. He first appears in the third instalment, when 'Alice Morning' describes sitting in the Café de la Rotonde with 'the bad garçon of a sculptor' talking about 'a grand ball next Saturday at which everyone is going to perform something'.[13] Modigliani appears here only as 'the pale and ravishing villain'.[14] Hastings first mentions him by name a month later, when discussing her reaction to some works by Henri 'Le Douanier' Rousseau, seen at an exhibition that also included a 'large painting' by Picasso looking like 'a well-dressed Colossus'.[15] Hastings finds Rousseau 'bourgeois, sentimental and rusé' and cannot understand why an artist such as Modigliani should praise his work:

> What beats me is when, for instance, an unsentimental artist like Modigliani says, Oui, très joli, about him. One of Modigliani's stone heads was on a table below the painting of Picasso, and the contrast between the true thing and the true-to-life thing nearly split me. I would like to buy one of those heads, but I'm sure they cost pounds to make, and the Italian is liable to give you anything you look interested in. No wonder he is the spoiled child of the quarter, enfant sometimes-terrible but always forgiven – half Paris is in morally illegal possession of his designs. 'Nothing's lost!' he says, and bang goes another drawing for two-pence or nothing, while he dreams off to some café to borrow a franc for some more paper![16]

Modigliani is described here as 'a very beautiful person to look at, when he is shaven, about twenty-eight, I should think, always either laughing or quarrelling à la Rotonde'.[17] Hastings ends this 'Impression' by humorously recounting how Modigliani 'horrifies some English friends of mine whose flat overlooks his studio by tubbing at two-hour intervals in the garden, and occasionally lighting all up after midnight apparently as an aid to sculpturing [the Tower of] Babel'.[18]

Modigliani is next mentioned in the following issue of the periodical, when Hastings tells of leaving Paris for a brief trip back to England after 'someone wrote me that some women were up to something, so I had to go to see what it was'.[19] She describes him stopping her taxi as it was crossing the boulevard Montparnasse and imploring her 'to be allowed to ride with me'.[20] After arriving at the station, Modigliani 'fainted loudly against the grubby side of the carriage and all the English stared at me':

> Modigliani was gasping, 'Oh, Madame, don't go!' I said, 'Modigliani, someone says you've been three years fiddling about with one type of head, and you'll be another three on the new design.' He came round. 'Cretin!' he glared at me as though I had said it. 'Mais, ma-a-a-is, ma petite, he is right! I might have grown asparagus in the time.'[21]

It was during Modigliani's time with Hastings that he decided to shift his focus from sculpture to portrait painting, and her part in encouraging this shift is evident here. She remained impressed by his sculptures, however. The last time he is mentioned in her 'Impressions', in February 1915, she writes:

> I possess a stone head by Modigliani which I would not part with for a hundred pounds even at this crisis: and I rooted out this head from a corner sacred to the rubbish of centuries, and was called stupid for my pains in taking it away. Nothing human, save the mean, is missing from the stone. It has a fearful chip above the right eye, but it can stand a few chips. I am told that it was never finished, that it never will be finished, that it is not worth finishing. There is nothing that matters to finish! The whole head equally smiles in contemplation of knowledge, of madness, of grace and sensibility, of stupidity, of sensuality, of illusions and disillusions – all locked away as matter of perpetual meditation. It is as readable as Ecclesiastes and more consoling, for there is no lugubrious looking-back in this effulgent, unforbidding smile of intelligent equilibrium. [...] I will never part with it unless to a poet; he will find what I find and the unfortunate artist will have no choice as to his immortality.[22]

The 'Impressions of Paris' series changed from a humorous travelogue to the diary of a city under siege when war was declared in the Summer of 1914, with Hastings describing the 'frenzied faces laughing for war' in the initial weeks before the misery of food shortages and the continual threat of Zeppelin raids set in.[23] At this time of 'crisis', as the quotation above highlights, Modigliani's art provided consolation, and Hastings shows herself to be an astute, perceptive critic of his achievement, noting that the unfinished quality of the sculpture is part of its aesthetic 'grace'. Years later, in 1925, Hastings would look back at this time with Modigliani with not insignificant bitterness, revising her earlier endorsement of the artist by writing that 'my own admiration of his talent was strictly limited since I discovered that one thing I had raved over – a stone head – was a copy of some Italian sculpture!'[24]

Anecdotes about Hastings and Modigliani in this period abound. At the Quat'z' Arts ball she appeared in a 'dress' that he had painted directly on to her naked body. At another event, Hastings went dressed as an eighteenth-century shepherdess, complete with a tall crook, long-ribboned hat and basket of live ducks. Modigliani made innumerable drawings and at least fifteen portraits of Hastings in their time together. The two portraits that were included in the Tate Modern exhibition in 2017–18 conveyed her shape-shifting character. In 'Madam Pompadour' (1915), she is caricatured as Louis XV's mistress, fair-haired and virtually unrecognisable from the portrait that hung next to it in Tate Modern (Fig. 7), which tenderly captures both Hastings's dark beauty and the intelligent mind behind her piercing gaze. In a proto-surrealist novella, *Minnie Pinnikin*, which she recited in parts at a literary and musical matinee on 21 July 1916, organised by Guillaume Apollinaire, Hastings celebrates her relationship with Modigliani. The novella tells of the love between Minnie (Hastings) and Pâtredor (Modigliani) in a hallucinatory prose that alternates between the real-world cafés of Paris and an idyllic dream-world space in which the characters jump into a void as a 'means of knowing the future'.[25] In reality, however, the relationship was anything but ideal. Living together from the beginning of 1915 in Hastings's flat at 13 rue Norvins, a side street in Montmartre beyond the then recently completed Sacré-Cœur basilica, Hastings and Modigliani frequently clashed; both were prone to alcohol-fuelled violence, and the poet Max Jacob was often forced to assume the role of mediator between the two lovers. There are stories of Hastings turning up at Le Dôme restaurant in Montparnasse with a ripped dress, only to explain: 'Modi's been naughty.'[26] The Russian painter Maria Vorobieff Marevna tells of Modigliani throwing Hastings through a window after she provoked him.[27] And Katherine Mansfield provides a vivid and detailed eyewitness account of Hastings during this period in her letters to John Middleton Murry, composed when she was staying in Paris in March 1915:

> Beatrice's flat is really very jolly. She only takes it by the quarter at 900 francs a year – four rooms & a kitchen – a big hall a cabinet and a conservatory. Two rooms open on to the garden. A big china stove in the salle à manger heats the place. All her furniture is second hand & rather nice. The faithful Max Jacobs [*sic*] conducts her shopping. Her own room with a grey self colour carpet – lamps in bowls with Chinese shades – a piano – 2 divans 2 armchairs – books – flowers a bright fire was very unlike Paris – really very charming. But the house I think detestable – one *creeps* up and down the stairs. She has dismissed Dado [*sic*] & transferred her virgin heart to Picasso – who lives close by. Strange and really beautiful

though she is still with the fairy air about her & her pretty little head still so fine – she is ruined. There is no doubt of it – I love her, but I take an intense, cold interest in noting the signs. She says – 'it's no good me having a crowd of people. If there are more than four I go to the cupboard & nip cognacs until its all over for me, my dear'. – or 'Last Sunday I had a fearful crise – I got drunk on rhum by myself at the Rotonde & run up & down this street crying and ringing the bells & saying 'save me from this man'. There wasn't anybody there at all.[28]

'Dedo' was Modigliani's nickname. Mansfield's account not only highlights Hastings's problems with alcohol but also her volatile, on–off relationship with the Italian artist. As Pierre Sichel argues, however, it is unlikely that Hastings left Modigliani for Picasso; whilst she often met with Picasso in these years, he was not 'close by' to her flat in Montmartre but living at 5 rue Schoelcher in Montparnasse; Sichel instead suggests the Italian sculptor Alfredo Pina as the artist whom Hastings briefly 'transferred her virgin heart to'.[29] This break in the relationship with Modigliani is materially recorded on the manuscript of *Minnie Pinnikin*, where the name Pinarius, for Pina, is often crossed out by Hastings and replaced with Pâtredor. Hours after writing the above letter, Mansfield left for Hastings's apartment to attend a gathering. The following day she wrote to Murry again, detailing how the night had 'ended in a great row':

> I enjoyed it in a way, but Beatrice was very impossible – she must have drunk nearly a bottle of brandy & when at 9 o'clock I left & refused either to stay any longer or to spend the night [t]here she flared up in a *fury* & we parted for life again.[30]

Mansfield surmises that her dancing with 'a very lovely young woman – married & curious – blonde – passionate' had provoked this outburst from Hastings: 'she was drunk and jealous and everybody knew it'.[31] After parting from Hastings 'for life again', Mansfield later drolly wonders 'if Beatrice Hastings has maxed her jacob yet or if she flew to Italy with her Dado. I am not really curious and I'll *never* seek to know.'[32]

Hastings ended her relationship with Modigliani in late 1916, at which point she and Pina became a couple. Hastings and Pina saw in the New Year of 1917 together at a banquet held in Montparnasse, ostensibly to welcome Georges Braque home from the war. Everyone was in high spirits until a drunk Modigliani showed up and Pina produced a revolver, taking aim at his compatriot and love rival; Modigliani was hurriedly rushed out by Picasso, who locked the door after him. When her time with Pina ended, Hastings embarked on another passionate affair, this time with the much younger writer Raymond Radiguet (who was simultaneously involved with Jean Cocteau). During this on–off affair, Hastings was admitted to a hospital ward in the Autumn of 1920, possibly because of a miscarriage or botched abortion. The diary that she kept at this time, titled *Madame Six*, was written only months after Modigliani's death in January from tubercular meningitis, and in it she looks back on their life together. She writes that he was 'inspired every day with something about me' but was 'always suspicious': 'Modigliani suspected me; but he never knew distinctly of what until I abandoned him. Then, he knew that much, that I was capable of abandoning him.'[33] Hastings reflects on her role as both lover and muse, asserting that 'I never posed, never let him "do" me, as he pleased.'[34] She recounts how Modigliani 'used to come [home] drunk and break the windows to get in' and there would be 'a great scene': 'Once, we had a royal battle, ten times up and down the house, he armed with a pot and me with a long straw brush.'[35] She was always his equal.

Madame Six was published far later than its moment of composition in 1920, serialised in a periodical edited by Hastings from January 1932, *The Straight-Thinker*. Hastings was the primary and often sole contributor to issues of this periodical, commenting on world affairs in the turbulent interwar years, printing scathing attacks on her contemporaries in a regular 'Pastiche' column, and serialising a 'Psychic Diary' titled *The Picnic of the Babes in the Wood*. For one month, in February 1933, the subtitle of *The Straight-Thinker* changed from 'A Fortnightly Review' to 'A Literary and Modernist Review'; this intriguing early use of the term indicates that Hastings clearly viewed herself as a 'modernist' writer. After spending time in Dieppe, Switzerland and the Riviera, Hastings had returned to England in the early 1930s to find herself excluded from the literary circles in which she had once been so prominent. She now used *The Straight-Thinker* to begin to put the record straight; in particular, she was provoked by the acclaim that was lavished on Orage after he became editor of *The New English Weekly* in April 1932. In the inaugural issue of this periodical, Orage printed letters of endorsement from a range of writers celebrating his abilities as an editor. Writing in *The Straight-Thinker* as 'T. K. L.', a pseudonym that she had used in *The New Age*, Hastings responded by noting that '[a]ll these songsters! – tootling to Orage how they would never have been Big Birds but for Him, would have mummified on the edge of their nests for lack of a worm' if it had not been for 'Alice Morning, D. Triformis, Beatrice Hastings' and 'a round dozen pseudonymous Pastischists, twelve dozen Reviewers and Lord knows how many Correspondents and Anons of all capacities': in other words, many roles and disguises that all amount to one writer, Beatrice Hastings.[36]

The Straight-Thinker contained advertisements for a bookshop on Red Lion Square in Holborn, London, owned by the anarchist Charles Lahr. In 1936, Lahr's Blue Moon Press printed Hastings's memoir, *The Old 'New Age': Orage and Others*, as one in a list of radical, esoteric pamphlets intended to upset the literary and political establishments. Writing only two years after Orage's death in 1934, Hastings did not pull her punches, accusing him and his circle of conducting a 'social cabale' [*sic*] against her, 'a literary boycott that does, or should, matter to every reading person'.[37] In this memoir, Hastings claims that it was she, rather than Orage, who had 'entire charge of, and responsibility for, the literary direction of the paper, from reading and selection of MSS. to the last detail of spacing and position', and that it was she who had discovered and then championed both Katherine Mansfield and Ezra Pound.[38] The actual position that Hastings occupied on the periodical is difficult to ascertain with absolute certainty, as all archival records for *The New Age* were lost to posterity when its offices in Cursitor Street were bombed in the Second World War. Recent scholarship, however, gives credence to many of her claims. My own book, *Katherine Mansfield and Periodical Culture* (reviewed on p. 195), for instance, looks to recuperate Hastings's centrality as an important figure in the emergence of early twentieth-century literary modernism by crediting her with a crucial role in the formation and development of Mansfield's first published writings in London; and, as her autobiographical 'Impressions' and hospital diary highlight, Hastings was also a noteworthy figure in the Parisian avant-garde art scene during the 'crisis' years of the First World War.

Recognition never came to Hastings in her lifetime, however. Reflecting on Modigliani's disregard for his own posterity at the time of their affair, Hastings had observed: 'I don't think artists understand or bother much about immortality. [. . .] They interpret their day with a kind of blind infallibility.'[39] Her own 'Impressions of Paris' were composed according to exactly this kind of artistic credo. In an instalment published in July 1915, for instance, she notes: 'one doesn't write Impressions with an eye on Immortality'.[40] And yet, towards the end of her life, Hastings was impelled to write her frequently vitriolic memoirs by the injustice she felt at having been overlooked. There is a distinct sense of faded glory in a letter that she sent to Charles Lahr's wife, Esther, now held in the archives at Senate House, which ends with Hastings signing herself: 'Beatrice Hastings, Modigliani's mistress for years'.[41] Suffering from worsening health and finding herself increasingly alone, Hastings committed suicide in 1943 after systematically destroying nearly all her personal papers, putting them to the fire after they were rejected by the British Museum. In her gas-filled flat in Worthing, Sussex, she was found clutching her dead pet mouse. Lahr's daughter, Sheila, later wrote about her feeling at the time that she was in some way responsible for Hastings's death, having kept her mother from making a visit to the older woman: 'Now, when in galleries, I avoid the eyes of Modigliani's paintings of women with long necks, in case one of them should prove to be Beatrice. For I could not face the reproach in her eyes.'[42]

Notes

This essay is an extended and revised version of an article first printed on 26 January 2018 in *The Times Literary Supplement*.

1. Photograph held in the H. P. B. Library, Toronto.
2. Philip Mairet, *A. R. Orage: A Memoir* (London: Dent, 1936), pp. 46–7.
3. Beatrice Hastings, 'Madame Six', *The Straight-Thinker*, 1:1 (23 January 1932), p. 6.
4. Jeffrey Meyers, *Katherine Mansfield: A Darker View* (New York: Cooper Square Press, 2002), p. 55.
5. Meyers, p. 58.
6. *Letters* 1, p. xi.
7. Antony Alpers, *The Life of Katherine Mansfield*, rev. edn (Harmondsworth: Penguin, 1982), p. 114.
8. Stephen Gray, *Beatrice Hastings: A Literary Life* (London: Viking, 2004).
9. Ann L. Ardis, 'Debating Feminism, Modernism, and Socialism: Beatrice Hastings' Voices in *The New Age*', in Bonnie Kime Scott, ed., *Gender in Modernism: New Geographies, Complex Intersections* (Urbana: University of Illinois Press, 2007), pp. 160–85; Ann L. Ardis, 'The Dialogics of Modernism(s) in *The New Age*', *Modernism/Modernity*, 14:3 (September 2007), pp. 407–34; Lucy Delap, 'Feminist and Anti-Feminist Encounters in Edwardian Britain', *Historical Research*, 78:201 (August 2005), pp. 377–99; Robert Scholes, 'Model Artists in Paris', in *Paradoxy of Modernism* (New Haven, CT, and London: Yale University Press, 2006), pp. 221–56; Carey Snyder, 'Katherine Mansfield and the New Age School of Satire', *Journal of Modern Periodical Studies*, 1:2 (2010), pp. 125–58.
10. Benjamin Johnson and Erika Jo Brown (eds), *Beatrice Hastings: On the Life and Work of a Lost Modern Master* (Warrensburg, MO: Pleiades Press, 2016).
11. Alice Morning [Beatrice Hastings], 'Impressions of Paris', *The New Age*, 16:12 (21 January 1915), p. 309.
12. Alice Morning [Beatrice Hastings], 'Impressions de Paris – II', *The New Age*, 15:4 (28 May 1914), p. 91.
13. Alice Morning [Beatrice Hastings], 'Impressions de Paris – III', *The New Age*, 15:5 (4 June 1914), p. 115.
14. Morning, 'Impressions de Paris – III', p. 115.
15. Alice Morning [Beatrice Hastings], 'Impressions de Paris – VII', *The New Age*, 15:10 (9 July 1914), p. 235.
16. Morning, 'Impressions de Paris – VII', pp. 235–6.
17. Morning, 'Impressions de Paris – VII', p. 236.
18. Morning, 'Impressions de Paris – VII', p. 236.
19. Alice Morning [Beatrice Hastings], 'Impressions de Paris – VIII', *The New Age*, 15:11 (16 July 1914), p. 259.

20. Morning, 'Impressions de Paris – VIII', p. 259.
21. Morning, 'Impressions de Paris – VIII', p. 259.
22. Alice Morning [Beatrice Hastings], 'Impressions of Paris', *The New Age*, 16:15 (11 February 1915), p. 401.
23. Alice Morning [Beatrice Hastings], 'Impressions of Paris', *The New Age*, 15:15 (13 August 1914), p. 350.
24. Beatrice Hastings, 'Madame Six', *The Straight-Thinker*, 1:1 (23 January 1932), p. 6.
25. Beatrice Hastings, 'Minnie Pinnikin', in Kenneth Wayne, *Modigliani & the Artists of Montparnasse* (New York: Harry N. Abrams, 2002), p. 210.
26. Quoted in Jeffrey Meyers, *Modigliani: A Life* (New York: Harcourt, 2006), p. 144.
27. See Meyers, *Modigliani*, pp. 144–5.
28. *Letters* 1, pp. 159–60.
29. Pierre Sichel, *Modigliani: A Biography of Amedeo Modigliani* (New York: E. P. Dutton, 1967), p. 161.
30. *Letters* 1, pp. 164–5.
31. *Letters* 1, pp. 164, 170.
32. *Letters* 1, p. 180.
33. Beatrice Hastings, 'Madame Six', *The Straight-Thinker*, 1:1 (23 January 1932), p. 6; Beatrice Hastings, 'Madame Six', *The Straight-Thinker*, 1:2 (6 February 1932), p. 14.
34. Beatrice Hastings, 'Madame Six', *The Straight-Thinker*, 1:1 (23 January 1932), p. 6.
35. Beatrice Hastings, 'Madame Six', *The Straight-Thinker*, 1:2 (6 February 1932), p. 14.
36. T. K. L. [Beatrice Hastings], 'On "The New English Weekly"', in *Straight-Thinker Bulletin*, 1:1 (May 1932), p. 2.
37. Beatrice Hastings, *The Old 'New Age': Orage and Others* (London: Blue Moon Press, 1936), p. 3.
38. Hastings, *The Old 'New Age'*, p. 3.
39. Alice Morning [Beatrice Hastings], 'Impressions of Paris', *The New Age*, 16:15 (11 February 1915), p. 401.
40. Alice Morning [Beatrice Hastings], 'Impressions of Paris', *The New Age*, 17:12 (22 July 1915), p. 277.
41. Beatrice Hastings to Esther Lahr, Charles Lahr papers, Senate House Library, University of London, MS985C/44.
42. Sheila Lahr, *Yealm*, available at <www.militantesthetix.co.uk/yealm/yealm13.htm> (last accessed 30 August 2018).

REVIEW ESSAY

Katherine Mansfield's Many Forms

Derek Ryan

Gerri Kimber and Janet Wilson, eds, *Re-forming World Literature: Katherine Mansfield and the Modernist Short Story* (Stuttgart: *ibidem*-Verlag, 2018), 325 pp., $40. ISBN 9783838211138

Vassiliki Kolocotroni and Olga Taxidou, eds, *The Edinburgh Dictionary of Modernism* (Edinburgh: Edinburgh University Press, 2018), 432 pp., £150. ISBN 9780748637027

Chris Mourant, *Katherine Mansfield and Periodical Culture* (Edinburgh: Edinburgh University Press, 2019), 320 pp., £80. ISBN 9781474439459

John Newton, *Hard Frost: Structures of Feeling in New Zealand Literature 1908–1945* (Wellington: Victoria University Press, 2018), 368 pp., $40. ISBN 9781776561629

C. K. Stead, *The Necessary Angel* (London: Allen & Unwin UK, 2018), 240 pp., £15.99. ISBN 9781760631154

When Katherine Mansfield writes to John Middleton Murry in May 1913 'there aren't any superfluous words: I mean every line of it [. . .] Im a powerful stickler for form in this style of work',[1] she is not simply refusing to cut down a satirical piece written for *The Blue Review* but is affirming what Chris Mourant describes in *Katherine Mansfield and Periodical Culture* as 'one of the best-known statements on the importance of form in her work' (p. 170). Mourant's monograph amply demonstrates that Mansfield's experimenting with the shapes and styles of the short story cannot be understood without attending to the formation of the various periodical magazines in which she published many of them for the first time. When this is read alongside the other books reviewed here, we are reminded that we can only understand Mansfield's modernist aesthetics if we also take seriously her role as essayist, poet, aphorist, editor and translator. These books show, too, how Mansfield continues to inspire critical and creative works of many forms (a novel, essay collection, critical study, monograph and even dictionary entries), with each of them reflecting on different versions of her that have formed over the past hundred years in presenting us with the New Zealand, the English, the French, the transnational and, at times, the missing Mansfield.

In his ground-breaking study, Mourant makes the compelling claim that the magazine form was used self-consciously by Mansfield to forge transnational identities and writing styles, as well as to pose challenging questions concerning the nationalist and imperialist foundations of modernity. In looking at a wide range of Mansfield's output, including lesser-known writings and archival discoveries, he also, as he puts it in his well-judged introduction, aims to 'recover and interrogate the many different literary forms that Mansfield used throughout her career' (p. 24). The book is neatly divided into substantial chapters on *The New Age*, *Rhythm* and *The Athenaeum*, which chart Mansfield's experiments with multiple forms, followed by a briefer but no less important account of Mansfield's 'afterlives' as shaped by *The Adelphi*. For a study so rich in detail, the broadly chronological approach makes it easier to navigate for the reader, and allows a coherent, though far from linear, story to be told about Mansfield's career and life. Across these chapters, readers are provided with patient contextualising of her publication history, insight into her textual politics, and careful consideration of the intertextual relationship between her work and those of other contributors to these magazines. Evidence of Mourant's meticulous research is on display in the very helpful list of Mansfield's periodical publications, and readers are also treated to the full text of Mansfield's 1909 story, 'A Little Episode', and her 1911 series of aphorisms, 'Bites from the Apple'.

Nowhere is the multiplying of Mansfield's literary forms more evident than in the book's substantial opening chapter, in which Mourant focuses on numerous contributions to *The New Age* in order to trace, as he provocatively states, her 'emergent radical version of individualist feminism constituted in clear opposition to the suffrage movement and shaped by contemporary discourses about nationhood and empire' (p. 33). At the heart of this claim are the fascinating connections between the writings of Mansfield and Beatrice Hastings, with Mourant delineating their 'coterminous ideas' about women, albeit acknowledging their markedly divergent view of eugenics: Hastings, we are told, 'subscribed to the eugenicist beliefs of her day' even as she put forward her often contradictory 'renegade feminism', whereas Mansfield's feminism was tied to 'a piercing critique of nationalism and empire' (p. 40). As well as nuancing our understanding of Mansfield's early feminist politics, the chapter recuperates Hastings as a significant, if controversial, modernist writer and an important influence on Mansfield's own nascent modernism. While providing examples of how aspects of Hastings's work are echoed in Mansfield's, the highlights of the opening chapter are the two above-mentioned archival discoveries at the *Adam International Review* collection, which forms part of the King's College London Archives holdings. First, in what would become a motif in Mansfield's writings, the story 'A Little Episode' contrasts Yvonne Mandeville's '*caged*' (p. 278) life with her husband to her feeling of being 'alive and loving' (p. 279) during an encounter with charismatic pianist Jacques Saint Pierre. In so doing, it contains the kind of love triangle found in the first five instalments of Hastings's novella *Whited Sepulchres*, published in *The New Age* between August 1908 and June 1909, when Mansfield was 'highly likely' to have read it in London (p. 51). Second, 'Bites from the Apple' showcases Mansfield's experimentation with the aphoristic form, and demonstrates a further instance of how her writing was influenced by a magazine she published in. These fifty aphorisms wear the Nietzschean influence of the magazine's editor, A. R. Orage, and many of its contributors, with Mansfield characterising man 'as a fixed, fallen and limited species without hope of redemption' – a view that Mourant suggests counters the image cultivated by Murry of her as a Romantic (p. 70). Despite their somewhat gloomy subject matter – 'If you wish to live you must first attend your own funeral,' Mansfield writes – the series will surprise and delight readers, as well as adding another layer to our understanding of her emerging modernist style.

Mourant's second chapter turns to Mansfield's role in the short-lived but significant little magazine *Rhythm*, focusing particularly on her self-fashioning through negotiation between her position as a colonial outsider and 'adopting a pose of the centred, authoritative metropolitan artist' (p. 113). The chapter argues that she upsets hierarchies of race and gender, showing in the process how attuned she was to the association between modernism and the ideology of imperialism in the period 1912–13. While the broader claim Mourant makes here is well-worn territory for Mansfield scholars, its value comes through the evidence provided for the case study of *Rhythm*, which deepens our understanding of her career. Especially important is Mourant's turn to Mansfield's poetry, specifically the handful of 'parodic translations' published under the pseudonym Boris Petrovsky, also explored in the *Katherine Mansfield and Translation* edition of this yearbook (2015).

Correcting the long-held view that these poems are literal translations of a Russian poet by that very name (though its origins, Mourant tells us, are actually Polish), the chapter details how they are, in fact, the same poems she initially tried to publish in *The New Age* and that several were intended for her 1910 cycle, *The Earth Child*, discovered by Gerri Kimber in the Newberry Library archive in Chicago in 2015. Fitting into the 'constructed image of the magazine's internationalism', to which fascination with Slavic arts were central, Mourant asserts that, despite their 'debatable artistic merit', Mansfield 'deliberately positioned' them in *Rhythm* both to associate herself with an international avant-garde and to set them 'in a parodic relation to translations in *The New Age*' (p. 132). The chapter then considers short stories that Mansfield published in the magazine, especially 'The Woman at the Store' and 'How Pearl Button Was Kidnapped', to suggest that they appropriate the primitivism and orientalism of *Rhythm* – which Mourant illustrates through a discussion of drawings by Anne Estelle Rice – precisely to disrupt them: 'Mansfield appropriates the tropes of imperial discourse, of the wild and animalistic colonial "other", in order to turn these stereotypes back on to the imperial centre' (p. 159). Mourant closes his discussion with a sustained and illuminating reading of one of Mansfield's later, best-known stories, 'Je ne parle pas français', which he reads as continuing her mode of parodying the magazine's imperialist posturing. In this chapter, then, we see one of the greatest strengths of the study in that the even-handedness of Mourant's approach to these magazines allows him to expose their prejudices as much as celebrate their literary exploits.

The remaining chapters of *Katherine Mansfield and Periodical Culture* seek to wrest Mansfield from Murry's hold on her legacy. Considering her reviews for *The Athenaeum* in his third chapter, which he argues were seen by Mansfield as 'a vital post-war project of cultural rejuvenation' (p. 186), Mourant underlines how her commitment to the magazine exceeded obligations she felt towards its editor, Murry, even as she redeployed terminology first explored, alongside D. H. Lawrence, in their earlier venture, *The Signature* (p. 190). Throughout her reviews, Mourant notes, Mansfield used *The Athenaeum* to link 'the "new word" of modernist formal experimentation with the spatial imaginary of a "new world"' (p. 183). Part of this project of creating 'a new word' was the dynamic between Mansfield and Virginia Woolf that played out in the magazine's pages. Refusing to view it within the usual paradigm of jealous rivalry, Mourant revisits Mansfield's review of *Night and Day*, positing that it resulted from 'a firmly held belief that fiction should register the impact of the war and that writers must look to create new forms able to express this profound change in consciousness' (p. 199). Adding to existing work on their relationship, most notably by Angela Smith but also in the essays on the topic in *Katherine Mansfield and Virginia Woolf* (2018), edited by Christine Froula, Gerri Kimber and Todd Martin, Mourant explains it was through their critical essays in this period that 'Mansfield and Woolf established a dialogue in print, each echoing the terms of debate and conceptual ideas advanced in the literary reviews written by the other' (p. 213). The final chapter of the book turns to a rebuke of Murry's forming of the Mansfield myth after her death, a project that may have meant that her work found a larger posthumous readership but was also 'arguably responsible for placing her outside the developing canon of modernist literature that took shape throughout the 1920s and '30s that encompassed Woolf, Eliot and Joyce' (p. 256). While attacks on Murry's 'saintly idealisation' are now commonplace among Mansfield critics, what makes Mourant's approach valuable is his exposing of how this myth 'owed much to the periodical contexts in which it was first formulated' (p. 257). The witty, innovative and mature writings of Mansfield are displaced by publication in *The Adelphi* of material that emphasised her nature as childlike or innocent, and 'erased' or 'smoothed over' the feminist Mansfield of *The New Age*, the (post)colonial Mansfield of *Rhythm*, and the modernist critic of *The Athenaeum* (p. 257). It is all of these Mansfields that Mourant expertly stages in his study, with this final chapter serving as a powerful reminder that what was primarily lost with Mansfield's death was access to her most radical achievements.

The nexus between feminism, transnationalism and modernism is explored in *Re-forming World Literature: Katherine Mansfield and the Modernist Short Story*, a collection of thirteen essays edited by Gerri Kimber and Janet Wilson. Centred on Mansfield's experiments with the short story, a literary form that, according to the editors, remains 'an under-researched and overlooked genre in the current understanding of world literature' (p. 11), chapters are divided into four sections, under the headings 'Global Modernisms', 'UK and US Modernisms', 'Poetry, Suffering and the Self' and 'Fairy Stories and War'. Several essays adopt thematic approaches, covering topics including energy (Duffy); postcolonialism (Mundeja); class (Boscagli); mysticism (Baldt); fairy tales (Kimber); the politics of food (Högberg); preservation and bequest (Gasston); and symbolism (Kascakova). Others pair Mansfield with specific writers: A. S. Byatt, Janice Galloway, Ali Smith and Tessa Hadley (Cox); Woolf (Wilson); Margery Latimer (Kaplan); Heinrich Heine (Davison); and Robert Browning (Martin). However, as this list and the section titles themselves suggest, the book is uneven in its exploration of the global dimensions of Mansfield's writing. Influences and intertexts, often international, are evident across the chapters, though they tend to remain within English, American, French and Russian contexts. That the publication largely consists of papers expanded and repackaged from a conference held in Bandol, France, in 2016 on 'Katherine Mansfield and the Art of the Short Story' may explain why the emphasis on 'World Literature' can feel a little forced on to what are, in their own rights, very interesting, informative and clearly argued pieces. Therefore, if the book might disappoint readers hoping for a reconceptualisation of global literatures through analyses of Mansfield, it should please those keen to follow skilful readings of the twists and turns of her prose.

While it is not possible in the space allowed here to summarise each of the chapters, there are three – by Enda Duffy, Claire Davison and Elsa Högberg – that deserve special mention for the manner in which they open up Mansfield studies to new critical terrain. In 'Mansfield, Soma, and the Burning Dress of Modernism', Duffy beautifully captures the juxtapositions of bodily states found in what he calls Mansfield's 'energy writing', in which both adrenaline and stress condition her 'intense tenderness' (p. 48). To illustrate these features of Mansfield's writing, Duffy uses her touching letter to Murry, in which she describes how she 'loved [his] body with such tenderness' (*Letters* 1, 86), as an example of Mansfield moving towards a 'language of intimacy' that is built around 'sensation and affect' (p. 31). Following this with a reading of 'Bliss', Duffy makes a plea for thinking of Mansfield, like Joyce and Woolf, as having the primary aim 'to record with an unprecedented accuracy the physical sensations, the spasms, the reactions of bodies to stimuli' (p. 33). Claire Davison's standout essay, 'On First Looking into Mansfield's Heine: Dislocative Lyric and the Sound of Music', focuses on the volume of Heine's *Buch der Lieder* [*Book of Songs*] that she received as a present from Thomas Trowell in 1903. Through close reading of Heine's poems and his lyrical mode alongside Mansfield's early writings, Davison's persuasive argument is that this volume furnishes Mansfield's aesthetic imagination with the emotion, tone and rhythm that she would adapt for her short stories. In the process, she cautions that 'the type of resonance to be found is different to what might be labelled "intertextuality", "pastiche" or "influence", which imply a more conscious anchoring in another author's textuality or style', a point that sits well alongside Mourant's borrowing of the term 'parafluence' to describe Hastings's impact on Mansfield (p. 51). Turning from poetics to politics, Elsa Högberg homes in on Mansfield's depictions of food as a kind of portal into socio-historical events. In a fascinating analysis,

Högberg asserts that in Mansfield's pre-war story 'Germans at Meat' she 'links gluttony to political dominance and aggression', whereas in the post-war 'A Suburban Fairy Tale' the 'tables are turned' and Mansfield instead 'uses the figure of the hungry sparrow to highlight the Allied nations' exacerbation of the humanitarian crisis caused by food shortages in Germany during the blockade'. Again, with echoes of Mourant, we are given in this essay a sense of the politics embedded in Mansfield's aesthetics.

In contrast to the efforts to place Mansfield in an international network, John Newton's deeply engaged and engaging study, *Hard Frost: Structures of Feeling in New Zealand Literature 1908–1945*, aims to return Mansfield to the cultural history of New Zealand. The first in an ambitious project of three volumes that attempts to retell the story of New Zealand literature, it is Mansfield's pivotal place in the opening volume, where she is given the first chapter, and her influence (or lack thereof) on New Zealand writers, that will be of most interest to Mansfield scholars. In order to explore this literary history, Newton works with Raymond Williams's 'Structures of Feeling', which, he explains in his introduction, brings to mind three aspects of his experience of reading critically: a 'constant alertness' to his own positionality; a sensitivity to generational shifts in sentiment or 'repertoire of feeling' that affects what is written; and – most significantly, perhaps – 'a mapping of literary–historical development onto a generational grid marked by changes in the climate of feeling: a genealogy of feelings; or, better, a seismology of feelings' (p. 24). Tooled with this critical apparatus, Newton grapples with two central problems in this first volume: on the one hand, the formation of a literary nationalism at the precise moment that an international modernism was in full swing; on the other, the gendered nature of nationalist writing, which he characterises as 'a masculine affair' (p. 15). As New Zealand's foremost international modernist woman, it is clear to see how Mansfield is an important point of departure for this book. Newton is concerned with how New Zealand's most famous writer was, in fact, not read by the nationalists of the 1930s, such as short story writer Frank Sargeson and poet Allen Curnow, astutely observing that she was 'a writer whom it seems they were obliged to forget in order to invent a literature that began with themselves' (p. 40). He uncovers how Mansfield – and, by extension, modernism and gender – 'haunts' the literature that followed, though for Newton it is modernist 'interiority' and 'psychological intelligence', rather than the more bodily reading of Mansfield that we find, for example, in Duffy, that the nationalists eschew (p. 61). What this chapter says about Mansfield's experiments with the short story form itself – and it is squarely with her short stories that Newton is concerned – will be more familiar to Mansfield readers than the material covered by Mourant or some of the essays in Kimber and Wilson's collection. But what we learn about her place within New Zealand's literary canon makes it a very welcome addition to Mansfield studies.

What all three of the above books foreground, to different extents, is Mansfield's innovative, modernist aesthetics over and above her biography. It is initially sobering, then, to turn to two very different texts where her artistic achievements drop out of view: a novel that resurrects, however knowingly, a mythologised Mansfield, and a critical dictionary of modernism, where Mansfield in any shape and form is largely absent. Following a lifetime of critical responses to Mansfield's writings and more recent creative works inspired by her, most notably his 2004 novel *Mansfield* covering the period 1915–18, C. K. Stead's *The Necessary Angel* brings the ghost of Mansfield into the present. Set in Paris, the novel explores the entangled passions of protagonist Max Jackson, a professor living in the lower floor of a townhouse inhabited by his estranged wife, Louise, and with split desires for his younger academic colleague at the Sorbonne Nouvelle, Sylvie Renard, and an English student, Helen – all of which takes place against the backdrop of contemporary social and political events that include Barack Obama's presidency, the rise of Marine Le Pen, and the months running up to and including the *Charlie Hebdo* terrorist attack of January 2015. Mansfield arrives in the story via Helen's fascination with the writer, though this is, from the beginning, through the lens of her death at Gurdjieff's Institute for the Harmonious Development of Man at Fontainebleau-Avon rather than her writing. Given that Stead has, as Kimber summarises in her 2014 reflection on Mansfield's influence on his career, taken Murry to task for his 'hagiographic tone',[2] we are surely meant to read Helen's desire to visit this 'nice little village' and experience the 'mini-tour' as a sign of youthful naïvety (p. 29). The tourism around Mansfield's death is deftly exposed by Stead in the scene where Max and Helen are shown the stairs where she suffered a fatal haemorrhage. We are first told that 'Max hung back at the bottom of the oak-brown stairway with its heavy banister, and Helen waited at a discreet distance, thinking she was respecting an observance,' but rather than being moved by this poignant moment, 'when he turned and hurried to catch up she saw he'd been checking his cell phone' (p. 66). It is Max's pretensions that are then revealed during a phone call with Louise, who, learning about the trip, refers to Gurdjieff as 'that fraudulent Russian', and surprises him by, in fact, knowing that Gurdjieff had an 'Armenian mother. Greek father' (p. 70). Just after this call, the narrator describes Max's visit to the graves of Gurdjieff and Mansfield: 'The inscription said "Katherine Mansfield, Wife of John Middleton Murry". It didn't mention that she was a writer' (p. 71). This cleverly prefigures a scene towards the end of the book, when two *livres de poche* of Mansfield's stories make an appearance, only for Helen's to respond immediately: '"I've seen her grave," Helen said, as if these were books that needed an excuse' (p. 187). It may be Mansfield's ghost, rather than her work, that captivates Helen, but there is undoubtedly something of Mansfield's style in Stead's finely tuned exploration of confused desires and complex emotion; command of irony; skilfully crafted transitions between multiple narrative perspectives; and, not least, in his depiction of Paris. If these are not reason enough to read his latest novel, there is also a surprisingly gripping plot about a missing Cézanne painting.

Where its engagement with Mansfield is concerned, *The Edinburgh Dictionary of Modernism* has the opposite problem to Stead's novel: Mansfield, either mythical or modernist, is rarely to be found. This weighty volume, meticulously edited by Vassiliki Kolocotroni and Olga Taxidou, and featuring a stellar group of established and emerging scholars, offers a companion to their earlier *Modernism: An Anthology of Sources and Documents* (co-edited with Jane Goldman), which remains one of the finest textbooks on its subject. Like that anthology, the *Dictionary of Modernism*'s biggest strength is its international approach, covering key figures, movements and contexts of modernism and the avant-garde with authoritative entries that also contain reading suggestions – a feature that will be particularly useful to students. Many of the best entries provoke with arguments and questions rather than repeating standard or settled definitions, with some longer sections – Sophie Vlacos's 'Realism', Dominic Paterson's 'Surrealism', Adam Piette's 'War' – reading as concise essays. Mansfield enters under 'Feminism', where Jana Funke recognises her alongside Stein and Woolf as a writer who 'sought to re-evaluate the gendered and erotic possibilities of domestic spaces, explored women's novel experiences of public spaces and modes of transportation and addressed how women have been excluded from literary and political history' (p. 146) – though it is noticeable how frequently Mansfield's name is absent from lists of women modernists given elsewhere in the volume. There is a welcome mention of Mansfield in Piette's entry on 'Translation' for her 'reading in Henri Bergson, Marcel Proust and Anton Chekhov' (pp. 379–80), followed by a note on her *In a German Pension* stories, but nothing is said of her own translations as explored in Claire Davison's 2014 monograph, *Translation as Collaboration*. In Piette's 'War' entry, Mansfield's famous vision of 'the ghost-body of her dead brother' is alluded to (though Mourant reminds us that Murry's publication in *The Adelphi* of this material from her journal and her poem 'To L. H. B. (1894–1915)' contributed to the sanctified image of her; p. 251). This very limited focus on Mansfield is largely due to the book's expansive scope, of course, but there are none the less entries within which we might have expected her name or works to appear: for example, 'Colonialism', 'Everyday', 'Exile', 'Global Modernisms', 'Little Magazines' – all live topics in Mansfield studies. Then again, given the many forms of Mansfield and ways of reading her that are opened up by the books under consideration here, it is perhaps apt that she would escape definition.

Notes
1. *Letters* 1, p. 124.
2. Gerri Kimber, 'The Influence of Katherine Mansfield on the Work of C. K. Stead', in Gerri Kimber, Todd Martin, Delia da Sousa Correa, Isobel Maddison and Alice Kelly, *Katherine Mansfield and World War One* (Edinburgh: Edinburgh University Press, 2014), pp. 145–59 (p. 146).

Notes on Contributors

Richard Cappuccio has presented papers at various Katherine Mansfield Society conferences as well as the Virginia Woolf International Conference. His most recent article appears in *Katherine Mansfield and the Bloomsbury Group* (2017). He enjoys tending his garden alongside his wife and setting type by hand at the Center for the Book in Charlottesville, Virginia.

Charlotte Fiehn is a PhD student at the University of Texas, Austin. She completed her undergraduate degree at the University of Cambridge. She has published articles on Shakespeare, George Eliot and Charlotte Brontë. Her graduate research focuses on questions of form and gender in relation to George Eliot and Virginia Woolf.

Aimee Gasston is Reviews Editor and Editorial Assistant of Katherine Mansfield Studies. She is also a Postdoctoral Visiting Research Fellow at the Institute of English Studies, School of Advanced Study, University of London, where she is researching modernist short fiction and aesthetics.

Alison Hennegan became a Fellow of Trinity Hall, Cambridge, in 2006, where she was also Director of Studies in English, retiring in September 2018. Previously, her working life was spent in gay and feminist literary journalism, publishing and broadcasting. She has published widely on areas where literature, gender and sexuality intersect, especially the English Decadence and the Great War.

Karina Jakubowicz, an adjunct lecturer at Florida State University, completed her PhD at UCL on the subject of gardens in the work of Virginia Woolf. She is the author of *Garsington Manor and the Bloomsbury Group* (2016), published by Cecil Woolf. She is currently researching the evolution and applications of the Eden Myth in early twentieth-century culture.

Gerri Kimber, Visiting Professor at the University of Northampton, is co-editor of Katherine Mansfield Studies and Chair of the Katherine Mansfield Society. She is the deviser and Series Editor of the four-volume

Edinburgh Edition of the Collected Works of Katherine Mansfield (2012–16), and is the author or editor of a further twenty volumes on Mansfield.

Sarah Laing has written short stories, novels and comics. Her most recent graphic memoir is *Mansfield and Me* (2018), published by Lightning in the UK and Victoria University Press in New Zealand. She lives in Karori, Wellington, and two of her three children go to Katherine Mansfield's old primary school.

Isobel Maddison is a Fellow of Lucy Cavendish College, University of Cambridge, where she is a College Lecturer and the Director of Studies in English. She has published on Dorothy Richardson and Katherine Mansfield and is the author of *Elizabeth von Arnim: Beyond the German Garden* (2013), the first full-length treatment of this author. She is President of the International Elizabeth von Arnim Society.

Ann Herndon Marshall earned her BA from Hollins College and her doctorate from the University of Virginia. She taught for twenty-five years at The Hill School in Pottstown, Pennsylvania. She has published on Oscar Wilde, Elizabeth von Arnim and Katherine Mansfield. She lives in Charlottesville, Virginia.

Todd Martin is Professor of English at Huntington University and has published articles on John Barth, E. E. Cummings, Clyde Edgerton, Julia Alvarez, Edwidge Danticat, Sherwood Anderson and Katherine Mansfield. He currently serves as the Membership Secretary of the Katherine Mansfield Society, and is the editor of *Katherine Mansfield and the Bloomsbury Group* (2017).

Chris Mourant is a Lecturer in Early Twentieth-Century English Literature and Co-Director of the Centre for Modernist Cultures at the University of Birmingham. He is the author of *Katherine Mansfield and Periodical Culture* (2019).

Noreen O'Connor is an associate professor at King's College in Pennsylvania. Currently Vice-President of the International Elizabeth von Arnim Society, she was co-organiser of the joint Elizabeth von Arnim and Katherine Mansfield conference, held at the Huntington Library in 2017. Her research focuses on women modernists, narrative and war trauma.

Nina Powles is a writer from Aotearoa, New Zealand, currently living in London. She is the author of two poetry pamphlets, *Field Notes on a*

Downpour (2018) and *Girls of the Drift* (2014) and a set of five chapbooks titled *Luminescent*, published by Seraph in 2017. She is Poetry Editor for the *Shanghai Literary Review* and was the 2018 winner of the Jane Martin Poetry Prize.

Juliane Römhild is a lecturer at La Trobe University, Melbourne, where she works on British and German interwar literature. She has published widely and is the author of *Femininity and Authorship in the Novels of Elizabeth von Arnim: At Her Most Radiant Moment* (2014).

Derek Ryan is Senior Lecturer in Modernist Literature at the University of Kent. He is author of *Virginia Woolf and the Materiality of Theory: Sex, Animal, Life* (2013) and *Animal Theory: A Critical Introduction* (2015), and co-editor of *The Handbook to the Bloomsbury Group* (2018) and the Cambridge Edition of Virginia Woolf's *Flush*. His recent article on 'Katherine Mansfield's Animal Aesthetics' was published in *Modern Fiction Studies*.

Bonnie Kime Scott is Professor Emerita at San Diego State and the University of Delaware. Her books include *Joyce and Feminism* (1984), *The Gender of Modernism* (1990), *Refiguring Modernism* (1996), *Selected Letters of Rebecca West* (2000), *In the Hollow of the Wave: Virginia Woolf and Modernist Uses of Nature* (2012), and the monograph *Natural Connections: Virginia Woolf and Katherine Mansfield* (2015).

Angela Smith is Professor Emerita in English Studies at the University of Stirling. Her books include *East African Writing in English* (1989), *Katherine Mansfield and Virginia Woolf: A Public of Two* (1999), *Katherine Mansfield: A Literary Life* (2000), an edition of Jean Rhys's *Wide Sargasso Sea* and of *Katherine Mansfield Selected Stories*.

Andrew Thacker is Professor of Twentieth Century Literature at Nottingham Trent University. He is the author or editor of several books on modernism, including *Moving Through Modernity: Space and Geography in Modernism* (2003), *Geographies of Modernism* (2005), *The Oxford Critical and Cultural History of Modernist Magazines* (2009–13), and the forthcoming *Modernism, Space and the City* (2019).

Index

Acton, Carol, 14
Adam International Review, 197
The Adelphi, 196, 199, 204
'The Advanced Lady' (Mansfield, K.), 90
After Leaving Mr Mackenzie (Rhys, J.), 176
Agnes Grey (Brontë, A.), 134
All the Dogs of My Life (von Arnim, E.), 66
'The Aloe' (Mansfield, K.), 118, 172
Alpers, Antony, 183
America *(and Americans)*, 5, 15–16, 37, 77, 94, 115–18, 120–6, 133, 163–4, 199–200
American Journal of Psychology, 133
Anderson, Sherwood, 164
    Poor White, 164
    The Triumph of the Egg, 164
    Windy McPherson's Son, 164
    Winesburg, Ohio, 164
Apollinaire, Guillaume, 187
April Baby's Book of Tunes (von Arnim, E.), 95
Ardis, Ann, 184
von Arnim, Beatrix (*Trix*), 11, 13–18, 20–2, 79–81, 94, 122
von Arnim, Elizabeth
    All the Dogs of My Life, 66
    April Baby's Book of Tunes, 95
    The Benefactress, 110, 115, 127
    The Caravaners, 102–3, 108, 119
    Christine, 4–5, 12–14, 16, 19, 87, 93–4, 96, 115–20, 125, 127–8
    Christopher and Columbus, 15, 29, 124
    Elizabeth and Her German Garden, 1, 29, 32–4, 73, 76, 86–7, 99, 102, 108, 115, 117, 128
    The Enchanted April, 1, 29, 33, 35, 49, 55, 61–2, 66–8, 125
    Expiation, 102–3, 105, 107–8, 110–13
    Father, 5, 101–3, 105–6, 108, 111, 113
    Fräulein Schmidt and Mr Anstruther, 100–1, 103, 110–11
    In the Mountains, 4, 12, 17–22
    The Jasmine Farm, 22, 66
    Love, 22, 108
    Mr. Skeffington, 66, 108, 123, 125–6
    One Thing in Common: Three Famous Novels in One Volume, 116
    The Pastor's Wife, 16, 22, 102–4, 106–10, 113, 115, 142
    The Solitary Summer, 87, 132
    Vera, 4, 6, 21–2, 41, 49–50, 52, 76, 99, 102, 116, 126, 132–3, 138–43
von Arnim, Elizabeth (*Liebet*), 13, 16, 18, 115, 117, 119–21, 123–4, 126–7
von Arnim, Felicitas (*Martin*), 11–16, 116, 119, 122, 127
Asheham, 30
'At Lehmann's' (Mansfield, K.), 106, 142
'At the Bay' (Mansfield, K.), 4
The Athenaeum, 41, 196, 198–9
Austen, Jane, 2, 21, 109
Australia, 36, 99

Bach, Johann Sebastian, 95
Bad Wörishofen, 87
Baker, Ida Constance, 41, 166
Baldt, Erika, 119, 199
Beach, Sylvia, 6, 163–6, 178
Beauchamp, Charlotte (*Chaddie*), 79
Beauchamp, Leslie (*Chummie*), 11–12, 14–15, 19, 22, 32
Beauchamp, Vera, 11, 32, 49, 77
Beauvoir, Simone de, 164
Beerbohm, Max, 27
Beethoven, Ludwig van, 14, 95–6
The Benefactress (von Arnim, E.), 110, 115, 127
Bennett, Arnold, 27
Benstock, Shari, 166
    Women of the Left Bank, 166

Index

Bergson, Henri, 203
Berlin, 13, 15, 95, 117, 119, 121, 167
Bigelow, Poultney, 117
Birch-Pfeiffer, Charlotte, 133
   Die Waise von Lowood, 133
'A Birthday' (Mansfield, K.), 142
'Bites from the Apple' (Mansfield, K.), 196–7
'Bliss' (Mansfield, K.), 6, 29, 38, 55, 60–3, 67, 132–8, 140–1, 143, 169–71, 176, 200
Bliss and Other Stories (Mansfield, K.), 97, 134, 164
The Blue Review, 195
bohemian, 164, 173
Boscagli, Maurizia, 199
Braddon, Mary Elizabeth, 133
Braque, Georges, 188
Brett, Dorothy, 2, 29–31, 49, 71, 77–9, 140, 163, 166
The Brimming Cup (Fisher, D.), 164
Brontë, Anne, 6, 132–4, 139–40, 142–3
   Agnes Grey, 134
Brontë, Charlotte, 6, 132–40, 142–3
   Jane Eyre, 6, 132–40, 143
   Villette, 134
Brontë, Emily, 6, 51, 132–3, 139–40, 142–3
   Wuthering Heights, 21, 51, 109, 132, 139, 143
Broughton, Rhoda, 133
Brown, Erica, 133
Browning, Robert, 199
Buch der Lieder (Heine, H.), 200
Burgan, Mary, 19–20, 56–7
Burney, Fanny, 109
Byatt, A. S., 199

'The Canary' (Mansfield, K.), 4, 23
Cappuccio, Richard, 5, 118
The Caravaners (von Arnim, E.), 102–3, 108, 119
Carco, Francis, 175–8
   Perversité, 177
'Carnation' (Mansfield, K.), 81
Chalet des Sapins, 2, 49
Chalet Soleil, 3, 30, 32
Chanler, Archie, 125
Chanler, Beatrice, 125–6
Charlotte Brontë: A Monograph (Reid, W.), 133
Charlottesville, 115–16, 123–5, 127

Chekhov, Anton, 203
Chelsea Flower Show, 30
Christine (von Arnim, E.), 4–5, 12–14, 16, 19, 87, 93–4, 96, 115–20, 125, 127–8
Christopher and Columbus (von Arnim, E.), 15, 29, 124
Clover Fields, 5, 115, 120–2, 125, 128
Cocteau, Jean, 189
The Collected Letters of Katherine Mansfield (O'Sullivan, V.; Scott, M.), 7n, 23n–5n, 39n–40n, 53n, 83n–5n, 98n, 129n, 143n–4n, 178n, 180n, 191n–2n, 200, 204n
Country Life, 78
Craik, Dinah, 133
Cran, Marion, 73
   The Garden of Ignorance: The Experiences of a Woman in the Garden, 73
Crans-Montana, 2, 70
Crozier, W. Ray, 174
'A Cup of Tea' (Mansfield, K.), 29
Curnow, Allen, 201

'The Daughters of the Late Colonel' (Mansfield, K.), 42, 46–7, 49–50, 119, 159
Davison, Claire, 199–200, 203
   The Edinburgh Edition of the Collected Works of Katherine Mansfield: Vol. 4 – The Diaries of Katherine Mansfield, including Miscellaneous Works, 53n, 128n–9n, 180n
   Katherine Mansfield and Translation, 197
   'On First Looking into Mansfield's Heine: Dislocative Lyric and the Sound of Music', 200
   Translation as Collaboration, 203
Delap, Lucy, 184
Dickinson, Violet, 28
   'Friendship's Gallery', 28
Dickson, Polly, 58
Dictionary of Modernism, 203
'The Doll's House' (Mansfield, K.), 4
A Doll's House (Ibsen, H.), 109
Don Quixote (Cervantes, M.), 184
von Donnersmarck, Graf Henschel, 28
Dooley, Lucile, 133
   'Psychoanalysis of Charlotte Brontë, as a Typical Woman of Genius', 133

Duffy, Enda, 199–201
  'Mansfield, Soma, and the Burning Dress of Modernism', 200

'The Earth Child' (Mansfield, K.), 198
Edgeworth, Maria, 109
The Edinburgh Dictionary of Modernism (Kolocotroni, V.; Taxidou, O.), 195, 203
The Edinburgh Edition of the Collected Works of Katherine Mansfield: Vols 1 and 2 – The Collected Fiction (Kimber, G.; O'Sullivan, V.), 53n, 68n, 85n, 97n–8n, 179n
The Edinburgh Edition of the Collected Works of Katherine Mansfield: Vol. 3 – The Poetry and Critical Writings (Kimber, G.; Smith, A.), 53n
The Edinburgh Edition of the Collected Works of Katherine Mansfield: Vol. 4 – The Diaries of Katherine Mansfield, including Miscellaneous Works (Kimber, G.; Davison, C.), 53n, 128n–9n, 180n
Eliot, T. S., 30, 173–4, 199
  'The Love Song of J. Alfred Prufrock', 173
Elizabeth and Her German Garden (von Arnim, E.), 1, 29, 32–4, 73, 76, 86–7, 99, 102, 108, 115, 117, 128
The Enchanted April (von Arnim, E.), 1, 29, 33, 35, 49, 55, 61–2, 66–8, 125
England, 11, 14, 20–1, 30, 32, 34–5, 77, 90, 92, 100, 121–2, 126, 181, 185, 189
Ernst, Heinrich, 95
  Pathétique Concerto, 95
'The Essence of Religion' (Russell, B.), 65
Expiation (von Arnim, E.), 102–3, 105, 107–8, 110–13

fantasy, 15, 20, 28
Father (von Arnim, E.), 5, 101–3, 105–6, 108, 111, 113
feminism, 6, 27, 48, 70, 72–4, 76, 81, 83, 92–3, 100, 107–8, 164, 183–4, 196–7, 199, 203
'Feuille d'Album' (Mansfield, K.), 172–7
Fiehn, Charlotte, 5–6

Finnegans Wake (Joyce, J.), 31
Firedamp (Rives, A.), 126
First World War *see* World War One
Fisher, Dorothy Canfield, 164
  The Brimming Cup, 164
flowers, 2, 5, 27–34, 36–8, 45, 57, 59–60, 70–2, 74–83, 88, 126, 175, 187
  acacias, 28, 33
  anemones, 33, 36
  asters, 2, 31, 78–9
  camellias, 31
  carnations, 38, 82
  celandines, 33
  chrysanthemums, 79, 81
  daffodils, 28
  daisies, 34, 88
  forget-me-nots, 36, 82
  geraniums, 28, 32, 34
  hepaticas, 33
  hyacinths, 31, 71, 75
  lilacs, 31, 33, 36, 74, 89
  lilies, 37–8, 118
  marigolds, 34, 78, 127
  nasturtiums, 34, 71, 78
  pansies, 32, 36, 87
  peonies, 33
  periwinkles, 33–4
  petunias, 2, 31, 71, 78–9
  primroses, 35, 78, 80–1
  roses, 28, 30–4, 36–7, 70–1, 75, 80–1, 87, 126
  snapdragons, 34, 71
  sweet peas, 2, 31, 78–9
  tulips, 75, 78
  violets, 31, 33, 70–1, 77–8
'The Fly' (Mansfield, K.), 4, 15, 23
Fontainebleau, 202
Ford, Ford Madox, 166, 177–8
Forster, Edward Morgan, 27, 33
France, 32, 45, 78, 115, 119, 123, 163, 200
'Frau Brechenmacher Attends a Wedding' (Mansfield, K.), 111
'Frau Fischer' (Mansfield, K.), 36, 88, 90
Fräulein Schmidt and Mr Anstruther (von Arnim, E.), 100–1, 103, 110–11
The Freewoman, 184
Freud, Sigmund, 15, 22, 108, 137, 166
'Friendship's Gallery' (Dickinson, V.), 28

Index

Froula, Christine, 199
  Katherine Mansfield and Virginia Woolf, 199

Galloway, Janice, 199
Gana, Nouri, 22
'The Garden' (Marvell, A.), 89
The Garden of Ignorance: The Experiences of a Woman in the Garden (Cran, M.), 73
'The Garden Party' (Mansfield, K.), 4, 37, 141–2
The Garden Party and Other Stories (Mansfield, K.), 164
gardeners, 28, 32–4, 37, 70, 75, 77–8, 87
gardens, 2, 4–5, 20, 27–39, 57–8, 60, 62, 73–5, 77–9, 83, 87, 89, 101, 126–7, 141, 185, 187
  German gardens, 4, 33–6, 87
  Asheham, 30
  English gardens, 28
  Garsington, 28, 30
  Kensington Gardens, 28
  Kew Gardens, 28, 30
  Luxembourg Gardens, 171
  Spade House, 30
  Thornfield Hall, 140
  Wellington Botanical Garden, 28, 36
Garsington Manor, 30
Gasston, Aimee, 199
Gender in Modernism: New Geographies, Complex Intersections (Scott, B.), 184
The Gender of Modernism (Scott, B.), 27
George, W. L., 118
Gerhardi, William, 49
'Germans at Meat' (Mansfield, K.), 13, 87, 201
Germany *(and Germans)*, 11–14, 16–19, 21–2, 34, 36, 86–8, 90–2, 94, 100, 102–3, 115–19, 121–2, 125, 127, 142, 201
  Anglo-German, 15, 88, 142
  anti-German, 17, 22, 94
Ghosts (Ibsen, H.), 58
A Gift of the Dusk (Prowse, R. O.), 4, 41–2, 46–7, 49
Girard, René, 60
'God's Grandeur' (Hopkins, G.), 89
Good Morning, Midnight (Rhys, J.), 167
Gordon Square, 66
Gothic, 21, 41, 47–8, 51–2
Gray, Stephen, 184

Greenaway, Kate, 72
  The Language of Flowers, 72
Gurdjieff, George Ivanovich, 202–3

Hadley, Tessa, 199
Hall, Radclyffe, 106
  The Well of Loneliness, 106
Hamlet (Shakespeare, W.), 174
Hamnett, Nina, 185
Hapgood, Lynne, 73
Hard Frost: Structures of Feeling in New Zealand Literature (Newton, J.), 195, 201
Harriet Hume (West, R.), 28
Harris, Dianne, 73
Harris, Frank, 118
Hastings, Beatrice, 6, 91, 181–91, 196–7, 200
  Madame Six, 189
  The Maids' Comedy, 184
  Minnie Pinnikin, 187–8
  The Old 'New Age': Orage and Others, 190
  Pages from an Unpublished Novel, 183–4
  The Picnic of the Babes in the Wood, 189
  pseudonyms, 183, 189
  Whited Sepulchres, 184, 197
  Woman's Worst Enemy: Woman, 184
Heine, Heinrich, 92, 199–200
  Buch der Lieder, 200
Hemingway, Ernest, 164
Hennegan, Alison, 5
von Hirschberg, Anton, 17–18, 21–2
Hitler, Adolf, 22, 123
Hogarth Press, 30
Högberg, Elsa, 199–201
Hopkins, Gerard Manley, 89
  'God's Grandeur', 89
'How Pearl Button Was Kidnapped' (Mansfield, K.), 198
Huxley, Aldous, 30

Ibsen, Henrik, 58, 92, 109
  A Doll's House, 109
  Ghosts, 58
In a German Pension (Mansfield, K.), 1, 13, 36, 86, 91, 93, 119, 132, 140, 203
'In the Botanical Gardens' (Mansfield, K.), 36
In the Mountains (von Arnim, E.), 4, 12, 17–22

Index

'An Indiscreet Journey' (Mansfield, K.), 175
Italy *(and Italians)*, 33, 35, 62, 70, 77, 185–6, 188

Jacob, Max, 185, 187
Jakubowicz, Karina, 5
Jameson, Frederic, 68
Jane Eyre (Brontë, C.), 6, 132–40, 143
Japanese, 92
The Jasmine Farm (von Arnim, E.), 22, 66
'Je ne parle pas français' (Mansfield, K.), 173, 176, 198
Jekyll, Gertrude, 30, 34
Jensen, Meg, 22
Jones, Kathleen, 15, 76
The Journal of Horticulture and Cottage Gardener, 33
Journal of Katherine Mansfield (Mansfield, K.; Murry, J. M.), 164
Joyce, James, 31, 59, 164, 199–200
  Finnegans Wake, 31
  Ulysses, 31, 164
Jüngling, Kirsten, 22

Kaplan, Sydney Janet, 92, 167, 169–70, 172, 199
Kascakova, Janka, 199
Katherine Mansfield and Periodical Culture (Mourant, C.), 190, 195, 198
Katherine Mansfield and Translation (Davison, C.; Kimber, G.; Martin, T.), 197
Katherine Mansfield and Virginia Woolf (Froula, C.; Kimber, G.; Martin, T.), 199
The Katherine Mansfield Notebooks (Scott, M.), 39n, 178n
Katherine Mansfield: Novels and Novelists (Mansfield, K.; Murry, J. M.), 164
Kavanaugh, Julia, 133
Keats, John, 33
Kennedy, Kate, 19
'Kew Gardens' (Woolf, V.), 30
Kimber, Gerri, 6, 59, 82, 195, 198–9, 202
  The Edinburgh Edition of the Collected Works of Katherine Mansfield: Vols 1 and 2 – The Collected Fiction, 53n, 68n, 85n, 97n–8n, 179n
  The Edinburgh Edition of the Collected Works of Katherine Mansfield: Vol. 3 – The Poetry and Critical Writings, 53n
  The Edinburgh Edition of the Collected Works of Katherine Mansfield: Vol. 4 – The Diaries of Katherine Mansfield, including Miscellaneous Works, 53n, 128n–9n, 180n
  Katherine Mansfield and Translation, 197
  Katherine Mansfield and Virginia Woolf, 199
  Re-forming World Literature: Katherine Mansfield and the Modernist Short Story, 195, 199
Kolocotroni, Vassiliki, 6, 195, 203
  The Edinburgh Dictionary of Modernism, 195, 203
Komura, Toshiaki, 16
Koteliansky, Samuel, 15
Kristeva, Julia, 42, 52

Lacan, Jacques, 137, 164
Lady Betty Across the Water (Williamson, A.), 77
Lahr, Charles, 190–1
Laing, Sarah, 6
The Language of Flowers (Greenaway, K.), 72
The Language of Flowers: With Illustrative Poetry (Schoberl, F.), 72
Latimer, Margery, 199
Lawrence, D. H., 30, 112, 170, 198
  Women in Love, 112
The Left Bank (Rhys, J.), 166–7, 177
The Letters of Katherine Mansfield (Mansfield, K.; Murry, J. M.), 164
Lewis, Wyndham, 183
The Life of Katherine Mansfield (Mantz, R.; Murry, J. M.), 164
liminal *(space)*, 67–8
'A Little Episode' (Mansfield, K.), 196–7
'The Little Governess' (Mansfield, K.), 6, 132–5, 143
Love (von Arnim, E.), 22, 108
'The Love Song of J. Alfred Prufrock' (Eliot, T. S.), 173
Lukács, Georg, 54, 56–7
  The Theory of the Novel: A Historico-Philosphical Essay on the Forms of Great Epic Literature, 54

Index

Macaulay, Rose, 27
McDonnell, Jenny, 91
Madame Six (Hastings, B.), 189
Maddison, Isobel, 51, 61, 86–7, 94, 97, 118, 139–40, 142
The Maids' Comedy (Hastings, B.), 184
Mairet, Philip, 183
Mandeville, Yvonne, 197
Mansfield, Katherine
   'The Advanced Lady', 90
   'The Aloe', 118, 172
   'At Lehmann's', 106, 142
   'At the Bay', 4
   'A Birthday', 142
   'Bites from the Apple', 196–7
   'Bliss', 6, 29, 38, 55, 60–3, 67, 132–8, 140–1, 143, 169–71, 176, 200
   Bliss and Other Stories, 97, 134, 164
   'The Canary', 4, 23
   'Carnation', 81
   'A Cup of Tea', 29
   'The Daughters of the Late Colonel', 42, 46–7, 49–50, 119, 159
   'The Doll's House', 4
   'The Earth Child', 198
   'Feuille d'Album', 172–7
   'The Fly', 4, 15, 23
   'Frau Brechenmacher Attends a Wedding', 111
   'Frau Fischer', 36, 88, 90
   'The Garden Party', 4, 37, 141–2
   The Garden Party and Other Stories, 164
   'Germans at Meat', 13, 87, 201
   'How Pearl Button Was Kidnapped', 198
   In a German Pension, 1, 13, 36, 86, 91, 93, 119, 132, 140, 203
   'In the Botanical Gardens', 36
   'An Indiscreet Journey', 175
   'Je ne parle pas français', 173, 176, 198
   Journal of Katherine Mansfield, 164
   Katherine Mansfield: Novels and Novelists, 164
   The Letters of Katherine Mansfield, 164
   'A Little Episode', 196–7
   'The Little Governess', 6, 132–5, 143
   'Marriage à la Mode', 110
   'A Married Man's Story', 52, 110
   'The Modern Soul', 91, 93
   'My Potplants', 80–1
   'Prelude', 30–1, 118, 172–3
   'The Singing Lesson', 96
   'The Sister of the Baroness', 36
   'The Stranger', 41, 46, 50
   'Study: The Death of a Rose', 81
   'A Suburban Fairy Tale', 201
   'The Woman at the Store', 198
   'The Yellow Chrysanthemum', 81
'Mansfield, Soma, and the Burning Dress of Modernism' (Duffy, E.), 200
Mantz, Ruth Elvish, 164
   The Life of Katherine Mansfield, 164
Marevna, Maria Vorobieff, 187
'Marriage à la Mode' (Mansfield, K.), 110
'A Married Man's Story' (Mansfield, K.), 52, 110
Marsden, Dora, 184
Marshall, Ann Herndon, 5
Martin, Carolyn, 125
Martin, Todd, 87, 199
   Katherine Mansfield and Translation, 197
   Katherine Mansfield and Virginia Woolf, 199
Marvell, Andrew, 89
   'The Garden', 89
Maugham, Somerset, 27
Menton, 41, 78
Meyers, Jeffrey, 132, 183
A Midsummer Night's Dream (Shakespeare, W.), 140
Miller, Thomas, 72
   Poetical Language of Flowers, 72
Minnie Pinnikin (Hastings, B.), 187–8
Miss Tiller's Vegetable Garden and the Money She Made By It (Warner, A.), 73
'Modern Fiction' (Woolf, V.), 49
'The Modern Soul' (Mansfield, K.), 91, 93
modernism *(and modernist)*, 5, 21, 27, 29–31, 49, 54–5, 68, 83, 86, 88, 97, 99, 163–4, 166–7, 172–3, 183, 189–90, 196–9, 201–4
Modernism: An Anthology of Sources and Documents, 203
Modigliani, Amedeo, 6, 181–3, 185–91
Moffett, Alex, 118
Moine, Fabienne, 72
Montmartre, 177, 187–8
Montparnasse, 177, 184, 186–8

Moran, Patricia, 29
Morrell, Ottoline, 1, 28, 30, 66
Mourant, Chris, 6, 195–203
   Katherine Mansfield and Periodical Culture, 190, 195, 198
mourning, 4, 12, 15, 19–20, 22–3, 50
Mozart, 29
Mr. Skeffington (von Arnim, E.), 66, 108, 123, 125–6
Mundeja, Ruchi, 199
Murry, John Middleton, 2, 4, 12, 21, 27, 30, 41–2, 45–6, 78–9, 109, 118, 143, 164, 171–2, 175–6, 184, 187–8, 195, 197–200, 202–4
   Journal of Katherine Mansfield, 164
   Katherine Mansfield: Novels and Novelists, 164
   The Letters of Katherine Mansfield, 164
   The Life of Katherine Mansfield, 164
'My Potplants' (Mansfield, K.), 80–1

Nardin, Jane, 140–1
Nassenheide, 28, 32–3, 115–17, 126
nationalism, 14, 197–9, 201
The Necessary Angel (Stead, C. K.), 195, 202
The New Age, 6, 87, 91, 181, 183–4, 189–90, 196–9
The New English Weekly, 189
The New Statesman, 49
New York, 117, 120–1, 125, 164, 183
The New York Times, 93, 120, 139, 167
New York Times Book Review, 139
New Zealand, 12, 20, 22, 28, 37, 87, 90, 128, 163, 173, 196, 201–2
Newton, John, 6, 195, 201–2
   Hard Frost: Structures of Feeling in New Zealand Literature, 195, 201
Nietzsche, Friedrich, 197
Night and Day (Woolf, V.), 21, 198
A Note on Charlotte Brontë (Swinburne, A.), 133

O'Connell, Rachel, 74
O'Connor, Noreen, 5
The Old 'New Age': Orage and Others (Hastings, B.), 190
'On First Looking into Mansfield's Heine: Dislocative Lyric and the Sound of Music' (Davison, C.), 200

One Thing in Common: Three Famous Novels in One Volume (von Arnim, E.), 116
Orage, A. R., 183, 189–90, 197
O'Sullivan, Vincent, 119, 183
   The Collected Letters of Katherine Mansfield, 7n, 23n–5n, 39n–40n, 53n, 83n–5n, 98n, 129n, 143n–4n, 178n, 180n, 191n–2n, 200, 204n
   The Edinburgh Edition of the Collected Works of Katherine Mansfield: Vols 1 and 2 – The Collected Fiction, 53n, 68n, 85n, 97n–8n, 179n

Pages from an Unpublished Novel (Hastings, B.), 183–4
Paris *(and Parisians)*, 6, 123, 163–4, 166–8, 170–8, 181, 184–7, 190, 202–3
The Pastor's Wife (von Arnim, E.), 16, 22, 102–4, 106–10, 113, 115, 142
Pathétique Concerto (Ernst, H.), 95
patriarchy, 48, 51, 62, 68
patriotism, 13, 121
Perlman, Itzhak, 95
Perversité (Carco, F.), 177
Peter Whiffle: His Life and Works (Van Vechten, C.), 164
Picasso, Pablo, 185, 187–8
The Picnic of the Babes in the Wood (Hastings, B.), 189
Pina, Alfredo, 188
Pitts, Charity, 115, 124–5
Poetical Language of Flowers (Miller, T.), 72
The Politics of Modernism: Against the New Conformists (Williams, R.), 54–5
Poor White (Anderson, S.), 164
Pound, Ezra, 184, 190
Powles, Nina, 6
'Prelude' (Mansfield, K.), 30–1, 118, 172–3
Preston House, 115, 124
Proust, Marcel, 203
Prowse, R. O., 4, 41–2, 45–6
   A Gift of the Dusk, 4, 41–2, 46–7, 49
'Psychoanalysis of Charlotte Brontë, as a Typical Woman of Genius' (Dooley, L.), 133

Quartet (Rhys, J.), 167, 177–8
The Quick or the Dead: A Study (Rives, A.), 125–6

Radiguet, Raymond, 188
Re-forming World Literature: Katherine Mansfield and the Modernist Short Story (Kimber, G.; Wilson, J.), 195, 199
Reid, Wemyss, 132–3
  Charlotte Brontë: A Monograph, 133
Rhys, Jean, 6, 163–4, 166–8, 171, 176–8
  After Leaving Mr Mackenzie, 176
  Good Morning, Midnight, 167
  The Left Bank, 166–7, 177
  Quartet, 167, 177–8
  'A Spiritualist', 166
  'Vienne', 92, 166
Rhythm, 184, 196–9
Rice, Anne Estelle, 198
Rives, Amélie, 5, 115, 120, 125–8
  Firedamp, 126
  The Quick or the Dead: A Study, 125–6
Roßbeck, Brigitte, 22
romance, 36, 59, 63, 65–6, 72, 80–2, 91, 96, 107, 112, 115, 120, 133, 139–40, 175–6, 197
Römhild, Juliane, 4, 66, 142–3
A Room of One's Own (Woolf, V.), 100–1
Rousseau, Henri, 123, 185
Russell, Bertrand, 27, 30, 65–6, 99
  'The Essence of Religion', 65
Russell, Francis, 30, 65–6, 99, 128
Ryan, Derek, 6

Sackville-West, Vita, 28, 30, 34
St James's Park, 28
Sargeson, Frank, 201
satire, 27, 61, 184
Schoberl, Frederic, 72
  The Language of Flowers: With Illustrative Poetry, 72
Scholefield, Guy H., 86, 90
Scholes, Robert, 184
Scott, Bonnie Kime, 4, 58, 66, 184
  Gender in Modernism: New Geographies, Complex Intersections, 184
  The Gender of Modernism, 27
Scott, Margaret, 183
  The Collected Letters of Katherine Mansfield, 7n, 23n–5n, 39n–40n, 53n, 83n–5n, 98n, 129n, 143n–4n, 178n, 180n, 191n–2n, 200, 204n
  The Katherine Mansfield Notebooks, 39n, 178n
Seaton, Beverly, 72
Second World War *see* World War Two
Shakespeare and Company, 6, 163–6
Shakespeare, William, 140, 174
  Hamlet, 174
  A Midsummer Night's Dream, 140
Sichel, Pierre, 188
The Signature, 134, 198
Sinclair, May, 27, 133
  The Three Brontës, 133
  The Three Sisters, 133
'The Singing Lesson' (Mansfield, K.), 96
'The Sister of the Baroness' (Mansfield, K.), 36
Smith, Ali, 199
Smith, Angela, 4, 29, 167, 199
  The Edinburgh Edition of the Collected Works of Katherine Mansfield: Vol. 3 – The Poetry and Critical Writings, 53n
Smyth, Ethel, 27
Snyder, Carey, 184
The Solitary Summer (von Arnim, E.), 87, 132
spiritual, 19, 21, 55, 63, 125
'A Spiritualist' (Rhys, J.), 166
Stead, C. K., 6, 195, 202–3
  The Necessary Angel, 195, 202
Stein, Gertrude, 163–4, 203
  Tender Buttons, 163
  Three Lives, 163–4
Stephen, Caroline Emilia, 28
Stoneman, Patsy, 133
Strachey, Lytton, 30
The Straight-Thinker, 189–90
'The Stranger' (Mansfield, K.), 41, 46, 50
Stuart, Charles Erskine *(Cousin William)*, 122–3
'Study: The Death of a Rose' (Mansfield, K.), 81
'A Suburban Fairy Tale' (Mansfield, K.), 201
Swinburne, Algernon Charles, 133
  A Note on Charlotte Brontë, 133
Switzerland, 2–4, 18, 28, 30, 32, 44, 49, 61, 71, 76, 78, 122, 189

Tate, Claudia, 63
Tate Modern, 181, 187
Taxidou, Olga, 6, 195, 203
   The Edinburgh Dictionary of Modernism, 195, 203
Tender Buttons (Stein, G.), 163
Thacker, Andrew, 6
The Theory of the Novel: A Historico-Philosphical Essay on the Forms of Great Epic Literature (Lukács, G.), 54
Thomson, Lachlan, 181
The Three Brontës (Sinclair, M.), 133
Three Guineas (Woolf, V.), 100
Three Lives (Stein, G.), 163–4
The Three Sisters (Sinclair, M.), 133
The Times, 61–2
Tomkins, Silvan, 174–6
The Transatlantic Review, 166
Translation as Collaboration (Davison, C.), 203
Tristan und Isolde (Wagner, R.), 121
The Triumph of the Egg (Anderson, S.), 164
Trowell, Garnet, 80, 170
Trowell, Tom, 80, 200
tuberculosis, 42, 44–5, 61, 189
tyranny, 102–4, 106, 112, 122

Ulysses (Joyce, J.), 31, 164
United States *see* America

Van Vechten, Carl, 164
   Peter Whiffle: His Life and Works, 164
Vera (von Arnim, E.), 4, 6, 21–2, 41, 49–50, 52, 76, 99, 102, 116, 126, 132–3, 138–43
Vienna, 167
'Vienne' (Rhys, J.), 92, 166
Villette (Brontë, C.), 134
Virginia *(USA)*, 5, 115–17, 120, 123, 125, 128

Wagner, Richard, 107, 121
   Tristan und Isolde, 121
Die Waise von Lowood (Birch-Pfeiffer, C.), 133
Walker, Jennifer, 22, 28–9, 66
Walpole, Hugh, 13, 27
Warner, Anna, 73
   Miss Tiller's Vegetable Garden and the Money She Made By It, 73

Washington DC, 117–18
Waterlow, John, 11
Webb, Mary, 72
The Well of Loneliness (Hall, R.), 106
Wellington, 6, 79, 132
Wells, H. G., 27, 30
Wells, Jane, 30
West, Rebecca, 27–8, 35, 49, 53
   Harriet Hume, 28
Whited Sepulchres (Hastings, B.), 184, 197
Wilde, Oscar, 81, 92–3, 126
Williams, Patrick, 167
Williams, Raymond, 54–5, 68, 167, 172, 201
   The Politics of Modernism: Against the New Conformists, 54–5
Williamson, Alice Muriel, 77
   Lady Betty Across the Water, 77
Willing, James, 133
Wilson, Janet, 6, 173–5, 195, 199, 202
   Re-forming World Literature: Katherine Mansfield and the Modernist Short Story, 195, 199
Windy McPherson's Son (Anderson, S.), 164
Winesburg, Ohio (Anderson, S.), 164
Winter, Jay, 21
'The Woman at the Store' (Mansfield, K.), 198
Woman's Worst Enemy: Woman (Hastings, B.), 184
Women in Love (Lawrence, D. H.), 112
Women of the Left Bank (Benstock, S.), 166
Woolf, Leonard, 30, 32
Woolf, Virginia, 21, 27–30, 32, 38, 49, 89, 100–1, 198–200, 203
   'Kew Gardens', 30
   Night and Day, 21, 198
   Three Guineas, 100
Wordsworth, William, 28, 30
World War One, 4, 12, 14, 54, 61, 190
World War Two, 5, 122, 190
Wuthering Heights (Brontë, E.), 21, 51, 109, 132, 139, 143

'The Yellow Chrysanthemum' (Mansfield, K.), 81

Zadkine, Ossip, 185

Also available in the series:

Katherine Mansfield and Continental Europe
Edited by Delia da Sousa Correa and Gerri Kimber
Katherine Mansfield Studies, Volume 1

Katherine Mansfield and Modernism
Edited by Delia da Sousa Correa, Gerri Kimber and Susan Reid
Katherine Mansfield Studies, Volume 2

Katherine Mansfield and the Arts
Edited by Delia da Sousa Correa, Gerri Kimber and Susan Reid
Katherine Mansfield Studies, Volume 3

Katherine Mansfield and the Fantastic
Edited by Delia da Sousa Correa, Gerri Kimber, Susan Reid and Gina Wisker
Katherine Mansfield Studies, Volume 4

Katherine Mansfield and the (Post)colonial
Edited by Janet Wilson, Gerri Kimber and Delia da Sousa Correa
Katherine Mansfield Studies, Volume 5

Katherine Mansfield and World War One
Edited by Gerri Kimber, Todd Martin, Delia da Sousa Correa, Isobel Maddison and Alice Kelly
Katherine Mansfield Studies, Volume 6

Katherine Mansfield and Translation
Edited by Claire Davison, Gerri Kimber and Todd Martin
Katherine Mansfield Studies, Volume 7

Katherine Mansfield and Psychology
Edited by Clare Hanson, Gerri Kimber and Todd Martin
Katherine Mansfield Studies, Volume 8

Katherine Mansfield and Russia
Edited by Galya Diment, Gerri Kimber and Todd Martin
Katherine Mansfield Studies, Volume 9

Katherine Mansfield and Virginia Woolf
Edited by Christine Froula, Gerri Kimber and Todd Martin
Katherine Mansfield Studies, Volume 10

www.edinburghuniversitypress.com/series/KMSJ

Join the Katherine Mansfield Society

Patron: Professor Kirsty Gunn

Annual membership starts from date of joining and includes the following benefits:

- Free copy of Katherine Mansfield Studies, the Society's prestigious peer-reviewed annual yearbook published by Edinburgh University Press
- Three e-newsletters per year, packed with information, news, reviews and much more
- Regular email bulletins with the latest news on anything related to KM and/or the Society
- Reduced price fees for all KMS conferences and events
- 20% discount on all books published by Edinburgh University Press
- Special member offers

Further details of how to join are available on our website:
http://www.katherinemansfieldsociety.org/join-the-kms/
or email us:
kms@katherinemansfieldsociety.org

The Katherine Mansfield Society is a Registered Charitable Trust (NZ) (CC46669)

EU representative:
Easy Access System Europe
Mustamäe tee 50, 10621 Tallinn, Estonia
Gpsr.requests@easproject.com

www.ingramcontent.com/pod-product-compliance
Lightning Source LLC
Chambersburg PA
CBHW070351240426
43671CB00013BA/2468